THE REASON FOR OUR HOPE

THE REASON
FOR OUR HOPE

A Theological Anthropology

RICHARD VILADESAU

PAULIST PRESS
New York/Ramsey

Library of Congress
Catalog Card Number: 83-82019

ISBN: 0-8091-2574-9

Published by Paulist Press
545 Island Road, Ramsey, N.J. 07446

Printed and bound in the
United States of America

CONTENTS

to my parents

PREFACE

This book is intended as the first part of a Christian fundamental or "foundational" theology. It arises out of my experience of teaching both seminarians and lay people. Increasingly I have found that theological students today are coming to this study with little or no philosophical background. If theology for them is to be more than simply "dogma," there is a need to confront the fundamental issue of the *presuppositions* of religious faith: the meaning of human existence, the existence and knowability of God, the possibility and necessity of the salvation offered by Christianity. This book is an effort to meet that need. I have attempted here to provide a synthetic approach to the foundational questions of Christian faith which will meet the need to "give answer" for the option of belief, and provide a background for the further study of theology.

Materially then, much of the content of this study falls within the domain of the traditional field of "apologetics." The point of view I have adopted, however, is "anthropological"; that is, the question of faith is approached from the starting point of the experience of the subject. The first chapters pose the problem for contemporary belief and suggest a method for examining that problem. After a brief consideration of transcendence revealed in personal experience, and the alternatives for finding a ground of transcendence, the central two chapters propose an approach to the existence of God. The traditional "ways" to God and the modern critique are followed by a modern approach based on transcendental method. The final two chapters establish the need for salvation and our hope for receiving a "word" from God.

The method of the book develops from the problem itself. The general idea of correlating Christian faith with the contemporary situation leads to a preliminary examination of the problems which must be faced by a modern "answer" for faith. These problems are met by a turn of the subject as the starting point for the justification of belief. The phenomenology of the subject reveals the fact of transcendence and raises the question of God. From this arises a double movement of dialectics and of foundational reflection: "dialectics" to examine the possible alternatives for grounding our experience; "foundational reflection" to examine transcendentally the bases of transcendence.

Both in content and method this work owes much to the writings of Karl Rahner and of Bernard Lonergan. In the use of transcendental method, I have attempted to synthesize their approaches. At the same time, I have integrated material from other theologians, traditional and modern, insights from literature, and references to non-Christian traditions, to broaden the base for understanding and dialogue.

I have stated that this is the "first part" of a foundational theology. It reaches as far as the affirmation of God's existence and the recognition of the need and expectation of salvation from God. In a second volume, now in preparation, I hope to continue with an examination of the reasons for *Christian* faith. The expectation of salvation, with which this book ends, leads to a turn to history and to the phenomenology of religions, to examine the actual claims to have encountered a saving revelation from God. In the context of the convergences and the dialectic of world religions, the absoluteness of the Christian claim is discussed, and an attempt is made to justify Christian conversion by means of the same dialectical-transcendental method used here.

The anticipation of a second volume will explain what might otherwise be seen as major lacunae in this treatment. World religions have barely been touched upon here; the Hindu and Buddhist traditions in particular are represented only minimally, and mostly in atypical forms. They will be dealt with more fully in the consideration of the dialectic of religions. Students of Lonergan will perhaps miss more references to his later works especially *Method in Theology;* these will form a major part of the basis of the examination of the act of conversion. Finally, the specifically Christian dimensions of faith will come to light more fully only in the context of the examination of Christian conversion.

A few words are in order concerning matters of style. I have attempted to be sensitive to the feelings of those who see the use of the pronoun "he" for the common gender as "sexist" by replacing it with he/she (except of course in quotations, where I have not altered the authors' words). This leads, I fear, to a certain stylistic awkwardness, for which I beg the reader's indulgence. I have retained the use of the word "man," in the sense of "humanity," without any sexual differentiation, and with the pronoun he/she. This represents the original and primary meaning of the word (as for example in the etymology of "woman," from the Anglo-Saxon "wif" = female, and "mann" = human being). I have accordingly avoided using the word to mean a male human being. A difficulty in this regard occurs with the word "God." After some consideration, I have decided to retain the traditional pronoun "He," not so much because the reigning metaphor for God in the Christian tradition is "Father" (one could also legitimately speak of God, as is common in some forms of Hinduism, as "Mother"), as because the alternatives seemed either to introduce sexuality into God or to present the Absolute as impersonal. It goes without saying, however, that the use of this pronoun is meant to indicate God's personhood, with no sexual connotations.

Within the text there are sections which are printed within brackets. These represent elaborations or explanations which I considered too important to be relegated to the footnotes, but which are not absolutely crucial to the main line of thought of a section, and which can be skipped over without losing the continuity of ideas. The footnotes for each chapter are independent, so that citations of references are not carried over from one chapter to the next.

Since this book is above all an invitation to the reader to uncover and examine the bases of his/her own faith, to engage in an honest attempt to explore its foundations, it can only succeed to the extent that the reader brings to it a personal engagement and an appropriation of his/her own experience. My own experience in teaching and in studying has shown that this effort, demanding as it is, is rewarding not only intellectually, but also spiritually, for it places each person face to face with the most fundamental questions and the most ultimate realities of life. In this sense, the book is also addressed to the non-believer, for it takes its stand on our common humanity and proposes a dialogue based upon the shared experience of the mystery of human existence.

ABBREVIATIONS USED IN THIS VOLUME

MG = J.-P. Migne (ed.), *Patrologia Graeca (Patrologiae Cursus Completus, Series Graeca et Orientalis)* (Paris: J.-P. Migne, 1856).

ML = J.-P. Migne (ed.), *Patrologia Latina (Patrologiae Cursus Completus, Series Prima)* (Paris: J.-P. Migne, 1844).

HThG = Heinrich Fries (ed.), *Handbuch Theologischer Grund-
begriffe* (München: Kösel-Verlag, 1963).

SM   = Karl Rahner (ed.), *Sacramentum Mundi* (New York:
Herder and Herder, 1968).

I. GIVING ANSWER FOR OUR HOPE

THE PROBLEM

Reverence Christ in your hearts as Lord, and always be ready to give answer to anyone who asks the reason for the hope which is in you . . .

—1 Pet. 3:15

Only those who have experienced the shock of transitoriness, the anxiety in which they are aware of their finitude, the threat of non-being, can understand what the notion of God means.

—Paul Tillich: *Systematic Theology, I*

It has become increasingly clear in our day that the readiness to share the questionings and problems of the world is for the Christian not merely an "apologetic" necessity, a precondition for dialogue in the missionary sphere, but belongs to the very essence of genuine Christian faith.[1] The Christian can only be a hearer of God's word when he is attentive at the same time to the objections and difficulties of the "world," the human situation to which God's message is addressed. It follows that the basic character of all Christian theology is to "give answer": to manifest the human possibility of faith, to show its intelligibility as the interpretive key to the deepest questionings about man's existence and fate, strivings and desires. In a sense, faith can only understand itself in trying to make itself intelligible to the unbeliever: because the person of faith shares—or rather, constitutes—the same world and the same humanity with his/her non-believing brothers and sisters. Indeed, unless one has experienced in oneself, as Tillich states, the deepest questioning about finite existence, the anxious search for meaning in an ambiguous world, the very concept of God can have no sense.

It is the readiness of faith to give an intelligible accounting for itself and for its grounds for hope (1 Pet. 3:15) which distinguishes genuine faith from every "ideology,"[2] including the religious ideology of "blind" and unquestioning belief. If faith makes a claim upon the whole person, upon all of human existence, it must be able and willing to respond to the totality of our being, including our search for meaning and value; it must be able to lay claim to us on the basis of our own deepest strivings and questions. As the free act of man in response to God's word, faith must be grounded only in truth and love, and not in fear, imposition, or the suppression of authentic elements of the human mind and heart.

Faith's reflection on itself, or theology, necessarily implies a relation to non-theological questions and data. This relation derives in a particular way from the eschatological nature of Christian faith. In faith, that is, we are still "under way," we see only "darkly, through a glass"; we await the full manifestation of God's reign. On the other hand, Christian faith recognizes in Jesus God's final and supreme word to man. But if the Christ is "already" God's unique and culminating word of self-revelation, and if that revelation is directed to the salvation of all (1 Tim. 2:4), then the Christian message must somehow include a relationship to all human experience. If the entirety of the creation has Christ as its goal and explanation (Col. 1:15ff), and if this statement is not to be reduced to mere mythology, then the entirety of the creation must be really related to Christ; the Christian message must have a universal relevance for man, and, conversely, man's universal experience must have a relevance for Christianity. In a sense, then, Christian faith is "not yet" the full manifestation of God's reign precisely because the relating of all things to Christ has not yet taken place. This is true not only on the historical and social levels, but also in the case of each individual; there remain portions of my life and of my always growing experience which are as yet unconverted, which have not been enlightened by my faith commitment or reflection. Christian faith therefore remains in some sense incomplete until the world and history have become fully integrated into the economy of salvation. The theological and missionary attempts to accomplish consciously a relation of the Christ event to man's concrete being, individually and socially, in its full extension in time and place, belong essentially to the eschatological movement of the Christian community which not only awaits the coming of its Lord, but is called to further that coming by "building" the body of Christ.

THE TASK OF CHRISTIAN ANTHROPOLOGY

It follows that Christian theology must include a correlation (to use Paul Tillich's term) of faith to human experience.[3] God is the "answer" to man's questions—and it is under the impact of God's answer, existentially if unreflectively present to all persons, that man asks about our ultimate destiny and meaning. We may say, indeed, that man *is* the question before ever we ask;[4] our very being calls out for meaning and explanation. It is the task of theology to formulate the question implied in man and, guided by this essential question, to bring to light God's "answer" in intelligible terms. Such a "correlation," then, will include an analysis of the human situation out of which existential questions arise and a reflection on the symbols of the Christian message which claims to answer those questions.

Theology, then, by its very nature must be ready to face the contemporary human situation: science, art, economics, politics, ethics, philosophy, and every other form of man's self-interpretation and self-expression.[5] It is these which permit faith to formulate its own content and to find a language in which to speak the "answer" to the ultimate questions contained in human self-understanding. This notion of the relationship of theology to the human situation in general implies a methodical principle of great importance: theology cannot by itself, and in isolation, determine what questions it will ask and answer; its content and direction will depend largely upon the full human context out of which it arises, and upon the dialogue-partners to whom it is addressed, whether within or outside the faith community.

There are several immediate and practical consequences for the function of a fundamental theological reflection today. Because it arises from faith's facing the "world," theology must look for its content and means of expression to contemporary man's formulations about the meaning of life. In the past, this has generally meant that theology is especially related to the philosophy of its period, since philosophy has traditionally been the repository of man's deepest and most articulate formulations on the sense of his/her existence.[6] In the contemporary world, however, we find ourselves in a situation in which there is no longer any single philosophical tradition offering a universally acceptable language for theology to use. The radical questioning about man's identity, our possibility for knowledge of reality, our ultimate destiny, no longer takes place

within a uniform philosophical framework which theology can presuppose. If such issues—which are crucial to the foundations of
theological thought—are to be raised for modern faith, they must
become an internal moment in the theological task itself. Theology
today must have the courage to philosophize. The old separation
between philosophy and theology, based on the classical presupposition of a universal culture, can no longer stand.[7]

The situation of the non-theological world is no longer adequately epitomized or described by philosophy alone; hence the
need for a "philosophical" analysis of man and of our concrete
situation within theology. But how, concretely, can such an analysis
take place? The data needed by the philosopher-theologian are not
immediately available within his/her field of competence. Hence,
the theologian must be ready to receive much of the data from
other specialized sciences, particularly from the studies of sociolo-
gists, historians, economists, anthropologists, literary scholars, art-
ists, and others whose analyses provide specific insights into the
human situation, as well as from those fields of inquiry more specifically and traditionally associated with the theological task: biblical
criticism, Church history, archaeology, etc.

Finally, the situation which faith faces through theology will
determine not only what questions theology asks, but also how it
approaches them. The general notion of "correlation" provides us
with a heuristic understanding of the theological task: its concrete
procedure is not an *a priori* method, but is determined by the
character of the correlative realities. The first step in a foundational
theology, therefore, must be a preliminary analysis of the present
situation, in order to uncover more specifically the method which
will meet its problems.

PRELIMINARY ANALYSIS OF THE CONTEMPORARY SITUATION

Our task at this point must be clearly delimited: our goal is not a
thoroughgoing analysis of the contemporary world in all its aspects,
but merely the consideration of those general characteristics which
will allow us to formulate the problems which faith today faces, and
therefore will also permit the formulation of a method which will
address those problems. Again, the "contemporary situation" envis-
aged is not universal in its scope, nor can we attempt to determine
the method for all of foundational theology in every circumstance;

we are addressing only that context which prevails generally in the Western and "developed" world: the European and American cultural sphere. Within this area, we will consider five factors which unfold problems for the Christian faith, and which our theological method must be prepared to meet.

The Epochal Consciousness

As contemporary people, who have seen unprecedented advances in technology—the development of long-range communications; startling breakthroughs in medicine; the beginnings of the nuclear and space ages, to name but a few—all within a single generation, we have been made extraordinarily aware of our own "modernity." The uniqueness of the contemporary world with regard to all past history has become a commonplace, one of the unreflected presuppositions of our time. Modernity in consequence frequently becomes not merely a temporal, but a value category: it is supposed that modern man's unique position in history places us beyond and above every previous stage in human development.[8] Such an attitude easily tends to become a form of chiliasm: our own times are seen as being the unique turning-point to a new era in which for the first time man is "come of age,"[9] a period so radically new in history that no norm can apply to it but its newness itself. We are then in danger of losing sight of our factual continuity with the past. For no one is ever a product only of his/her own age.[10] What characterizes our lives as peculiarly "modern" must not be thought of or lived as though it were the totality of our humanity—even if our modern situation does in some measure leave its mark on the whole of our being. That man must not lose sight of rootedness in the past is more than a mere platitude; it is a warning against a real, although hidden danger. Man's desire to unify experience exposes us to the perpetual temptation to determine everything in life as the function of a single principle (in this case, "modernity"), instead of facing the complexity of the actual world.[11] But such a reductionism would falsify our perception of reality and lead to a narrowing of horizons.

The chiliastic tendency of modern man results in a curious contradiction within the contemporary mind. While it is itself the product of the historical consciousness which marks modern philosophy and culture,[12] at the same time it tends to devaluate the importance of history. For the philosophical and scientific community, the past remains mere fact, without existential relationship to man,[13] while the popular mentality is prone to judge that "history is just one damn thing after another," or, in the famous words of Henry Ford, "history is bunk!"

The contemporary valorization of modernity and the unhistorical bias of many contemporary forms of thought and imagination pose a particular problem for Christian faith. Christianity, in fact, appears to be rooted in the past, in an utterly unmodern situation. It seems to insist upon the relevance of old truths for the new world. An older apologetic attempted to answer the question, "*cur tam sero?*": why did God wait for so long before sending the world's savior? Modern man's objection is precisely the opposite: why so early? *If* human salvation is tied to a particular historical event, why did such a vitally significant event take place at such a comparatively primitive stage of human history? To believe that all existence is related to Jesus seems to mean relating everything to an event and a person which are now utterly outside the realm of human experience, stemming from a period which was totally foreign in mentality to our own, immersed in a pre-scientific, mythical way of thinking, and lacking even the concept of scientific history. Can such a belief be tolerated by the modern mind?

The objection lies yet deeper. The value criteria of modern man are in large part derived from the influence of the scientific and technological mentality. But for the method of empirical science, the individual as such is not ultimately important. What is "objective," permanent, definitive, and hence "true" is what can be verified.[14] But what can be verified scientifically is what can be repeated in experiments. The unique and merely individual belongs to the "empirical residue": what is unimportant and can be disregarded in the search for the universally valid and useful.[15] Christianity, on the contrary, seems to insist that the key to the truth and the future of man and the world is tied to an individual, irrepeatable past event.

A fundamental theological method which will attempt to correlate faith to the present situation must therefore face the *problem of relevance*. It must be able not only to overcome the hidden anti-historical bias, but also to find some basis to reconcile the uniqueness of the historical Christ-event with its claim to universal validity in the determination of the meaning of human existence. It must, in short, be able to justify an approach to man based on a continuity in history and community.

The Plurality of Worlds

In speaking of the "modern mentality," we have already made a generalization which is only in part justifiable. For in fact only one part of our world can be considered "modern" in the evaluative sense of the term. We are chronologically contemporary with a plurality of "periods" or of "worlds." Although they are fast diminishing in number because of increasing contacts, there still exist even at this moment cultures which belong to a stone-age phase of development. More numerous are those parts of the world which have come to be known as "underdeveloped"—the huge masses of people who constitute the "third world," and who live only on the margins of the "modern" situation as known in Europe and America.

Even within the "developed" nations, however, there exists an enormous diversity. The "modern" world is in reality a composite of many sub-worlds, each manifesting to a different degree the characteristics we label "contemporary." Even within modern Western culture, there is a vast plurality, not only of psychic states and consciousness, but also of objective material situations, of human self-interpretations, and of horizons. Thus, in modern America biblical fundamentalism co-exists with the sophistication of nuclear technology, traditional ethnic ghettos with the cosmopolitan internationalism of the metropolis, the heritage of Puritan morality with free-wheeling hedonism. There is no longer any single, highly integrated and cohesive culture; rather, we face today a plurality of coexistent "worlds." This is true not only in the cultural sphere, but also within the sciences, technology, and politics.

Furthermore, the phenomenon of pluralism occurs not only on the social level, but even within individuals. Modern people frequently find themselves subject to a split or fragmented consciousness, a single subject living simultaneously in different environments which have little in common with each other. Thus the suburban commuter may find him/herself in one world, with its own complex presuppositions and rules and behavior, in his/her daily job in the city; in another when he/she returns home to his/her family; in yet another in church on Sunday mornings; and so on. The beliefs and morals of business life may be quite foreign to what the congregation professes in church, which may in turn have little to do with leisure activity or family code. In short, the plurality and complexity of the world have become such that the situation is, in Karl Rahner's words, "in the highest degree incapable of analysis and incapable of being grasped and apprehended as a whole."[16]

Finally, this situation is not only a fact, but a fact which has come to consciousness in society: the situation of plurality gives rise to the thought-form of plural*ism*. People have increasingly come to recognize and to accept plurality; they find that they can live together in some kind of social order without a single unifying view of life. Our age is witnessing for the first time in history a culture built on the presupposition that it is not vital to the functioning of society to attain a consensus on the ultimate questions of human existence; a pragmatic union can be formed without agreement on our world-view. So, for example, the principle of religious tolera-tion—including the equal rights of non-belief—in the Western de-mocracies presupposes that it is not crucial for the functioning of the state for people to agree on the existence of God, a universal code of morality, or a final reason behind human rights or society itself.[17]

The pluralist context of the modern world has important reper-cussions for theology—especially when the explicit goal of the latter is "correlation." For when we speak of "God," we necessarily at-tempt to address all of reality, in its wholeness, and to relate it to a single supreme Reality.[18] But such an attempt seems to stand at odds with the pluralism and consequent relativism of the age. The problem is aggravated in the Christian context. Pluralism seems to mark the singular and individual as merely relative, historically conditioned and contained. From the time of the decline of Roman-ticism, the future of man has been seen increasingly in social, deprivatized, non-individual terms. The Christian claim to relate all of human existence, or even all being whatsoever, to the finite and relative history of a single individual can easily appear as Romantic and mythological.[19] A fundamental theological method, therefore, which attempts to address this situation, must be able to get beyond the absence of any single general philosophical analysis of the world, and to account for the possibility of some underlying unity which can be affirmed despite the plurality of concrete human existence.

The problem, however, is even wider. There is not only an "exterior" plurality of "worlds" in which we live, but also a plurality which is interior to ourselves as subjects. This plurality consists of a lack of personal integration of the elements of an individual's own world-view. We live in the age of the "knowledge explosion": there are more data, more to be known, than can be synthesized by any one person. We live, therefore, in a time of specialization. Hence, although the total share of human knowledge is greater than at any

previous time, that knowledge is dispersed in the minds of special-
ists in multiple fields; the totality of human knowledge is never
"together," except, to a certain degree, in the memory banks of
computers.

This situation of the dispersal of human knowledge, and the
consequent inability of any individual to have at his/her disposal all
the knowledge necessary to integrate life, is what Rahner calls
"gnoseological concupiscence":[20]

> In previous ages, an educated person could *himself* have at least
> an approximate over-all view of the whole field of insights and
> questions relevant to a world-view.... He was thus able ... to
> form more or less adequately *direct* judgments about world-view
> questions....

Now, however, the amount of human knowledge has so expanded
that no individual can possibly enter into direct contact with the
whole range of questions bearing upon his/her life-situation.[21] In
the sciences and in technology, the problem is solved by teamwork;
the scientist simply accepts the results achieved by others, without
having to pose each question anew and reverify the results. The
computer, which can quickly synthesize information from many
sources more than could possibly be available to the individual, is
the great symbol of this form of collaboration.

This kind of teamwork, however, does not seem possible when
the question is one of a person's faith, one's most basic world-view,
and one's free disposal of his/her life; such questions are matters of
ultimate concern, and form the basis for all other faiths, beliefs, and
commitments; they cannot be settled simply by accepting the answers of others, even presupposing that there were a consensus of
"experts" about the meaning of human life. The result is that all
individuals, including philosophers and theologians, when outside
their areas of special knowledge, find themselves in the position of
those whom an older theology called *"rudes"*—those simple people
who were unable to attain an adequate knowledge of the reasons for
their belief. And yet the demand for a rational justification of one's
stance toward life—one's basic "faith"—remains.

A theology which attempts to "give answer" for Christian faith,
then, must find a method which can justify the right and duty to
believe despite the fact of "gnoseological concupiscence." In short,
our method must meet the problem of *integration.* Christianity
makes a claim to universal validity; but knowledge of the universal

situation is no longer attainable, either on the social or the individual level. Our method must therefore correlate the deprivatized and pluralistic situation with both the individuality and the universality of the Christ-event, and, at the same time, must somehow transcend the inability of the individual to gain access to the material whole of questions relevant to a fundamental decision about his/her being.

The Secularization of the West

A great deal has been written on the theme of the "secularization" of the modern world.[22] It is not our purpose here to enter into a detailed discussion of the subject, which has been thoroughly treated elsewhere, and which is furthermore a part of the daily experience of anyone living in the mainstream of Western culture. The extent of "secularization," versus the survival of "sacral" experiences, cannot detain us.[23] Nevertheless, we must give a brief account of the phenomenon only insofar as it bears upon our problem of determining a method of correlation in theology.

The relative independence of the world of human affairs from the sphere of the sacred may be said to have begun with the disappearance of the "God of explanations" from Western thought: first from science, then from philosophy, history, and politics.[24] As progress made it possible to explain the world and to function within it without reference to the divine—a process whose course is marked by the thought-revolutions of Copernicus, Marx, Darwin, and Freud—the idea of God eventually became superfluous to everyday life. Philosophy, art, and literature turned from the transcendent to ordinary experience as the normal source of their inspiration. Man came in time to be regarded as the planner and master of the world; we began to live in a context where we encounter primarily our own products; our environment has become increasingly self-made. In such a situation, "nature," long regarded as God's direct determination of the world, has come to play less and less of a role in man's life. We find ourselves in control and responsible for the world, in which we create meaning for our living.[25] The idea of God is relegated to the "margins" of life, to the specialized field of religion, if, indeed, it survives at all. Although notable exceptions may exist, both in the larger community and in sub-communities, it is clear that the basic logic of the modern world, especially in its politics and philosophy, is "secular" and godless. The practical and public lives even of religious people are led in a context of secularity, whatever may be their more intimate and private convictions. As the psychologist Eugene Rolfe states: "Almost all of us nowadays conduct our lives for all practical purposes as if God did not exist."[26]

From the time of Hegel it has frequently been noted that this process of the secularization of the West is largely a result of attitudes rooted in the Judaeo-Christian religious heritage itself.[27] The transcendence of the biblical God desacralizes the world: the gods of nature are eliminated. Nature is seen as God's creation ("you spoke, and they were made"—Jdt. 16:14) rather than being itself divine. The biblical God is invisible, not merely in the sense that electrons or radio waves are invisible, but in being essentially beyond the realm of sensation.[28] God does not "occur" within the spatio-temporal area that defines the living space of man. Therefore, what happens in the world can no longer be experienced directly as the action of God; the world is demythologized, secularized, humanized.[29]

Furthermore, biblical religion presents man as responsible for the world; man is in some sense God's co-creator, commanded to subdue and fill the earth (Gen. 1:28). In the New Testament, all the powers of nature and history are dethroned by Christ, and man is freed from slavery to the powers of the cosmos:

> Formerly, in your ignorance of God, you were slaves to gods that really did not exist, but now that you know God, or rather have come to be known by him, how can you turn back to old, crude notions, so poor and weak, and wish to become slaves to them again? (Gal. 4:8f)

> It is in Christ that all the fullness of God's nature lives embodied, and in union with him you too are filled with it. He is the head of all your principalities and dominions. . . . He disarmed the principalities and dominions and displayed them openly, triumphing over them through him. (Col. 2:9f, 15)

For the Judaeo-Christian tradition, then, the world is other than God; nature is not the awe-full and numinous presence of the sacred, but is rather man's possession as God's co-creator, man's legitimate domain and field of labor.

It follows that, even though *de facto* the process of secularization has often been connected with humanistic atheism, its basic premises of hominization and demythologization are in thorough accord with Christian faith. There is a legitimate independence of the "world" from the sphere of the sacred and religious. This does not of course mean that the world is irrelevant to man's salvation, or that "grace" is not operative in it. It does mean, however, that God is present and operates in the world in a non-apparent way; he operates in the world *as secular*. In Rahner's terminology, the profane world is "sanctified," but not "sacralized"; grace remains hidden in order to leave room for human freedom.[30] The distancing of man's field of *explicit* relation to God (religion) from the really but *implicitly* God-related field of the world means that man's symbols and concepts for dealing with the Ultimate do not give us a means of dealing with the concrete world.[31] This fact is the basis for the independence of both the political sphere and the profane sciences from religion and theology. Not only the "separation of Church and state" but also the separation of empirical science from the theological depends upon the recognition of this principle.[32] The consequences of its neglect will be brought to mind if we recall Galileo before the Inquisition, the horrors of the European wars of religion, or the injustices of the penal laws in English-ruled Ireland.

The principle of secularity applies also on the individual, personal level. The independence of the "world" means that man cannot determine the *whole* of life, of consciousness and action, from the single starting point of faith. That is, *man cannot live by faith alone.* Faith relates us to our ultimate destiny, but does not provide, as it were, a blueprint for living; our concrete decision making and behavior in the world must be based on other factors besides those operative in religious faith. Faith is not a total *Weltanschauung,* a world-view in which all of a man's actions and thoughts can be integrated and systematized.[33] To attempt to make one's religion—the symbol system by which one relates to the ultimate Other, the Ungraspable—into the *sole* context or motivation in life is to mistake the nature of faith and to fall into a false integralism or "ultrasupernaturalism,"[34] with its attendant danger of fanaticism. As Rahner points out:

> A phenomenon frequently apparent in the history of the church is a false integralism. By comparison with this the process of secularization is, judged by genuinely Christian standards, right and just. . . . The Church is never, and never intends for one moment to be, the total and exclusive force determining and administering human conduct and morality in the world. She is not the sum total of this, but rather an element in the sum total made up of many factors, for at basis and of its very nature the sum total of all that determines human morality is essentially "pluralist". . . .[35]

If all this is true, however, it poses a further problem for a theology which is "giving answer." Christianity—and, indeed, religion in general—claims to speak to man's most intimate being, and to be vital to human authenticity. Furthermore, it makes of man an ultimate and total demand: "You shall love the Lord, your God, with your whole heart, your whole soul, your whole strength, and your whole mind" (Lk. 10:27). How can this be reconciled with a legitimate secularization in which the world is left free in its worldliness, with its own independent and profane norms and responsibilities? In order to correlate faith with such a situation, our method must be able to meet the *problem of radicality:* i.e., must be able to go beyond the legitimate distinction between the sacred and the secular, and show the radical nature of the God-relation and of faith *within* secularity.

The Demand for Praxis[36]

In the secularized and pluralist world, there is no unified theory or philosophy of life: man's criteria for truth and value are no longer given by the cultural situation; each must decide what will be productive of authenticity. At the same time, as we have seen, it has become impossible for any individual to control all the data necessary for a thoroughly personally validated *theoretical* stance toward the world and toward the ultimate meaning of reality. Increasingly, therefore, it is the *practical* relevance of ideas, their relationship to actual concrete life conditions, their ability to change the world, to work, which becomes man's guide in the decision to place trust in a system of thought or belief. Marx's remark that "the philosophers have only *interpreted* the world, in various ways; the point, however, is to *change* it,"[37] has become perforce a general norm of judgment.

Man's question to religion, therefore, is no longer simply rational and historical, but also (and principally) pragmatic: in what sense does this system of beliefs and symbols afford light and wisdom for the pressing questions and needs of myself, of my society, of man's future? Moreover, the world's questioning of Christianity does not stop with the practical spiritual value of the churches' beliefs, nor with the historical figure of Jesus; it involves also the practice of Christians: to what extent has Christianity, as lived in history and in the present, embodied salvific attitudes, and to what extent does the practice of believers betray and contradict the norms and values they proclaim?[38] The believability of any system can no longer be founded simply on its message. As Werner Heisenberg remarks, we have learned from recent history—especially the rise of ideologies like Nazism and Marxism—that any political system must be judged not by the aims it professes, no matter how loudly and sincerely, but by what it actually does in attempting to accomplish those aims.[39] The same criterion is applied to religion. It is in the book of deeds rather than that of words that contemporary people seek to read the meaning of religious attitudes. But a glance at the history of the "Christian" West will suffice to indicate that the application of the criterion of practice to the Church could have very ambiguous and even embarrassing results. Chesterton's famous dictum notwithstanding, it appears to many in the modern world that Christianity has indeed been tried, and has failed.

The demand for *praxis* makes itself felt even more dramatically when we turn from the individual to the global dimension of contemporary life. Already in 1958 the philosopher Karl Jaspers declared: "Facing us—we must repeat this again and again—is the possible and intellectually probable end of mankind." The context in which he wrote was the threat of a nuclear holocaust, made ever more likely by the stockpiling of atomic weapons. In our own day, nuclear weapons with their devastating capabilities are no longer the exclusive possession of the "superpowers"; the nuclear "club" has expanded to include secondary powers, and the requisite technology is almost universally available. The possibility of nuclear war—or even of a terrorist use of nuclear weapons—seems even more present. Moreover, we have come to realize that nuclear war is only one of the major threats to the survival of mankind. The as yet unchecked population explosion; the limitations of world food production in the face of constantly increasing demand; the depletion of available energy sources, and the consequent menace to technology and world economy; the inequity in the distribution of world wealth, and the potentially explosive discontent of the "have nots"; the still continuing pollution of the biosphere all over the globe: all these point to a crisis in which the very existence of the human race may be at stake. In the course of history, plagues, wars, and natural catastrophes have destroyed nations and civilizations; now for the first time our entire race seems to be on the brink of destruction, not as a result of the violence of nature, but from our own creations. In the course of evolution, whole species have perished because of lack of adaptation; now for the first time a species on the verge of destruction has been given a choice about survival

—and yet seems unable to make the decisions which would reverse the course of destruction.

The world situation is desperately in need of salvation in the practical order. The decisions which we must make in order to survive are possible, but they demand a change in behavior and in motivations on an enormous scale: the reversal of many priorities, the adoption of rational and global policies, the setting aside of short-term self-interest and immediately profitable goals in favor of the long-term good of all, the appropriation of a spirit of collaboration, self-sacrifice, and altruism. The values which must animate man in order to survive are, in fact, the basic values of biblical religion. But, ironically, the churches which embody and preach those values find themselves, for the most part, helpless in the face of the world crisis. The biblical religions today "encompass only a fraction of mankind, and this Western fraction has largely lost faith in the churches."[40] Even where the influence of religion has remained significant, it has been more in the realm of private devotion than in that of public policy. What seems to be needed, then, is a universally accessible philosophy of action, based on an appeal of human reason.[41] An appeal to revealed religion will not serve; contemporary man in his social situation must be addressed on a simply human level, without reference to any authority but that due to every rational being.

Faith today, then, must face the *problem of praxis*. It must first of all honestly admit and attempt to explain the disturbing disjunction between Christian preaching and practice; it must show itself capable of meeting the individual's need for a practical course of action in daily life, without usurping the place of legitimately secular values; and it must correlate the salvific claims of religion to the needed secular philosophy of action which will meet the present world crisis.

The Turn to the Subject

As we have already indicated, there is no single philosophical movement in the modern world which adequately articulates the full human "situation" of our time. Nevertheless, there is an overall context of the whole of modern philosophy which, on the one hand, reflects and expresses, and, on the other hand, helps create, a major feature of the contemporary thought-world.[42] That context is the turn of philosophical thought to the primacy of the human subject as its starting point and universal point of reference. This subjective or anthropological turn of philosophy since the time of Kant can perhaps best be explained in terms of the "realms" and "stages" of meaning described by Bernard Lonergan.

Meaning, for Lonergan, is the matter of man's intentionality of being.[43] The types of meaning can be divided systematically into diverse "realms," each created and governed by a different need and process of human intellect.[44] There is first of all a realm of undifferentiated consciousness. It is the field of "common sense." It results from the exigence of the practical point of view, the necessity of getting along in daily life. In it, the subject functions intelligently and reaches true judgments, but he/she is not concerned with distinguishing between the types of knowledge used, nor with how they are reached. The realm of common sense is concerned with the experiential, the particular, the relative and the imaginable. Its object is the "thing-for-me," i.e., things as they present themselves to my senses. It is therefore descriptive rather than explanatory. It does not clearly distinguish between the subject and the objects of perception; rather, it joins them as an experiential whole.[45] It does not aim at universally valid knowledge, or attempt an exhaustive articulation of reality; its only concern is to master individual life situations as they arise.[46] Because its basic referent is the sensible world, it expresses man's relation to non-empirical reality in mytho-poetic form, i.e., in terms of analogies drawn from sense experience.

Beyond "common sense," however, there is a "systematic" exigence of mind, creating the realm of "theory." In it, we attempt not merely to describe, but to explain the world. This demands a certain intellectual detachment of the subject from its objects. Within this realm, intellect is concerned with the abstract and universal, the comprehensive, which is therefore, by its nature, unimaginable. Its objects are things "in themselves"; it deals with the relations of objects to each other, rather than to the human senses.[47] If it considers the subject at all, it does so in a detached, objectifying manner. This is the realm of classical science and classical philosophy. While common sense provides the insights necessary for daily living, "theory" explains the world in the light of mind's natural tendency to ask what things "really" are.

The differentiation of consciousness into the realms of common sense and theory, however, gives rise to problems. How can the same object—a desk, for example—be at the same time heavy, solid, substantial, palpable, as common sense tells me, and also be composed mainly of empty space separating infinitesimally small and invisible atomic particles, as I am told by modern science?[48] How can I reconcile the daily common sense experience of seeing the sun rise and set over a plainly stationary earth with the notion that the earth is actually revolving around the sun, and that both earth and sun are hurtling through space at enormous velocity? From such contrasts arises the "critical" exigence of mind: man is forced to inquire about the nature, kinds, and value of knowledge itself. For the only way to relate the world of common sense to the world of science, without devaluating one or the other, is to understand why there must be different and yet equally valid cognitional procedures in each. And so we are led to reflect on our own knowing process, on our experience of consciousness itself. We are drawn to explore the theory of cognition and epistemology, in order to answer the three basic questions: "What am I doing when I am knowing? Why is doing that, knowing? What do I know when I do it?"[49]

In asking these questions, we pass from the realms of "external" knowledge by common sense and theory into the realm of "interiority," in which we attend to our own subjectivity. We reflect now on our own conscious experience in order to discover the bases of knowledge. Consciousness is now differentiated consciously through the subject's appropriation of his/her own conscious activities in the various realms of meaning.

Finally, there is a "transcendent" exigence of mind, through which man recognizes that there is a possibility of experience beyond the incomplete (although true) answers of common sense, science, and interiority; and in the transcendent realm we allow ourselves to be drawn into mystical religious experience.[50] This realm by its nature can have no "language" properly its own, but co-exists with any other realm of meaning, using their languages to articulate symbolically its fundamentally supra-rational experience.

On the basis of the degree of differentiation or undifferentiation of consciousness, Lonergan also distinguishes three idealized historical "stages" of meaning. These are temporally successive in that the appearance of the later presupposes the former; but they can also co-exist in a single pluralistic historical period, in different subjects. There is first a stage of common sense, with no differentiation of the various kinds of knowledge; religion and science mix freely with myth and with insights into everyday life. Then there is a stage of theory, controlled by logic. In it, the domain of thought (science, philosophy, theology) is separated from common sense. This stage is exemplified by the "classical" and especially the Aristo-

telian period of Western thought, in which the sciences are a pro-
longation of philosophy.[51] Finally, there is a stage in which the
development of the empirical method permits the sciences to become independent of philosophy. Since the criteria of scientific
truth are now sensible data, philosophy is faced with a dilemma. It
may either recognize its own futility as a "science" and disappear
altogether, or it may confine itself to the clarification of language
and become a branch of logic or even of mathematics, or, finally, it
may recognize the empirical world as the domain of the sciences
and turn to the experience of consciousness itself for its proper
data.[52] This last has been the direction of critical metaphysical
philosophy since the "Copernican revolution" of Kant forced the
shift in philosophical attention from "substances" to the conscious
subject.

Insofar as philosophical thought both reflects and influences
culture, the history of modern Western philosophy represents the
reflective form of those tendencies we have dealt with above under
the headings of epochal self-consciousness, plurality, secularity, and
pragmatism. From the time of the Renaissance, philosophy has
become increasingly estranged from the realm of the transcendent.
When, in the nineteenth century, Nietzsche proclaimed the "death
of God," he was giving expression to an alienation which had long
been in process in philosophical thought. Already with Descartes
the autonomy of reason from faith in confronting the problem of
God is declared; yet for Descartes, as for Malebranche, Spinoza, and
Leibniz, the concept of God remains necessary as the ultimate
explanatory principle of the philosophical system. As those systems
were rejected, however, so was the "God of explanations" they had
defended. The Kantian critique of human knowing lent force to the
process by throwing into doubt the very possibility of certain and
scientific knowledge of transcendent being. Increasingly man
looked for explanations of the world to the immanent, the "natural." Rather than positing God as the ultimate explanation of man,
thinkers begin to see man as the explanation of God: the thought of
Feuerbach, Marx, Freud expresses the common theme that God is a
projection of man's ideals or wishes, and that faith in God therefore
results in an alienation of man from our own humanity.

The philosophical turn to the subject, then, poses for Christian
faith the *problem of verification*. The explanation of the finite
world has become the domain of empirical science, for which
"God" is an unnecessary hypothesis.[53] Philosophy must turn to the
realm of interiority, to the data of human consciousness as such, to

find its own basis and validity. If the notion of God is to have meaning in this context, it must be shown that human consciousness is in some way capable of apprehending a being which by definition transcends the conditions of human knowing. That is, theological statements must be verified by appeal to the conscious experience of the subject.

INDICATIONS FOR A THEOLOGICAL ANTHROPOLOGY

In our attempt to formulate a sketch of the situation which must be faced in faith's effort to "give answer" to the world, we have uncovered several basic complexes of problems, which we have named relevance, plurality, radicality, and praxis. We have also noted that modern philosophical thought finds itself in the stage of "interiority," in which the question of the subject and the conditions of knowing takes priority and underlies every other reflective inquiry. This consideration is decisive for the determination of a basic method of our project. If theology must have the courage to confront the most radical questions as an interior moment of its own task, then it seems clear that theology must make its own the turn to the subject which we have uncovered as a basic presupposition of modern thought.[54] Theology, then, will take the form of anthropology, in the sense that its starting point and basic referent will be the concrete subject, and its basic assertions will be in principle *verifiable* by each person through the examination of his/her own experience.

The main efforts of faith to "give answer" for its hope have in the past been associated principally with the "theoretical" realm of consciousness: i.e., in "classical" theology and apologetics.[55] Even prior to this, of course, Christian faith attempted to justify itself and to speak to contemporary people: not in scientific apologetics, but through personal witness and the appeal to God's working in the individual's life. It adopted a "heart to heart" approach, often framed in poetical or symbolic language, appealing to the whole person in his/her undifferentiated consciousness. The God who was proclaimed was likewise named symbolically, in the figurative language of religious tradition, and especially of the Bible: Father, King, Shepherd, Lord, etc. The rise of theoretical consciousness established a "scientific" approach to the justification of faith, centered on a double appeal to philosophy and to history. God now is described in terms of the causality which "demonstrates" his existence: he is the Absolute Being, the metaphysical source of the contingent world. Within the modern turn to the subject, theology faces the task of showing how an examination of the human subject in the unique act of self-possession, which is the condition for all objective knowledge, can establish man as a possible knower of God and recipient of revelation. It must find a way of speaking of God which refers not simply to objective causality or to anthropomorphic images, but which relates to the concrete active experience of the human spirit.[56]

The acceptance of the "turn to the subject" as its starting point provides, in principle, the means for theology to address itself to the problems of the modern situation we have described. It meets the problem of *relevance* by counterposing to the anti-historical bias a new historical consciousness. When man is seen as a concrete subject, it is clear that he/she is not simply a self-sufficient and independent "substance"; the subject is a self-with-others, in the world—a *je-avec-autrui-au-monde.* The subject experiences the self not as a separated "spirit" or as a self independent of its surroundings, but as (also) the product of the non-self. We recognize that our spiritual existence, our selfhood, arises in a social and historical context which is not of our making, and which transcends our individual life-projects both in space and time. The subject's *self*-understanding, therefore, can only take place with reference to the larger framework of the history of which each person is a part.

The turn to the subject meets the problem of *integration.* In a sense, each subject lives in both the world of history and in a "world" of one's own, a horizon determined by one's unique personal situation in the world, and therefore irrepeatable and incommunicable. By making subjectivity itself our starting point, however, we ask about precisely what is constant and universal within the plurality of subjects: namely, the very experience of being a unique subject, of having a "horizon" in life. Since all persons are subjects, this starting point provides a trans-cultural basis for anthropology,[57] one which reaches beyond particular social and historical differences to what is common to all. Moreover, we are speaking not of a turn to some particular theory of subjectivity, but to the concrete subject's living experience of selfhood; hence, we refer not to any culturally conditioned content or expression of subjectivity, but to personally verifiable conditions. Similarly, the situation of "gnoseological concupiscence" is met by an appeal not to the content of knowledge, or to individual facts, but to the *a priori* root structure and pre-condition of all knowledge: conscious subjectivity.

The turn to the subject meets the problem of *radicality,* posed by secularism. The study of the concrete subject includes the realm of decisions and actions. But it is always the same subject who acts and decides, whether in a religious or a secular sphere. Hence we have in human personality or subjectivity a kind of integrator of all experience. Man's root or radical relation to God takes place precisely on the level of being-person, in whatever context, secular or religious. Hence, subjectivity or personality provides the radical basis for finding the experience of God within "secular" experience.

The turn to the subject meets the problem of *praxis.* First of all, it is itself based on praxis: it is concerned not with the idea of the subject, but with the real, concrete subject attending to self; it therefore demands the active involvement of the investigator. If I am to find the basis for authenticity in my own subjectivity, I must myself be authentic. Hence, the turn to the subject implies a "conversion." The examination of the subject's actual practice, furthermore, allows us to go beyond the concepts which he/she uses; these concepts or formulations may be more or less true expressions of real lived attitudes and actions. As we shall see, the turn to the subject allows us to formulate a fundamental dialectic between concepts and performance. In the light of this dialectic the divergence between religious practice and religious preaching can be understood.

With regard to the concrete demand for praxis in the modern world crisis, the turn to the subject grounds the possibility of a relation of God to the world outside the confines of religious consciousness. Because it takes root in the subject's experience, and not immediately in biblical religion, it can speak to the non-theological world. It establishes the possibility of dialogue, rather than preaching, and can address itself to "all men of good will," whatever their religious stance, for the sake of a common practical commitment to the betterment of the world.[58]

By attempting to address the problems of meaning and verification posed by modern philosophy, then, we appear to have arrived at a starting point which will allow the correlation of faith to the modern "situation" in general. We shall attempt to find an opening to the transcendent within the experience of subjectivity, of conscious being. It remains now for us to determine more precisely a method for performing this task.

II. THE TRANSCENDENT
SUBJECT

CONSCIOUSNESS: LIFE AS "QUESTION"

What is man that thou art mindful of him, and the son of man that thou dost care for him?

—Ps. 8

To call man, in the basic structure of his being, a "question" seeking an answer is not simply a metaphor. . . . In questioning, man goes beyond the confines of the known and thereby also beyond his present horizon. Man's openness to the world expresses itself in his ability to ask questions at all, and in his living by means of a process of questioning which pushes him ever farther into openness. Insofar as man questions the reality which meets him . . . he ultimately is questioning about himself, his own meaning. And so it makes good sense to call man a question which drives always toward openness.

—Wolfhart Pannenberg,
"Die Frage nach Gott"

Faith, in order to "correlate" to the situation of modern man, takes as the starting point of its reflection the experience of being a subject. In taking its stand on the consciousness of the concrete individual, theology intends to clarify its foundations by showing that man is radically open to the transcendent, and that this openness is a fact of each person's experience, even if one does not advert to it. We propose that this openness can be in principle "verified" by each person in a personal experiment, in which he/she examines the conditions of his/her own subjectivity or conscious existence. This process constitutes a philosophical moment within the theological endeavor. In meeting the philosophical challenge of evidence or verification, reflective faith also lays the groundwork for a theology which can address man today, faced with the problems of relevance, integration, radicality, and praxis.

The basis of our method, then, is the "turn to the subject."[1] Our purpose is to show that the affirmation of transcendent being is somehow within man's horizon—that the concept of God, or the Absolute, has meaning, because it enters into our very experience of ourselves as conscious beings.

What, then, is the experience of "subjectivity," of being a subject? To be a subject is above all to live that extraordinary way of being in the world which we call "consciousness." What is meant by "consciousness" is ultimately an irreducible experience which each knows for him/herself; our words about it cannot adequately capture it, but can only point out the direction in which each subject must attend in order to grasp his/her own consciousness, heighten it, objectify it, become explicitly aware of it.

Consciousness is first of all what distinguishes the mode of being of the subject from that of mere "objects" or things. Things present themselves to me simply as being "there," over against me and independent of myself. Consciousness, on the other hand, is not simply "there"; it must be actuated.[2] It is not a permanent feature of my existence. While I may be at all times equally "there," equally a "substance," whether I am awake or sleeping, young or old, sane or crazy, I am a conscious subject in different ways and to different degrees, depending upon the state of my self-actuation and self-presence.[3] When unconscious, I am a subject only in potency; when dreaming, I am a subject in a minimal way; when awake and sentient, I am an empirically conscious subject—and so on. Consciousness is my "presence" to myself, the "luminous" quality of my being—that strange and unique reality which consists in existing *for* oneself: "All living is living-for-oneself, feeling oneself living, knowing that one exists—where 'knowing' does not mean an intellectual cognition, nor any special wisdom, but rather is that surprising *presence* which each person's life comports for that person."[4] A stone or a chair exists, but does not feel itself or know its own existence; it is blind to itself. But human life is a constant transparency, an illumination: a continuous process of discovery of self and of the world.[5] (For this reason Heidegger correctly insists that there is a crucial difference between the "existence" of a subject [Heidegger's *Dasein*] and the "existence" of objects—a difference which is often overlooked or forgotten because our ordinary language speaks of the two with the same term.)[6]

This primary illumination, this "finding" of the self as self, is what makes "my" life, what unifies experience and constitutes me as a subject.[7] Consciousness is the awareness, not simply of the objects of experience, but of the experience itself as "mine," and hence it is an awareness of myself, in the awareness of the other (the "object").[8] This self-consciousness is the most fundamental reality of my life: other things present themselves to me, but such a manifestation of the other always presupposes my "self," my subjectivity, to which it is present.[9]

It must be clear that "consciousness" denotes first of all an internal *experience* of the self, prior to any introspection or inquiry *about* the self. It is that *concommitant* experience by which the subject is present to self in the very act of attending to anything at all: that is, it accompanies every experience of an object. There is, therefore, a duality in every conscious act of the subject: each act of knowing or willing implies both a subjective and an objective pole—an *intending* and an *intended,* a *pensée pensante* and *volonté voulante,* on the one hand, and a *pensée pensée* and *volonté voulue* on the other;[10] an unthematic consciousness, and a thematic and objective consciousness. It is at the first, the intending, thinking, willing pole that the subject is immediately present to self—not as object, but precisely as the subject. Consciousness of self as concommitant is therefore not a matter of perception or confrontation; it is rather a self-illuminating identity.[11] Of course, it is also possible to reflect on reflection itself, to introspect to heighten our self-awareness by making the conscious self the object of thematic consciousness; but, in this case, there always remains an un-thematized, concommitant experience of the subjective pole, the self performing the reflection; the polarity is never resolved.[12] There is always a "unity in difference" between one's original self-awareness and the subsequent self-reflection or thematic self-appropriation. The originating (unthematic) consciousness requires subsequent reflection in order to become explicitly perceived and appropriated; yet the reflecting, objectifying moment can never "capture" fully the original unity of self-presence.[13]

It must also be noted that the subject comes to self-consciousness precisely in the consciousness of objects; one never encounters oneself simply in oneself, but always in the world, in other things,[14] as a knower and lover. There is no "pure" experience of subjectivity alone, without objects; rather, paradoxically, the subject is all the more "with" itself the greater its involvement with the other, the objective pole of consciousness.[15] The conscious "I" is an "I-in-the-world," an "I and my situation."[16] Our life, our subjectivity, is indeed given to us, but not as a pure "possession": it is rather given as a problem to be resolved. We must "find" ourselves without the horizon of the world.[17] Subjectivity is indeed the mystery of an incommunicable, objectively uncapturable self-presence; yet this self-presence only occurs as the accompaniment to presence to the world. We cannot possess ourselves within the other, the non-self. By myself, I am; but I do not "have" myself, I do not become present to myself, except in my movement toward the world.[18] My inner being by itself is dark; to see myself, to become luminous, I must go out from myself toward the other, from which the self becomes distinguished.[19]

Conscious life is, therefore, in a profound sense, a "question": not merely in that we must ask questions and seek to know the world intellectually, but more radically, in the sense that man's solitude, our subjectivity, calls out for dialogue, for the presence and response of the other,[20] and cannot "have" itself except in this movement outward. Subjectivity is the anticipation of some meaning, some sense, which will be an "answer" to our being. "Life," in Ortega's phrase, "is a perplexity."[21] To be conscious is to be in a state of "radical unrest,"[22] to be in our profoundest depths always tending, seeking.[23] Life is not simply what we are, but is a project, an involvement in our own being, in our own becoming; paradoxically, our being consists more in what it is not yet than in what it is.[24] Thus, in the fact of consciousness, the "question" that we *are*, the radical seeking for selfhood through a constant facing of the other, we may discern a first inkling of the meaning of *transcendence:* a fundamental "going beyond" the present horizon of my being.

THE QUESTION ABOUT THE WORLD

For creation is waiting with eager longing for the sons of God to be disclosed.... We know that all creation has been groaning in agony together until now. More than that, we ourselves, though we have in the Spirit a foretaste of the future, groan to ourselves as we wait to be declared God's sons, through the redemption of our bodies....

Rom. 8:18–23

I believe that the Universe is an evolution.
I believe that evolution progresses toward Spirit.

I believe that Spirit comes to perfection in the Personal.
I believe that the supreme Personal is the universal Christ.

Teilhard de Chardin: "Comment Je Crois"

The subject comes to light in confrontation with the world. One discovers oneself as a self-in-the-world-with-others, as one pole of the relationship subject-object. Our very being is in a sense a question toward the other. It is for this reason that man lives within a "horizon," and not simply, like an animal, within an environment: man is not merely "there" in the world, but *wonders.* In Lonergan's famous dictum, "When an animal has nothing to do, it goes to sleep. When a man has nothing to do, he may ask questions."[25] As we shall have occasion to see, man's ability to wonder, to question, the "hunger" for intelligibility, has an unrestricted extension;[26] our questions may be about anything, and extend beyond the objective and intellectual realm to the interpersonal and free. But the first and most natural object of our desire to know is the "world": that context in which life finds itself, from which the experience of the self appears inseparable, and over against which we recognize ourselves as subjects. The question is most immediately about "my" world: the immediate horizon of my life, the objects with which I am in daily contact and which I must learn about in order to survive. But man's curiosity takes us beyond the immediate world to question also about the larger world, the world of others, and finally about the world as such: its meaning, intelligibility, its dynamism, goal, and fate. The question about the world is the source not only of the common sense by which we get along in life, the technology by which we master it, and the arts by which we express our feelings and aspirations in it, but also of the whole complex body of knowledge in the empirical sciences, history, and philosophy. It is to this body of knowledge that we must turn first—albeit briefly and summarily—in our search for the experience of transcendence. What is the world? How does it relate to the remarkable fact of subjectivity which we have discovered, and to the question that we are?

What immediately presents itself is that man finds the world intelligible.[27] Man as the radical "question" finds the world in fundamental correspondence with the desire to know. We find ourselves at home in, or at one with, the world around us. Our drive for knowledge allows us, first of all, to get along in the world; on the level of "common sense," we are able to attain insight into concrete situations and to use the world for our immediate purposes, to support our survival and meet our bodily needs. But we find that we are also able to go beyond the level of immediately practical, manipulative knowledge; we are able to ask about the nature of things, to seek to understand what they are in themselves. In short, man seeks and attains scientific knowledge of the world. We are able to hone our questioning ability into a method, establish criteria for evidence, formulate and clarify our insights, and build a body of knowledge which in the course of time gives man an overall view of the world we inhabit.[28] Through this second, scientific mode of knowing, man enters into the world of theory.

Within this theoretical realm, man seeks the intelligibility immanent in the data which the senses provide about the world. We seek an insight which goes beyond the relation of things to ourselves as subjects, and which regards their inner structure, their own immanent being. This sort of insight clarifies the relations of things to each other, rather than to the knower; it aims at uncovering the "forms" of things, their nature, their "definition" or essence: the "what is" of things.

Scientific knowledge formulates its grasp of the world's intelligibility first of all in classical laws and in definitions. These laws and definitions are, by their nature, abstract; that is, they do not regard individual events in their limitations of time and space, but leave aside what is merely individual to grasp the universal and permanent.

[Lonergan points out that we may observe in the formation of the laws of science the correct notion of "abstraction." Abstraction is not a matter of constructing an "impoverished replica of the concrete"; rather, it is a process of enriching the data of sensibility. There is first of all the enriching anticipation of an intelligibility to be added to sensible presentations: the expectation that there is something to be known or understood, and not a mere "brute multiplicity" of sensations. Then there is the erection of what Lonergan calls "heuristic structures": the process of naming the unknown, working out its properties from the data given, and using those properties to direct and order the scientific inquiry.[29] These anticipatory structures allow the attainment of insights which reveal in the given data what is significant: the essential, the "nature" of things, the formal cause or "form." Finally, there is the formulation of the intelligibility reached by understanding. "Only in this third moment does there appear the negative aspect of abstraction, namely, the omission of the insignificant, the irrelevant, the negligible, the incidental, the merely empirical residue."[30]]

Abstract scientific laws tell us of the nature of things, how they are and how they operate, "all things being equal." However, in the concrete, all things are not equal; there are elements in the situation which are irrelevant to the "nature" of things, but which affect their factual occurrence and interrelation.[31] Classical laws leave unexplained the "empirical residue," the non-systematic, the coincidental, the merely factual elements or circumstances which follow no law or systematic pattern. However, there is in man a drive for *complete* explanation; we are not satisfied with knowing the "natures" of things; we wish to understand their actual occurrence. Hence there arises also a science of the concrete world, a science which attempts to gain an understanding of the actual concatenation of causes in their non-systematic plurality. This science is that of statistical law, the science of probability. It is based on the inverse insight that, even if the intelligibility of an abstract system is not possible, we need not abandon the quest for understanding; for we can estimate the ideal frequency of the occurrence of events; and although such an ideal frequency does not give an infallible prediction of their occurrence, nevertheless it gives us a norm from which the non-systematic cannot diverge in any systematic way.[32] Probability, then, gives us the general patterns (or laws) of the actual occurrence of events which are not systematized by abstract, classical laws, which can never take into account every aspect of a given situation, and therefore end up in a position of indeterminacy.[33]

What is most significant about the foregoing is the realization that the world is not to be understood by means of a single method, but by complementary methods; and these methods are not static, but dynamic in their relationship. What is unsystematic from one viewpoint or on one level may lend itself to systematization in a different way, or from a different perspective. Science understands the world, in fact, not from a single horizon, but as a series of dynamically related *higher viewpoints*.[34] This means that there are successive levels of scientific inquiry, each higher step of which is necessary in order to systematize what is merely coincidental on a lower level. That is, science must recognize a real hierarchy of intelligibilities in the world. An event which on the level of physical laws, for example, is merely chance or coincidental, may be subject to laws of its own, on a higher (e.g., biological) level.

[A concrete example may serve to clarify this notion. On the level of the physical understanding of the universe, there is a "law" of gravity: things do not spontaneously move upward, but stay in place. According to the first law of motion, bodies at rest tend to stay at rest. Since this law is abstract, however, it cannot take into account every concrete situation, with its plurality of factors. The law therefore holds in general; there is a small probability that a particular thing, because of a confluence of factors unforeseen by the "law," may at some particular moment be found "in opposition" to gravity or the first law of motion. Thus, Gilbert N. Lewis found in 1926 that an object of one-one hundred millionth of a gram, if observed once per second, will be found one ten-millionth of a centimeter above a table, 6.32 times in every million years.[35] The probability of a larger object rising from a table is so small that it is negligible. Yet this immensely improbable event (physically speaking) is in fact happening all the time; because there exist in the world biological agents who exert energy (work) in order to move objects which, physically speaking, should remain immobile. That is, the physical laws do not give us a complete picture of the world; they abstract (at this level) from the work which proceeds from living agents. The movements produced by such agents are, from the standpoint of the first law of motion, merely coincidental; the law abstracts from them. Yet they are not simply non-systematic; but to understand them, one must proceed beyond the merely physical, to the level of biological causality and its laws.]

There are therefore successive levels of scientific inquiry, each of which systematizes and understands what is merely coincidental, unexplained, on a lower level. At the same time, the lower levels remain intact when they are transcended by the higher. We may then understand the world as from a series of higher viewpoints, each adding to the last a further dimension of explanation:

???

↑

"spiritual" intelligibility

↑

psychological intelligibility

↑

biological intelligibility

↑

chemical intelligibility

↑

physical intelligibility

The importance of this understanding of the world's intelligibility is that it eliminates any form of reductionism, in which the explanation of the world would be *a priori* limited to some particular level, be it material, biological, or psychological. The higher levels of intelligibility truly depend upon the lower, but they cannot be fully explained in terms of the latter alone; there is a "surplus" which demands a new level of synthesis. As Lonergan puts it:

> If the non-systematic exists on the level of physics, then on that level there are coincidental manifolds that can be systematized by a higher chemical level without violating any physical law. If the non-systematic exists on the level of chemistry, then on that level there are coincidental manifolds that can by systematized by a higher biological level without violating any chemical law. If the non-systematic exists on the level of biology, then on that level there are coincidental manifolds that can be systematized by a higher psychic level without violating any biological law. If the non-systematic exists on the level of the psyche, then on that level there are coincidental manifolds that can be systematized by a higher level of insight and reflection, deliberation and choice, without violating any law of the psyche. . . . Again, an acknowledgement that the real is the verified makes it possible to affirm the reality no less of the higher system than of the underlying manifold. The chemical is as real as the physical; the biological as real as the chemical; the psychic as real as the biological; and insight as real as the psychic.[36]

Such an explanation defends against what Teilhard names *l'illusion matérialiste:* a world view which sees the elements of analysis as more "real" than the terms of synthesis. On the contrary, the notion of higher viewpoints implies that the whole is greater than its parts; there is a further intelligibility to human life, for example, than to the sum of its material, biological, and psychological components. Thus we must reject any system—such as a grosser form of materialism, reducing all being to physical reality and mechanics,[37] or a Freudian or behaviorist psychologism, reducing all human activity to the interplay of psychic forces—which sets an *a priori* limit to the explanation of reality, and thereby ignores a portion of the data of experience.

The recognition of a series of higher viewpoints as the mode of explaining the world also eliminates the opposite error to reductionism: what we might call "the spiritualist illusion." For the lower manifolds of intelligibility *remain intact* within the higher,[38] so that, in order to understand the higher, more comprehensive levels of existence, one must also account for the lower, upon which the higher continually depend. So the spiritual level of life in man as questioner and lover is always supported by corporeity, environment, spatio-temporal encounter, sense experience; its activities are never "purely" spiritual, but are the acts of spirit-in-matter. Thus no explanation of man as spirit can be complete or adequate which entirely subsumes the lower elements into the higher, neglecting the necessary aspects of bodiliness, intercommunion, sociability, sensibility and aesthetics; and no notion of man's goal and perfection can be correct which moves away entirely from material being, as though man were a "Platonic" pure spirit. Rather, spirit in man must be regarded as the perfection and higher synthesis *of* the material and psychological substrata.

Scientific explanation reveals, moreover, that the world is dynamic not only in intelligibility, but also temporally, i.e., it is a succession of higher steps. The world is a process, an evolution. The higher levels of existence not only depend upon the lower; they also come out of them. The world and its events form a progressive system which tends to ever greater complexity; from simple elements to more complex, from complex elements to compounds of ever increasing intricacy, until in matter there appears the possibility of life; and within the sphere of living matter, the process continues: from elementary forms, like viruses, which barely manifest themselves as living, through the multifarious species of the plant kingdom, to the strange one-celled creatures that seem to mediate between the plant and animal forms of life, to the various species of animals, with ever more intricate nervous systems, with rudimentary or more advanced social relationships, systems of communications, and abilities to manipulate their environment, until there arises the possibility of thought in the mind of man and society. As Teilhard points out, the process of evolution is an upward movement toward ever greater self-presence or self-possession: from the merely spatial and material provisional unity of inanimate objects, to the rudimentary perceptions of plants, to sensation and spontaneity in the higher animals, and finally to the real self-presence and self-determination, in openness to the other, which we experience in ourselves as persons. The interior unity which is present in the material becomes qualitatively different in each successive stage, until it attains to the level of subjectivity, interiority, in which reality becomes luminous, becomes for the first time a real "self."

The recognition that the world is dynamic and evolutionary

also means that we may see in the world a process analogous to what we experience in ourselves as "transcendence." That is, the world as a whole is "open"; it develops in stages that surpass themselves. Things are not merely themselves, but are in potency to go beyond themselves, to be the material for a new and higher form of being. The dynamic self-transcendence we have noted in man's nature as "question" is not entirely novel or foreign to the universe as a whole; there is, rather, a basic continuity, in that nature itself manifests a process of "seeking" newer forms of being and higher modes of self-possession. Man appears to be simply the highest point in this process in which matter progresses toward meaning.

The working out of this process seems to follow a pattern of what Teilhard calls "directed chance"; the possibility of higher forms arises from chance mutations, which attain survival and pre-dominance through Darwinian natural selection. Lonergan charac-terizes this world-order as a system of "emergent probability" ("the successive realization in accord with successive schedules of proba-bility of a conditioned series of schemes of recurrence").[39] That is, on each level of evolution there is a certain probability for the accidental mutations which would give rise to a new form of being. Once such changes take place, a new series of probabilities arises for yet higher forms, which had no chance of occurring from the lower level alone.

[For example: the probability of one-celled animals gathering together in an accidental grouping and forming the complex organ-ism of a man is nil. But there is a significant probability of such one-celled animals forming several-celled forms of life; and once multiple-celled life occurs, there *emerges* a new probability of spe-cialization of functions. From simple organisms with specialization, there emerges, on successive levels, the probabilities of higher organisms, until at last there emerges a form of being capable of the necessary mutations to produce man. Moreover, this process re-gards not simply individual entities, but whole series of interrelated entities which depend on each other—for example the cycle of plant life. Upon this recurrent cycle depends the whole cycle of animal life, with its own interdependencies; and upon this cycle depend the probabilities which permit the emergence of man.[40]]

The actual order of the world depends on the occurrence of events which are probable in evolution; but every probability is not present, so to speak, from the beginning. Rather, further probabilities emerge as the world becomes increasingly complex and ordered.

In this explanation of the world process, we see a universe which becomes increasingly systematic, with each level of systematization leading to the production of yet higher orderings of being. Yet, at the same time, the process admits of breakdowns and evolutionary "dead ends," because the emergence of each new level is only probably, and not absolutely necessary.[41] Nevertheless, on the whole, the process must go forward, because, given sufficient time, the probable collocations of circumstances necessary for progress must eventually occur.[42]

THE QUESTION ABOUT MEANING

> *You have made him little less than God,*
> *and crowned him with glory and honor.*
> *You have given him dominion over the works of your hands;*
> *you have put all things under his feet,*
> *all sheep and oxen,*
> *and also the beasts of the field,*
> *the birds of the air, and the fish of the sea,*
> *whatever passes along the paths of the sea.*   Ps. 8

There are two of us in the room: my dog and I. . . . Outside, a frightful storm is blowing. The dog sits near me and looks straight into my eyes. And I also look into its eyes. Without words, it wishes to say something to me. It can't speak; it has no words; it does not understand itself; but I understand it. I understand that at this instant there lives in it and in me one and the same feeling; that there is absolutely no difference between us. We are identical; in each of us, there burns and shines forth the same flickering flame.

Death flies by; flaps its cold, wide wings . . . and it's over. Afterwards, who can differentiate which flame burned respectively in each of us? No! It is not an animal and a man who exchange glances . . . it is two pairs of identical eyes directed at each other.

And in each of those pairs, in the animal and in the man, one and the same life huddles together, frightened, with the other.

Turgenev: "The Dog"

A world which is constituted by an upward dynamism appears to manifest finality; it seems to be going somewhere, to have a goal. Behind the whole process of natural selection and evolution—a process which works against the natural inertia of physics[43]—there appears to be some kind of purposiveness. The world is moving somewhere; but where? In the words of Teilhard:

> The unity of the world is of a dynamic or evolutionary nature. . . . Thus the whole Universe, as well as each element within it, is defined for me by a particular movement which animates it. But what can this movement be? Where is it taking us? In facing this question, I find the suggestions and the evidence gathered throughout the course of my professional researches moving and coming together. And it is as an historian of Life, at least as much as a philosopher, that I reply, from the depths of my reason and from the depths of my heart: "It is moving toward Spirit."[44]

In effect, it appears that the high point of evolution, the goal of its dynamism, is the production of man, of that creature in which evolution becomes conscious of itself, determinative of itself, and hence reaches the domain of "spirit." Man is that being in whom the world comes to itself, exists for itself; in man, matter attains to meaning. The whole striving of the physical world, its entire upward motion, seems to culminate in the production of an animal which is intelligent and free, and which therefore sums up and comprehends the world within itself.[45]

The evolutionary world-view, therefore, presents a perspective of great significance for the consideration of the relationship between human spirit and the material world. In the evolutive process, what transcends is always in strict continuity with what came before, so that even the highest being (despite its newness and real superiority) is to be seen as a change *in* something already existing prior.[46] The emergence of spiritual being in man is to be regarded not as an exception, but rather as a particular and highest case of a transcending which is observable in the universe as a whole (and all of which, not only man, calls out for explanation).[47] Human spirit and world are strictly interrelated: man is the highest product—thus far—of the world's striving. If man is the evolving world come to consciousness of itself, humanity in a sense "contains" within itself, by virtue of consciousness, the whole process which produced it.

[Thus Pascal writes, in a famous passage: "Thought is what constitutes the grandeur of man. Man is nothing but a reed, the most feeble in nature; but he is a thinking reed. It is not necessary for the entire universe to take up arms to crush him: a vapor, a drop of water, is enough to kill him. But, even if the universe were to crush him, man would still be more noble than what destroys him, because man knows that he dies, and recognizes the advantage that the universe has over him; and the universe knows nothing about it. . . . Spatially, the universe contains me, and swallows me up like a point; but in thought, I contain the universe."[48]]

The meaning of the world depends upon the meaning of man, for humanity is its summit, and its sole part which can reflect upon itself and others, and can therefore ask about meaning, can be a question to existence, seek for sense in being. It is this virtual infinity of his mind, this openness to meaning, by which man's life is a "question," that constitutes man's greatness:

> What a piece of work is man! How noble in reason! how infinite in faculty! in form, in moving, how express and admirable! in action how like an angel! in apprehension how like a god! the beauty of the world! the paragon of animals! (*Hamlet*, II ii)

It is this which constitutes man's essential difference from the rest of the universe, and mankind's right to mastery over nature.[49]

But, by the same token, man is—even as spirit—also a part of the world. Humankind contains within itself its own pre-history as matter, without which we cannot exist at all. Well did St. Francis speak of "brother" fire, "sister" water, earth our "mother," and "sister death." Man must remember that we belong to the material world; for all our crucial differences and our legitimate mastery, we must avoid the hybris of separating ourselves and setting ourselves outside and above the whole.[50]

[Boris Pasternak, in the great tradition of so much of Russian literature, represented by Turgenev, Fet, Alexei and Lev Tolstoi, Dostoievski, etc., combines a vivid appreciation of the existential difference of man from all unconscious being, with a deep sense of almost mystical unity with nature. Reflecting on the love of Zhivago (the name signifies "the living one" [cf. Lk. 24:5] in Old Church Slavonic) for Lara, he writes:

> Never, never, even in their moments of richest and wildest happiness, were they unaware of a sublime joy in the total design of the universe, a feeling that they themselves were a part of that whole, an element in the beauty of the cosmos.

> This unity with the whole was the breath of life to them. And the elevation of man above the rest of nature, the modern coddling and worshiping of man, never appealed to them. A social system based on such a false premise, as well as its political application, struck them as pathetically amateurish and made no sense to them.[51]]

Because he stands at the summit of evolution, man is not only master of the world, but also its servant: we exist for the world; our mission is to bring it to consciousness, to give it the unity of awareness, to extend its being into the world of spirit, the personal. Moreover, man must have a sense of humility in the realization that we alone can bring real tragedy into the world. For humanity can destroy the world which produced it. As our mastery of the world increases, man's intelligent action becomes more and more crucial to the working of nature's schemes of recurrence. As we harness nature to our own ends, the requisite probabilities for survival and further evolution no longer arise automatically, but as the result of human planning.[52] The very existence of lower cycles comes to depend largely upon human decisions; the survival or disappearance of species, the balance of agricultural cycles, the composition of the atmosphere, are in man's hands, for good or ill. If mankind were to bring calamity upon itself—by nuclear war, for example, or continued pollution of the biosphere, or unchecked depletion of natural resources—the whole of earth's life, and not only man's, would find itself in peril.

Man may also fail in his evolutionary purpose by refusing our own humanization—by failing to act as a person, in accord with the demands of consciousness for intelligence and love. As Lonergan notes, "to equip an animal with intelligence constitutes not only the possibility of culture and science, but also the possibility of every abomination that has occurred in the course of human history."[53] Man's inhumanity and evil behavior is often called "brutal," or animal-like; and, in a sense, this is so. Yet because of the essential difference of consciousness, man's failures do not merely reduce humanity to a lower (but in itself ignorant and innocent) level of animal life, but comport a tragic dimension not possible in the natural conflicts and breakdowns of an evolving world. If man alone can recognize existence and rejoice in it, it is also true that man alone can despair, and find nausea in being.

Finally, in man, the living question, the whole world becomes a question. Man not only asks about the factual structure of the world; we also ask about its ultimate intelligibility, the reason for its existence, and its relationship with our own conscious being, and our own reason for existing. The question about the world becomes the question of meaning. The meaning of the world, as we have said, depends in the last analysis upon the meaning of man. But does man have meaning?

The immanent intelligibility of the world raises for consciousness the problem of the sense of the transcendence we have uncovered. How and why is transcendence possible? How can a radically higher reality come out of a lower? How can matter be the prehistory of spirit? How is it possible for the goal of the world's development to be something irreducibly new, which would seem beyond the powers of the substratum to foresee or to produce? For as we have noted, it is not merely a question of a higher stage being "added on" to the lower; it must be enacted *by* the lower stage, which in this very act transcends itself. If we rejected reductionism, we must admit that the world process includes "quantum leaps": what Teilhard calls "thresholds," or "critical points," where a qualitatively different form of being comes into existence,[54] with an "ontological surplus value" over its antecedents.[55]

The world therefore seems to show an upward directedness: a finality. Lower beings are in potency to become actualized at a higher level, which in turn is a new potentiality. In short, the world seems to be a directed dynamism. But how can unconscious being have a finality, a purposefulness? How is it that the world be unconscious and unintelligent, and yet work toward the goal of conscious intelligence (spirit), entering into more complex and systematic forms, contrary to the physical laws of equilibrium and entropy, which demand that all systems tend toward their simplest and most diffuse state? Or is the whole notion of progress and finality in the universe merely a *projection* of man's mind onto an uncaring, unfeeling, and purposeless world?

Here we have reached the final question of meaning, or of the *ultimate* intelligibility of the world. It reaches its culmination in the question of man. Is the existence of human spirit, the apparent goal of the evolutionary process, meaningful, and therefore does the process itself manifest meaning—or is spirit itself ultimately unintelligible, and its intimations of purposefulness in the world likewise void of sense? Is the demand for intelligibility itself groundless? Is human consciousness the greatness and pride of the universe—or is it ultimately an aberration: is man a sick animal, who not only must die, but who is also condemned to the anguish of being conscious of it? Is man "at home" in a cosmos which is spirit-directed, or are we "thrown" into existence in an alien world,[56] condemned to consciousness and freedom? Is our perspective to be that of Psalm 8, with its elevation of man, or of Turgenev's solitary thinker, meditating on the final equality of all life, which must end in annihilation?

The question of meaning asks where the world is finally going through its highest product, spiritual being. Does spiritual life —consciousness—have a purpose, a goal, an intelligibility—or is its evolution a senseless accident, with no ultimate meaning? Must we finally agree with Bertrand Russell:

> That man is the product of causes which had no prevision of the end they were achieving; that his origin, his growth, his hopes and fears, his loves and his beliefs, are but the outcome of accidental collocations of atoms; that no fire, no heroism, no intensity of thought and feeling, can preserve an individual life beyond the grave; that all the labor of the ages, all the devotion, all the inspiration, all the noonday brightness of human genius, are destined to extinction in the vast death of the solar system, and that the whole temple of man's achievement must inevitably be buried beneath the debris of a universe in ruins—all these things, if not quite beyond dispute, are yet so nearly certain that no philosophy which rejects them can hope to stand. Only within the scaffolding of these truths, only on the firm foundation of unyielding despair, can the soul's habitation henceforth be safely built.[57]

Or is there, in Teilhard's phrase, an "Omega point," beyond the apparently inevitable fate of the physical world: an ultimate transformation of man to a higher form of being, a new stage of transcendence or evolution which gives an ultimate direction, purpose, and intelligibility to the whole?

The question of ultimate meaning, then, in the last resort comes down to the question of a ground for the reality and intelligibility of transcendence, both in the world and in man. This ground would be the answer not merely to man's questions about the world, but, more profoundly, the answer to the question which humanity itself is, and which results in our radical drive to know and love. The question about a transcendence beyond the world and man, a reality which might give sense to the world-process and to man's own search for meaning, does not occur in an intellectual vacuum. From immemorial times and in all cultures people have affirmed an answer to this question in the form of metaphysical and religious convictions. The question of ultimate meaning, in short, raises the question of God, the absolute ground of being.

THE QUESTION ABOUT GOD

Then Moses said to God, "If I come to the people of Israel and say to them, 'The God of your fathers has sent me to you,' and they ask me, 'What is his name?' what shall I say to them?" God said to Moses, "I AM WHO I AM." And he said, "Say this to the people of Israel, 'I AM has sent me to you.'"

Ex. 4:13–14

The crisis of the human situation, the ground of our need, is God.

Emil Brunner

Prior to the scientific, critical question about the meaning and value of human life, there exists the extistential question which life itself *is;* and prior to the philosophical-theological attempt to respond to the thematic question, there are already profound convictions and hopes regarding the existence of an "answer" to man's being, an absolute ground of being, value, and meaning. This absolute ground or ultimate Reality is called in many different ways in diverse cultures and epochs: God; Being; the "really Real"; the gods; Nirvana; the "Way"; "Heaven"—these are among the words which have been used to speak of it. It has been conceived as personal and as impersonal, or as supra-personal; as singular or plural; in both religious and metaphysical terms; in the language of myth and symbol and in that of technical thought; in affirmation and in negation. What unites all of these expressions, on a level beyond the conceptual and linguistic differences, is that they *intend* or refer to the source and meaning of the *totality* of existence: the most ultimate reality, the "answer" to man's deepest question.

THE EXISTENCE OF THE WORD "GOD"

As Karl Rahner points out in his brief but profound "meditation" on the word "God,"[58] the very existence of such a word—or words[59]—is of great significance. For by its very nature the absolute ground of reality cannot be an "object" of human experience in the way that "things" in the world are. The objects of empirical experience "force" themselves upon us, and demand to be named if we are to deal with them effectively; we must have words for them because they are "there." God, on the other hand, is not "there"; an ultimate ground or explanation and goal of transcendence is not obvious or palpable; it does not "force" itself upon our awareness. Yet the fact remains that man has—and throughout recorded history, in every society, has always had—the word "God," in some form or other. Although God is not an object of human experience, the conception of God—at least as a question—seems unavoidable for man. As Rahner points out, even the atheist's position with regard to ultimate meaning (or meaninglessness) must be defined with reference to the notion and the word "God." To avoid it, one would have to remain entirely silent on the question of man's final status and the significance of existence.[60]

What Kind of Word is "God"?[61]

[The word "God" immediately causes problems, even from a linguistic point of view. (I refer, of course, not only to the English word and its equivalents, but to all words which intend the ultimate or absolute reality, *mutatis mutandis*). Any word which refers to the absolute being, transcendent to the empirical world and grounding its existence and meaning, must of necessity be a unique word; it designates a reality which is, by definition, not contained within or comparable to the things normally referred to by language. Hence, the word "God" is extremely difficult to categorize.

At first glance, "God" seems to be, or at least to show strong similarity to, a proper name: it is used grammatically as subject and object in sentences; it is spelled (in most Western languages) with a majuscule, as are proper names; it is used without a definite or indefinite article; it has no plural. Furthermore, the use of the word "God," at least in religious discourse, the "language game" of religious people, strongly parallels the way proper names are used. In prayer, the word seems to address another; in theological discourse, it is used to talk about him. It also seems, like names, to identify its referent by certain characteristics of his "personality." "God" has certain personal qualities which mark him, which make him *this* person; there are criteria for saying that God is or is not "like that" (in normal religious discourse, such "attributes" would include goodness, holiness, unity, power, etc.).

On the other hand, there are marked differences between the word "God" and normal proper names. First of all, we note that the word "God" can be translated from language to language, while proper names cannot. As we have already seen, there are many words which are commonly recognized as referring to the same divine reality, differing only verbally. The more basic difference of the word "God" from proper names is what lies behind its translat-ability: namely, the fact that "God" contains some kind of informa-tive content, which proper names (at least in modern languages) do not. A name, as we have said, identifies its referent; but it does so by "pointing" to him/her. The qualities which serve as criteria for identification are not contained in the name itself, which is merely a verbal sign or indicator. The word "God," however, clearly has some kind of content or *meaning,* as have concepts (as distinct from proper names).[62] Exactly what that "content" is, at this point, is not clear, and, indeed, may possibly vary with different languages and conceptual systems. Moreover, it is apparent that the word "God," if it has some "conceptual" elements, is nevertheless certainly not an ordinary concept or "common noun," but has unique and strange linguistic qualities, by the very fact of its unique referent.[63] At this point, however, we can at least say that the word "God" has meaning as a "heuristic" concept, whose "content" is the answer to the ultimate question about the meaning and value of existence.[64]

The characteristic of containing information about the subject it names might lead us to consider the word "God" as being more similar to a *title* than to a proper name. It is indeed similar in many respects to words which name functions and functionaries. (These, of course, are frequently very close to proper names, and often become them: names such as Smith [Schmidt, Kovac, etc.], Baker, Kaufmann, etc., are remnants of functional titles devolved into personal names). The similarity is heightened when we consider titles which designate a unique functionary: *the* King; *the* Pope. Such titles not only name, but also contain information concerning a person. Furthermore, they are relational: they tell us not only about the person "in se," but also about his/her relation to the speaker and about the context of discourse: the social situation or structure in which the title and function have meaning. We find that such "functional" titles are often used in religious language to describe further the functional word "God": God is King, Shepherd, Lord, Teacher, Maker, etc. Like these titles, the word "God" itself has meaning only in a relational context; as we shall see,[65] we cannot speak to God without speaking at the same time about ourselves and our relation to him. "God" therefore seems to combine the features of a proper name, in its uniqueness, and of a title, in its informative, functional, and relational character.

The word "God" also functions in some respects like a pronoun: I, you, he, she, etc. It is analogous to the experience of personality which pronouns express. What is meant by "God" is that which lies at the deepest level of selfhood, of person: God is the absolute "I," the absolute "self"—that which, in Augustine's formula, is closer to me than I am to myself (an intuition which is also expressed—albeit in a different metaphysical framework—in the Hindu statement of the fundamental identity of Atman and Brahman). Like the word "I," the word "God" does not refer to an object, but to a transcendental experience which is the condition of possibility for the experience of objects.[66] God is also the absolute case of a "Thou": the word refers not to an object or thing, but to a presence over against my subjectivity, a presence which presents itself as likewise "subjective" and as calling me to dialogue. In this sense, Karl Heim remarks that God can only properly be spoken of "in the second person, so that what I say is always said *to* him. . . ."[67] For the religious man, the referent of the word "God" is only really met when we stand in relation to that reality, when it meets us in the mystery of personal confrontation. Otherwise, we are missing the real meaning of "God."[68]

The notion of "God" as "pronoun" fits well with the tradition of "negative" theology: not only the word "God" itself, but all that we say "about" God fails to express what God is.[69] Nevertheless, what the word expresses is not "nothing"; not a mere void or absence; not a pure indeterminacy, nor an identity with the subject and the world (pantheism); but an experience which is *encounter* with mystery. In this sense, it is truly analogous to our experience of the "I" as the (transcendental) center of a world, or to the deepest experience of a "Thou" in dialogue. What is expressed is a transcendental experience, not an objective one; its "content," therefore, cannot be contained by a name or concept, but can only be "pointed to," confronted, and addressed. In this respect the word "God" is much like demonstrative words: "this," "that" (always remembering that the "this" referred to is an experience of the transcendent, which with regard to all objective experience can be qualified as *not* "this")—or even like adverbs such as "here," "there," "beyond," etc.]

What Does This Word Signify?

The word "God" is more than a mere "personal name"; it contains some kind of information. On the other hand, it clearly does not tell us what God *is*. In fact, the principal "content" of the word seems to be the indication that we are speaking here precisely about the unsayable, the "nameless," the transcendent one who (which) is "behind" or "beyond" the reality of the world, not "in" it as an element; that Reality which gives meaning and value, sense and purpose, to existence: the being which Rahner calls, in abbreviated form, the "Holy Mystery."[70]

If it is difficult to state precisely the conceptual meaning of the word "God," except in negative terms, it is more easy to define its *functional* meaning: how this word operates, what it does for man. The function of the word "God" is to place man before the whole of reality and the whole of our own existence; it contrasts man as "a" being with Being itself in its completeness. It thus confronts man with the question of the ultimate meaning and value of experience of consciousness, which is itself, as we have seen, a seeking for meaning and value; it concerns, therefore, the meaning of meaning, the value of value-seeking: the ground of what is deepest in man's experience of conscious subjectivity or spirit.

For this reason, as Rahner points out, the word "God" must be absolutely unique; it is not just a word among many, but *the* word which signifies the source of all intelligibility, and therefore the ground of all "words." Ultimately, it is the ability to speak the word "God" which separates man as "spirit"—intellect and love—from merely animal consciousness. Man can exist as man only when we say the word "God," at least as a question—even if only a negated or rejected question. As long as man remains human, therefore, the word "God" must continue to exist, even if its meaning is denied; for without this word, man would cease to embody the question which constitutes our very essence as a conscious, caring being. We may say, then, that man, whom we have characterized as a living "question," in being a conscious seeker of meaning and value, is and must be, in the last analysis, a "question" *about God.*

III. THE GROUNDING OF TRANSCENDENCE WITHOUT GOD

The fool says in his heart: "There is no God."

—Ps. 14:1

Now this God is dead! You higher men, this God was your greatest danger.

It is only since he lay in grace that you have risen again. Only now the great noontide comes; only now the higher man becomes Lord!

Do you understand this saying, O my brothers? You are frightened: do your hearts fail you? Does the abyss yawn at your feet? Does the hound of hell bay at you?

What of it? Forward! Higher men! Now at last the mountain of man's future is about to give birth. God is dead; now it is our will that the Superman shall live.

—Friedrich Nietzsche,
Thus Spoke Zarathustra (Part IV)

ALTERNATIVES TO FAITH IN GOD

The very existence of the word "God," taken in its deepest and most proper meaning, places before man's consciousness the experience of "transcendence"—the fact that man's project of being in the world takes place through a self-awareness which opens onto an apparently limitless horizon. The notion of "God" is the attempt to speak of the ground of that transcendent experience; and hence, as long as man is true to humanity, as long as we question about the meaning and value of existence as a whole, the idea of God must have a future, at least as man's deepest question. Nevertheless, the existence and perdurance of the word "God" does not, of itself and

44

without further ado, demonstrate that such a supreme reality and ground of transcendence does in fact exist. The *question* about God is a necessary component of man's humanity; but a positive answer to the question is not *eo ipso* assured.

In fact, despite the overwhelming preponderance of belief in a supreme reality of some sort in human history, there exist also agnostic and negative replies to the question about ultimate meaning. It is first of all possible for individual persons, if not for mankind as a whole, to avoid posing the question of God in its full seriousness.[1] People may neglect to advert to the experience of transcendence; or may take it and its traditional (religious) explanation for granted; or may more or less purposely avoid asking a question with so many profound and perhaps disturbing implications; or may indeed deny the reality of the experience itself, and thus the value of even asking about its ground and meaning. In any of these cases, the question of God is avoided only at the cost of the effective denial of man as "spirit" and as transcendence. On the other hand, there exist forms of thought which attempt to come to terms with man as "spirit" and to give a basis for "transcendence" without reference to an ultimate or absolute Transcendent, "God." Although we must later return to this subject at greater length, a brief look at several such attempts may serve for the moment to exemplify the tendencies of an explicitly non-theistic grounding of transcendence.

"ATHEISTIC" FORMS OF RELIGION IN THE HINDU AND BUDDHIST TRADITION

> *Yet these men are little to be blamed,*
> *for perhaps they go astray while seeking God and desiring to*
> *   find him.*
> *For as they live among his works they keep searching,*
> *and they trust in what they see, because the things that are seen*
> *   are beautiful.*
> *Yet again, not even they are to be excused;*
> *for if they had the power to know so much*
> *that they could investigate the world,*
> *how did they fail to find sooner the Lord of these things?*

Wis. 13:7–9

Proof of God's existence is not possible, because he can be neither free nor bound, nor anything else. . . . If bound, he cannot be Iśvara (God), owing to the conjunction of merit and demerit. If free, he cannot be the agent or doer, on account of the absence of particular cognitions and desire to act and effect. Hence Iśvara cannot be proven. Either way, also, he would be inefficient. If he were free, he would be unequal to the task of creation, etc., as he would not possess the will-to-be and the will-to-do, desires, etc., which instigate to creation. And again, if he were bound, he would be under delusion, and so unequal to the task of creation. . . .

The sacred texts which speak of God are either glorifications of the free self or homage paid to the perfect ones.

Sāṁkhya-Pravacana Sūtra, Vṛtti and Bhāṣya

Some forms of the non-theistic approaches to the grounding of human transcendence have been explicitly "religious." Several such "atheistic" religious interpretations of existence are found within Hinduism and Buddhism.[2] Of the six "orthodox" schools of Hindu theology or philosophy, the recognized interpretations of the Vedic religion, several are non-theistic, in the sense of not referring to, or even plainly denying, a supra-human Absolute or God as the ultimate explanation or cause or end of the universe and man. In one school (the Purva Mimamsa) we even find "proofs" of the non-existence of God. In the Sāṁkhya school of Hinduism, which we shall take as our example, we find an explicitly non-theistic system, in which there is no place for a supreme being. The Vedas are accepted as sacred books, and the existence of the lesser gods is presumed; but these are not the ultimate reality, and share the same basic lot as man. According to Sāṁkhya teaching (probably originating ca. the seventh century B.C.), there exist two eternal and uncreated substances: puruṣa, the "soul" or subject, and prakṛti, "matter" or nature or objective reality. "Souls" are conceived not as the creation of God, nor as participating in some ultimate and all-encompassing spiritual being, as in other Hindu systems, but rather as an infinite number of individual "monads," eternally self-subsistent. These souls do not change in themselves, but they enact change upon matter through their presence, thus effecting the evolutionary process of the world. It is the union of puruṣa with prakṛti which produces "life" as we know it: sentient individuals with self-awareness and knowledge of objects outside themselves. But the real "self" or individual is not the phenomenal self, the psychological ego, which is material and mutable; it is, rather, a "pure" spiritual consciousness, without objects, silent, alone, peaceful and eternal. Consciousness and individuality as we know them are laden with pain. The goal of religion is to release the real self from the bondage which causes pain, through the illuminating knowledge of the differentiation and independence of the soul from matter. When the bond of captivity to matter is broken, the pure puruṣa continues to exist; but it returns to a state of pure, objectless consciousness, with no material basis for any knowledge outside itself; it might be likened to a pure light, which shines but illumines nothing. The final and eternal reality is a multitude of unrelated, independent and eternal monads, each existing entirely for and in itself alone. The means for man to attain this state is the practice of meditation and Yoga, leading to a purified and empty consciousness. Sāṁkhya thus preaches a sort of transcendental egotism, interpreting man's deepest spiritual experience of transcendence over the world as a non-objective, non-dialogical escape from the material and illusory existence of this life. There is clearly no room for "God" in this system, since the ultimate reality is conceived of as plural and not united, and each puruṣa is a kind of "god" to itself: a self-caused and self-sufficient existence.

A religious yet non-theistic approach to the reality of spirit and transcendence also characterizes certain forms of Buddhism, in particular some associated with the "Hinayana" or Theravada schools.[3] This predominantly southern Asian form of Buddhism is probably closer to the teaching of the historical Buddha than is the more widely extended and later Mahayana tradition of China, Japan, and Tibet. The doctrine of the non-theistic forms is based upon the Buddha's pragmatic religious philosophy, in which transcendence is seen above all as escape from the pain of existence. Modern Hinayana teaching is, for the most part, ambiguous with regard to the existence and nature of ultimate reality; and this ambiguity may probably be traced to Gautama, the Buddha, himself.

A statement of the teaching of the historical Buddha (floruit ca. 500 B.C.) is made difficult by the fact that all of the sacred texts are considerably later than his lifetime; but the evidence of the scriptures is that the historical Buddha rejected and condemned speculation about metaphysics, the ultimate ground of existence, God, or the final state of human spirit. What he preaches is something better and more useful to man: a knowledge of the origin and end of sensation (i.e., pain), and the way of avoiding it (namely, the eradication of desire). The Buddha's teaching appears to be essentially a practical philosophy, and is agnostic on ultimate questions, including the precise nature of the state of "Nirvana" which is man's goal. Such matters are "questions which tend not to edification."[4]

That the Buddha was "agnostic" in his teaching about ultimate reality or God is undisputed; but there are diverse interpretations of the meaning of his silence. One reading would take Buddha's agnosticism literally: he really did not know or care about the ultimate; his doctrine was completely pragmatic, having no further metaphysical implications. The "Nirvana" which is the Buddhist's goal would refer simply to the achievement of the cessation of the pain of existence; it has no mystical or divine implications at all, nor should it be taken as some kind of cipher for "eternal life." This opinion is held principally by certain European historians and scholars; it is not that of practicing religious Buddhists. Even for the latter, however, the Buddha's real meaning is not unambiguous. A second interpretation would hold that the Buddha's silence hides a *positive* answer to the question about ultimate reality. In this view, which is that of most "popular" Buddhism as well as of some of the monks, the Buddha himself is a divine being, the Tathagata, who is omniscient. The doctrine of Gautama and his silence about God must be understood in the context of religious Hinduism, out of which he comes: although he proclaims no metaphysical doctrine, he presupposes a belief in an ultimate reality which is (in the broad sense, at least) theistic. In this interpretation, Nirvana would be a positive thing: not merely release from pain, but the attainment of (or union with) that being which is pointed to by the mystics. The Buddha's refusal to speak of "God" stems from the fact that the eternal Being is so transcendent to man's earthly life that no positive statement can be made about it. Like the Upanishads and the teachings of the Hindu mystics, Buddha's silence would represent a "negative theology." Moreover, since nothing positive can be said about the Absolute, even to raise the question becomes a distraction from man's salvation, which must be attained by the practical exercise of attention to the problem of pain and its solution by the extermination of desire.

Finally, in a third interpretation Buddha's agnosticism is held to cover a *negative* answer to the question of "God." The Buddha's teaching does indeed come out of Hinduism, but not the theistic Hinduism of the modern period, nor the pantheistic or monist schools of the Vedanta; rather, we must look for its context in the ancient Sāṁkhya philosophy discussed above. (It is in fact undoubtable that some of the present Buddhist scriptures bear notable similarities to the Sāmkhya doctrines.) Buddha therefore presupposes the ultimate unreality of the "ego" as lived on earth, and a notion of "salvation" whose content is essentially release or escape from the false "selfhood" of worldly existence. If this is so, then Buddha's silence about ultimate reality stems from the fact that no terms taken from this world, corrupted with matter, can apply to the pure final state of "spirit." The entirety of "reality" as we know it is mere illusion, produced by a temporary mixture of spirit with the elements of material being. In Nirvana, these do not exist; and hence, we have no ground whatsoever to speak of spirit's final condition (which, ultimately, is also its "real" present and eternal state, since the phenomenal ego and its world are illusory). According to this interpretation, the Buddha would be atheistic, like the Sāmkhya school; Nirvana means the annihilation of the phenomenal ego, being "blown out," as the word implies etymologically.[5] This interpretation is the one which seems best to fit the sacred texts of the Theravada as they now stand (although it is quite possible that the present scriptures, all much later than the Buddha, represent the addition of a Sāmkhya-like metaphysics to an original pure pragmatism); and it is the principal interpretation held by the order of monks in the strict Theravada tradition.

Whatever may have been the context and implication of the Buddha's original doctrine, it is in any case clear that his teaching is primarily pragmatic in intent. Whether one believes in an ultimate Reality and Ground of being or not, and whether that ground is "God" or not, it is plain that for Buddha this reality (if it exists) has no relation to the "salvation" of the individual. Each person must rely on his/her own unaided effort to attain enlightenment and thus escape the misery of the world. The question of God or the hereafter is of no importance in this task, and speculation about them is therefore to be discouraged. If there is any implicit theism in Hinayana Buddhism, it is of a "deist" variety; personal dialogue or relation with the supreme Being is not seen as the content or means of salvation. Although at least the lesser "gods" of the Hindu pantheon are accepted as existing, they are irrelevant to the attainment of Nirvana. Hinayana Buddhism therefore represents at least a "practical" non-theism, in which spirit attains its goal without reference to an ultimate ground of transcendence.

In both the atheistic schools of orthodox Hinduism and in the agnostic or atheistic types of Buddhism (and its derivatives—e.g., some schools of Zen), we encounter religious interpretations of existence which recognize the primacy of "spirit" and the experience of "transcendence" in man, but do not ground these in an ultimate transcendent reality or God. It must immediately be noted, however, that these non-theistic forms of oriental religion are by no means the norm, even within their own traditions. On the contrary, both in Hinduism and in Buddhism we find a dissatisfaction with the negative and agnostic responses to the question of final meaning, and a tendency for these philosophical approaches to evolve into a religious worship of God.

The Sāṃkhya school (which scarcely exists today as an independent tradition) represents a philosophical type of Hinduism which has never been the popular religion, which has, on the contrary, always tended to theism and even, in some cases, to monotheism. The Yoga school, which is regarded in India as the "practical" counterpart of Sāṃkhya philosophy, explicitly speaks of the love of God. Even where the Sāṃkhya tradition is accepted in Hindu thought, there is a tendency to amalgamate its dualism with the monist doctrine of the Vedanta, and to see in the former a kind of lower and incomplete viewpoint which is subsumed into and completed by the theistic (or monist) religion.[6]

It is clear that Hindu systems like the Sāṃkhya which do not admit "God" nevertheless affirm the reality of spirit, of salvation, and of an ultimate "real" which is not identical with the empirical world. Such ideas are clearly not "atheistic" in the modern Western sense. Indeed, to consider the Sāṃkhya system "atheistic" in the sense of a *denial* of god would be an anachronism, since the notion of a transcendent Absolute or God in the philosophical sense was a later development than the Sāṃkhya system. The latter's ideas might rather be called "trans-polytheistic," in the sense that the mythological gods of popular religion are devalued in favor of the proclamation of an ultimate and transcendent reality, beyond the world (of which the polytheistic gods are a part), a reality to which each individual can attain by ascetical practice. What separates the Sāṃkhya school from the mainstream of Hindu tradition (and to a certain extent the same could be said of Jainism) is the doctrine that the absolute transcendent reality is *plural.* In this regard, however, it must be remembered that the Sāṃkhya school (like Jainism) represents an extremely ancient, probably pre-Aryan stage in Hindu philosophical speculation. (It has been noted that there are similarities between the Sāṃkhya doctrines and the teachings of the very early Greek philosophers Empedocles and Anaxagoras.)[7] This early stage was to be surpassed and integrated in the development of Vedanta metaphysics. This at least is the view of Hindus themselves. Radhakrishnan notes in his history of Indian philosophy that the Sāṁkhya system, with its emphasis on human psychology, has practically the same account of the world as the later "monist" metaphysical systems: "Only a pluralist prejudice which has no logical basis asserts itself, and we have a plurality of souls. When the pluralism collapses, as it does at the first touch of logic, the Sāṁkhya theory becomes identical with the pure monism."[8] The *Bhagavad Gita,* for example, identifies the Sāṁkhya's indestructible life-monad as being actually a "particle" of the supreme and personal Divine Being—essentially identical with him. "Thus, with one bold stroke, the transcendental monism of the Vedic Brahman doctrine of the Self is reconciled with the pluralist life-monad doctrine of the dualistic, atheistic Sāṁkhya; and so the two teachings now are understood in India as descriptions from two points of view of the same reality."[9] As the metaphysics of the Hindu tradition developed, a pluralist and individualist interpretation of transcendence was found to be inadequate, and the human experience was seen to demand an ultimate grounding in the One, the reality to which we refer by the word "God."

Somewhat similar remarks may be made with regard to the non-theistic interpretation of Buddhism. First of all, it must be emphasized that it is only the Theravada or Hinayana tradition which adheres to the (probably) more primitive, "agnostic" doctrine; in its extension through Asia, this earlier form gave way to the more elaborate and complex doctrines of the Mahayana, in which we find a Buddhology which is definitely "theistic" in character and metaphysical in its explanations of existence. Secondly, even within the Theravada tradition it would be misleading to speak of a thoroughly "atheistic" approach. With regard to the Buddha's original teaching, it would again probably be more accurate to speak of "trans-polytheism" than of atheism or agnosticism in the modern sense. As Professor Geoffrey Parrinder states: "It used to be maintained that early Buddhism was atheistic, but it is now realized that there was no generally accepted belief in a supreme God for the Buddha to deny."[10] The doctrine of the Buddha, so far as it is available to us, ignores the existence of a personal creator-god of the world; it presupposes the reality of the lesser god of the Hindu pantheon; but it never declares itself with regard to Brahman, the supreme Absolute of the Upanishads.[11] Nevertheless, early Buddhist texts speak of "becoming Brahman" in a way parallel to "becoming truth (*Dhamma*)," in the sense of entering Nirvana.[12] A "Godless" and purely pragmatic philosophical interpretation of Buddhism, even in its earliest stages, appears to be for the most part the invention of nineteenth century Western students who never encountered the living religion.[13]

Theravada Buddhists today not only commonly worship the Hindu gods, but indeed worship the glorified historical Buddha himself; to the Buddha's doctrine is added (rather inconsistently, according to some) a theistic belief in his absolute supremacy and divine power, and worshipers on the popular level hope not only for Nirvana, but also for communion with the Buddha himself.[14] To this is joined (although to a lesser extent than in the Mahayana) a doctrine of merit, which implies not only a positive stance toward an eternal validity in human existence, but also some kind of dialogical relationship to the Absolute. The Buddhism of the Theravada monks is, in general, more consistent with the original doctrine; but even here there is a tendency to make the notion of Nirvana the practical equivalent of "God," expressed in the negative terminology of mystical theology. As the great student of Buddhism, Edward Conze, states: "When we compare the attributes of the Godhead as they are understood by the more mystical tradition of Christian thought, with those of Nirvana, we find almost no difference at all."[15] In its practice, Buddhism tends to become more a religion of mysticism and compassionate love than of self-sufficiency, isolation, and negativity.

Many Theravada Buddhists would today claim that it is above all the *name* "God" which they reject, rather than the reality.[16] In this they are joined by the Mahayana tradition as well.

[Thus the Buddhist abbot Soyen Shaku writes: ". . . Buddhism is not atheistic as the term is ordinarily understood. It has certainly a God, the highest reality and truth, through which and in which this universe exists."[17] However, he explains, Buddhists usually do not use the term God, because it has for them unfortunate Christian overtones. Daisetz Suzuki expands on the same idea: "Buddhism does not use the word God. The word is rather offensive to most of its followers, especially when it is associated in vulgar minds with the idea of a creator who produced the world out of nothing, caused the downfall of mankind, and, touched by the pang of remorse, sent down his only son to save the depraved. But, on account of this, Buddhism must not be judged as an atheism which endorses an agnostic, materialistic interpretation of the universe. Far from it. Buddhism outspokenly acknowledges the presence in the world of a reality which transcends the limitations of phenomenality, but which is nevertheless immanent everywhere and manifests itself in

its full glory, and in which we live and move and have our being."[18]
Suzuki explicitly identifies the "Void" or "Emptiness" of Buddhism
with the God of the Western mystics.[19]]

This "terminological non-theism" of the Buddhist tradition has
three important implications for our considerations. First, if we
have agreed with Rahner on the permanence and necessity of the
word "God," we must also insist that this does not mean the existence of any single *concept* of God, much less any single verbal
symbol. It is clearly possible to seek the ultimate ground of spiritual
experience in an absolute Transcendent without having an *explicit*
equivalent of the Western word "God," at least in its usual connotations and associations. The Buddhist concepts of "Nirvana," of
"Emptiness" or the "Void" may sound godless or even nihilistic to
Western ears, but we must be careful to understand them in their
proper context. As we shall see (below, Chapter VI), every statement about the Absolute Ground must in some sense be based in a
"negative theology," that is, a recogniton of the inadequacy of our
language to deal with the ultimate.

Second, in the light of the above, we must beware of making
hasty judgments or of indulging in an intolerant and conceptualist
dogmatism of the type which has too frequently characterized
encounters between—and even within—religions. Theravada Buddhists in Indonesia call their co-religionists in Sri Lanka atheistic;
many Hindus consider Buddhists of whatever type atheistic, because of the philosophical doctrine of the "Void" and the "non-
atman"; the Vedanta philosopher Śankara, who formulated his
system to combat Buddhist "atheism," was himself considered atheistic by some later Vedantists; followers of the non-dualist Vedanta,
with its philosophical and monist concept of the Absolute, are ac-
cused of atheism by *"bhakti"* Hindus;[20] and Westerners should not
forget that not only were Xenophanes and Socrates condemned for
"atheism," but that early Christians were sent to the arenas by the
Romans for the same offense.

Third, we must be aware that the context for human thought
also includes historical development. Earliest Buddhism as well as
the Sāmkhya system represents a thought context which had *not yet*
encountered the idea of "God" in an absolute sense, as the One and
ultimate ground of transcendence. In historical perspective, however, they can be seen to be going *toward* such an idea (however it
might be expressed), rather than *away* from it. (Similarly, the anthropomorphic conception of God in the "Yahwism" of the earliest

Hebrews had not reached to the point of monotheism, much less to a philosophical notion of Absolute Spirit; but it would be misleading on that account to characterize early Hebrew religion as philosophically materialistic or atheistic.)

In conclusion, our brief consideration of the non-theistic traditions within some forms of Hinduism and Buddhism makes it clear that it is possible to affirm human transcendence and spiritiuality without necessarily having an *explicit* or *clearly formulated* notion of "God." Religion can exist which is "more a transforming experience than a notion of God."[21] On the other hand, such non-theistic forms have been seen even within Hinduism and Buddhism to be incomplete as explanations of the ground of spirit; historically, they have been incorporated into explanations which are either theist, monist, or vaguely "mystical." In any case, these non-theistic forms of religion certainly point to a "higher" reality than man or the world. While they deny the ultimacy of the anthropomorphically conceived "gods" (and in this they may have a contribution to make to Western theologies, which frequently encounter the danger of anthropomorphic images of the Absolute[22]), they do not see human spirit as groundless or absurd, but seek an ultimate meaningfulness to existence in some transcendent principle. In this sense, although they may not have confronted the notion of God explicitly, they do not exclude the posing of the question about God. On the contrary, their own inner dynamic in affirming human transcendence—particularly in its dialogical aspect—seems to call out for grounding in an absolute and transcendent spiritual principle, which we refer to as God.

THE POSTULATORY ATHEISM OF EXISTENTIALISM: SARTRE

> *Whither shall I go from thy Spirit?*
> *Or whither shall I flee from thy presence?*
> *If I ascend to heaven, thou art there!*
> *If I make my bed in Sheol, thou art there!*
> *If I take the wings of the morning and dwell in the uttermost parts of the sea, even there thy hand shall lead me, and thy right hand shall hold me.*
> *If I say, "Let only darkness cover me, and the light about me be night," even the darkness is not dark to thee, the night is bright as the day; for darkness is all light with thee.*

> Ps. 139:7–12

Existentialism is nothing else but an attempt to draw the full conclusions from a consistently atheistic position. . . . Existentialism is not atheist in the sense that it would exhaust itself in demonstrations of the non-existence of God. It declares, rather, that even if God existed that would make no difference, from its point of view. Not that we believe God does exist, but we think that the real problem is not that of his existence; what man needs to find is himself again and to understand that nothing can save him from himself, not even a valid proof for the existence of God. In this sense Existentialism is optimistic, it is a doctrine of action, and it is only by self-deception, by confusing their own despair with ours that Christians can describe us as without hope.

Jean-Paul Sartre:
Existentialism and Humanism

If we find in oriental religion ancient traditions of thought which seek transcendence prescinding from the existence of God, we encounter in Western Existentialism a modern movement of thought which explicitly denies the existence of God, and precisely in the name of human transcendence. While "Existentialism" is a term which has been applied to many European philosophers, including theists like Martin Buber and Gabriel Marcel, there is a strong current of existentialist thinking which considers the denial of God central to its position and critical for man's attainment of true humanity.[23] Other forms of modern atheism—scientific positivism, materialism, or nihilism, for example—may deny the existence of an Absolute on the basis that "transcendence" itself is illusory, and that the intelligibility of man is reducible to the laws of the material world, so that the problems of ultimate "meaning" and "value" are themselves meaningless. Existentialism, on the contrary, insists upon man's ontological difference from the material world, and sees in the conscious subject, the seeker for meaning, the crucial and central fact of existence. Nevertheless, at least in its predominant spokesmen, it seeks to find the basis of man's unique place in the universe within human existence itself, without reference to God or an absolute principle of intelligibility.

We have already made mention of Martin Heidegger's critical distinction between the conscious being of man *(Dasein)* and the mere being of things.[24] It is in man that being is unconcealed and comes to light. Ontology, therefore, is necessarily anthropology: it must begin with *Dasein,* the being in which being is revealed, with the for-itself of the world. It is man who gives meaning to the world by going beyond beings to being itself. In this movement toward being, man is revealed as finite transcendence: transcendence because of the revelation of being; finite because man has a necessary beginning and end: his life is a "project" toward a future, is essentially temporal and never fully accomplished. The proper mode of self-realization of *Dasein* is *Existenz* (ex-sistere): a standing outside of self. The finite transcendence of man means that man, unlike things, is never complete, can never stand in place. Our being is marked by *freedom.* Man is the being who has care *(Sorge)* of the world; we must constitute ourselves in the world and make the world itself our project. The refusal of this task would imply the rejection of freedom and the reduction of life to the status of a thing.

Heidegger's "rediscovery" of the "ontological difference" between *Dasein* and the being of things leads him to criticize the idea of God in metaphysics; for this God, God as the ground of being, as *"causa sui,"* is "a being." Philosophical theology, with its metaphysical God, has become questionable because of its forgetfulness of the ontological difference: it has invented a God who is an object. Such a God has, in any case, nothing to do with the God of religion—who is, for Heidegger, necessarily and methodically excluded from the considerations of philosophy. According to Heidegger, anyone who has experienced the unity of being prefers in the realm of thought to remain *silent* about God. Nevertheless, Heidegger rejects the charge of atheism and insists that "the God-less thinking that is constrained to forego the God of philosophy, God as *Causa sui,* is perhaps nearer to the divine God," the God of religion.[25]

These principal themes of Heidegger's philosophy of existence can be recognized as having a profound influence on Sartre's existentialism. For Sartre, however, philosophy does not remain silent about God, but must on the contrary explicitly deny the existence of God if it is to affirm man's transcendence and freedom. Heidegger's "ontological difference" is found echoed in Sartre's phenomenological reduction[26] of all being to the two opposed elements of being for-itself *(être-pour-soi)* and being in-itself *(être-en-soi):* the being of consciousness or mind, and the being of things. The in-itself, the being of a thing, is solid, self-contained, lacking in relations; it is what it is, and encompasses no negation of itself; it is full positivity that harbors no otherness. It is merely factual being, with no significance or meaning.[27] Being for-itself, on the other hand, conscious being, is no-thing *(le néant);* its mode of being is the negation of thing-hood. Being for-itself, because it is no-thing, has no "essence," no stable and predetermined meaning; rather, it is that which confers meaning by the annihilation or negation of the world of the in-itself. Such being (for-itself) is always a project, totally undetermined except as a response to the moment of existence. For Sartre, this total lack of determination, in which man creates meaning and value, is the meaning of freedom, which is therefore identical with being for-itself. It is precisely this radical freedom of man which for Sartre necessitates the denial of God.

Sartre takes as his starting point Descartes' notion of God (more ultimately derived from Duns Scotus) as the being who is absolutely free, the creator of essences, unbound by any antecedents of a previous order.[28] This absolute and creative autonomy, according to Sartre, actually belongs to man, although Descartes, confined by his Christian faith and culture, could not recognize the fact. For on the Cartesian (and Christian) premise of God, man would be "free" for error and evil, but not for good. Only in negativity—sin—would man actually be able to create something properly man's own, while every achievement of goodness or positive value would be merely the ratification of values created and established by God.[29] Real freedom, however, must be productive of value, like the freedom attributed by Descartes to God; it can have no foundation other than itself. If God were to create man, then God's creativity would cover all of human life; all value and meaning would be fixed; man would be unable to be truly free, for-self, but would be reduced to a mere thing. However it is obvious, according to Sartre, that man is a free and self-realizing being, and therefore the hypothesis of God must be rejected, as a contradiction to that freedom.[30] Belief in God is thus a species of "bad faith,"[31] since the believer *eo ipso* accepts the status of being a thing, refusing radical responsibility to create the meaning of existence. In this sense, one might say that Sartre rejects God in the name of morality,[32] since, for him, real responsibility and subjectivity would be impossible if God existed.

The rejection of God also follows from Sartre's notion of the relation of the subject to the "other." The other is essentially one who looks, or stares, at me and, in so doing, reduces me to a "thing," an object.[33] All relations between people, for Sartre, ultimately amount to the one's reducing the other to a thing;[34] there is no possibility of a human "we," a unified subjectivity[35]—even though man always futilely strives for it. Sartre's view of man's relation to others is finally one of supreme pessimism: as he says in his play, *Huis-Clos (No Exit)*, *"L'Enfer, c'est les Autres"*—"Hell is other people." God, however, is conceived as the Absolute Other: the all-seeing yet unseen, the "Unstared Stare."[36] To accept the existence of God is therefore once more to be reduced to a thing, an object in God's world.[37]

The preceding considerations lead Sartre to what has been called a "postulatory" atheism: God is rejected on the grounds that his existence would mean a denial of man as subjectivity and self-creativity. Sartre also holds, however, that the very notion of God is in itself internally contradictory.[38] For "is not God a being who is what he is—in that he is all positivity and the foundation of the world—and at the same time a being who is not what he is and who is what he is not—in that he is self-consciousness and the necessary foundation of himself?"[39] The notion of God, in other words, unites the characteristics of being in-itself, the solid and complete positivity of being, with those of being for-itself, the non-being of consciousness or reflection. But such a combination is intrinsically impossible; there cannot be an "in-itself/for-itself," for the two states can only exist in mutual opposition. As we have seen, the for-itself is the negation, the annihilation of the "thing." But only the finite can be negativity; an infinite being, or "fullness of being," would have nothing to negate; it would be purely in-itself, and therefore not conscious. The notion of a pure creative liberty which is infinite and full is therefore a meaningless projection. Absolute liberty must be finite; the creative freedom which Christianity ascribes to God is in fact man's freedom.

The concept of God, then, is in reality nothing but a projection and hypostasization as "transcendence beyond the world"[40] of the human project of transcendence *in* the world. For human transcendence seeks always—and unsuccessfully—to attain the stability and security which characterize being in-itself, while not losing its characteristic of consciousness; it seeks to become perfect being, self-caused and self-grounded being, while remaining free:

> Imperfect being surpasses itself toward perfect being; the being which is the foundation only of its nothingness surpasses itself toward the being which is the foundation of its being. But the being toward which human reality surpasses itself is not a transcendent God; it is at the heart of human reality; it is only human reality itself as totality.

This totality is not the pure and simple contingent in-itself of the transcendent. If what consciousness apprehends as the being toward which it surpasses itself were the pure in-itself, it would coincide with the annihilation of consciousness. But consciousness does not surpass itself toward its annihilation; it does not want to lose itself in the in-itself of identity at the limit of its surpassing. It is for the for-itself as such that the for-itself lays claim to being-in-itself.

Thus this perpetually absent being which haunts the for-itself is itself fixed in the in-itself. It is the impossible synthesis of the for-itself and the in-itself; it would be its own foundation not as nothingness but as being and would preserve within it the necessary translucency of consciousness along with the coincidence with itself of being-in-itself. It would preserve in it that turning back upon the self which conditions every necessity and every foundation. But this return to the self would be without distance; it would not be presence to self, but identity with itself ... it would be this self as substantial being. Thus human reality arises as such in the presence of its own totality or self as the lack of that totality. And this totality cannot be given by nature, since it combines in itself the incompatible characteristics of the in-itself and the for-itself.

... When by a further movement of thought the being and absolute absence of this totality are hypostasized as transcendence beyond the world, it takes on the name of God.[41]

Human transcendence, in short, is constituted by the intrinsically impossible drive to be God.[42] Because this goal which energizes man's project is a self-contradiction, man can never be God, but only *un Dieu manqué*—a failed god. Man is finally nothing but a "useless passion":[43] freedom, exercising itself futilely in the void. Despite Sartre's call to "authenticity," his rejection of God as the ground of transcendence leaves human existence without any ground, since, as Sartre himself recognizes, humanity's attempt to ground its own being is doomed. Man's existence is an impossible, solitary, and ultimately meaningless struggle.

THE ATHEISTIC GROUNDING OF TRANSCENDENCE
IN DIALECTICAL MATERIALISM

What does it profit, my brethren, if a man says he has faith but has not works? Can his faith save him? If a brother or sister is ill-clad and in lack of daily food, and one of you says to them, "Go in peace, be warmed and filled," without giving them the things needed for the body, what does it profit? So faith by itself, if it has no works, is dead.

Jas. 2:14–17

The basis of irreligious criticism is; Man makes religion, *religion does not make man. In other words, religion is the self-consciousness and self-feeling of man, who either has not yet found himself or has already lost himself again. But* man *is no abstract being, squatting outside the world. Man is* the world of man, *the state, society. This state, this society produce religion,* a perverted world consciousness, *because they are* a perverted world. *Religion is the general theory of that world, its encyclopedic compendium, its logic in a popular form, its spiritualistic* point d'honneur, *its enthusiasm, its moral sanction, its solemn completion, its universal ground for consolation and justification. It is* the fantastic realization *of the human essence because the* human essence *has no true reality. The struggle against religion is therefore mediately the fight against* the other world, *of which religion is the spiritual* aroma.

Religious *distress is at the same time the* expression *of real distress and the* protest *against real distress. Religion is the sigh of the oppressed creature, the heart of a heartless world, just as it is the spirit of an unspiritual situation. It is the* opium *of the people.*

Karl Marx: Toward the Critique of
Hegel's Philosophy of Right

The existentialist morality of Sartre, Camus, and others calls forth a strong sense of human freedom and responsibility, but finally is unable to give any reason for human existence. It has the appeal of a kind of tragic heroism, since it proclaims human transcendence, but can offer no vision except that of absurdity and emptiness. It is not surprising that such a negative philosophy, for all its influence on modern thought, remains in essence the personal stance of very few. In stark contrast to the philosophy of the absurd presented by existentialism stands the major effort of modern times to construct or find meaning in human life without God: namely, the complex of thoughts and visions that are designated under the title of "Marxism," or, more technically, "dialectical materialism."[44]

Marxism attempts to offer to man not "nausea" and absurdity, but an "objective" ordering of the world; not an individualism in which the other is necessarily my foe, but a communal vision of people living in peace and harmony. Marxism offers no philosophy of the elite, but a synthesis which is understandable—at least in its broad lines—by all; not a mere theoretical system, but a concrete program and plan of action for human happiness. It intends to give man a goal to live and work for, a motive for hope, grounds for being.

[The contrast between the philosophical "mood" of Marxism and of Existentialism could hardly be more complete, despite their common rejection of God and religion. It is interesting that although Sartre and other existentialists have turned sympathetic eyes toward Marxism as a social doctrine, the admiration is not mutual. Party philosophy texts in the Soviet Union refer to Existentialism as "the philosophy of heroic irrationalism," a product of burgeois-capitalist society and its ideas. Sartre's flirtation with Marxist ideas is dismissed as being totally ignorant of the philosophical bases of Marxism, and as mixing it with absurdity and "idealism."[45]

Undoubtedly the name "Marxism" immediately provokes definite meanings and associations in the mind of the hearer. Upon close examination, however, it becomes somewhat difficult to define exactly what Marxism is, for the seemingly unified phenomenon disintegrates into a plurality of very different approaches to philosophy and social theory, all inspired—but to very different degrees and in various ways—by the thought of Marx (and usually also Lenin). The "Communism" which is frequently identified in the West with Marxism is in fact only one manifestation of the heritage. The wider designation must include many interpretations of Marx outside those of the "second world." There is, to begin with, the original thought of Marx himself. This in turn may be divided into the (comparatively recently discovered) philosophy of the "young" Marx (before 1844), and the writings of the mature thinker. There is secondly the "ontologization" of Marx's thought by Engels: a task partially accomplished in collaboration with Marx, but also largely realized without him; the extent of Marx's agreement with Engels' metaphysical dialectical materialism can only be surmised. There is then a whole series of Marxisms proceeding down to our own day: the "Kautskian" Marxism of the Second International (1889), based on the texts then known; the "official" or "orthodox" Marxism, more properly called "Marxism-Leninism," of the Soviet Union, with its variants, Stalinism and Trotskyism; the nationalist Marxisms of the Third International; and the recent rival claimant to the role of arbiter of orthodoxy, Maoism. Finally, there are the multiple philosophical and practical variants on Marxist thought:

the Frankfurt school; Titoism; the "unaligned" Marxism of the third world; Euro-communism; etc.]

Although there are many forms of "Marxist" thought and practice, some of which may even be compatible with theism, those who take the heritage of Marx and Engels as a complete view of the world are for the most part united, on the level of theory, by adherence to the philosophy of "dialectical materialism." This ideology of Marxism attempts to explain all of reality as "dialectical," thereby recognizing and preserving the transcendence of human existence, while it insists also upon the basically materialist nature of the world, thereby excluding any recourse to an ultimate "spiritual" principle as the ground of man's being.

The notion of "dialectic" in this context takes its origin in Marx's reformation of the very project of reflection on man and man's meaning, in reaction against the "idealist" dialectic of Hegel. Marxism begins above all as a philosophy of praxis—a practical program for the betterment of mankind's situation. As Marx proclaims in his famous dictum in the *Theses on Feuerbach* (1845), "The philosophers have only *interpreted* the world, in various ways; the point, however, is to *change* it."[46] In contrast to the philosophy of German Idealism, and particularly that of Hegel, Marx intends a theory of action, based upon the realities of human existence rather than upon *a priori* principles of abstract thought. His "overturning" of the Hegelian system[47] is founded on the principle that "it is not consciousness that determines life, but life that determines consciousness."[48] Man's reflection on the meaning of life necessarily flows from active material life itself. It is useless and indeed deceptive to ask about the meaning of life in abstraction from the concrete conditions of life which produce the question. One must, on the contrary, begin with real, existing humanity and the forces working upon it, in order to get at the true significance of the contents of consciousness:

> That is to say, we do not set out from what men say, imagine, conceive, nor from man as narrated, thought of, imagined, conceived, in order to arrive at man in the flesh. We set out from real, active men, and on the basis of their real life process we demonstrate the development of the ideological reflexes and echoes of this life process. The phantoms formed in the human brain are also, necessarily, sublimates of their material life process, which is empirically verifiable and bound to material premises.[49]

An inquiry into man which begins with the real sources of thought, i.e., material life, will eliminate much of the traditional content of philosophy as mere idle "speculation":

> Morality, religion, metaphysics, all the rest of ideology and their corresponding forms of consciousness, thus no longer retain the semblance of independence,[50]

but are seen as products, on the level of mind, of man's situation in the world. "Empty talk about consciousness ceases, and real knowledge has to take its place."[51] True philosophy does not preoccupy itself first of all with the analysis of mind, but with revolutionary practice, based on the analysis of man's social conditions, which produce different states of consciousness. For Marx, the analysis of society—especially the capitalist society of his day—takes the form primarily of consideration of the economic factors which influence social life and history.

The humanistic side of this pragmatic and "realist" approach to man may be observed most closely in the thought of the "young" Marx of the *Economic and Philosophical Manuscripts* (1844).[52] Marx sees the basic problem of man's existence in industrialized society as the product of a "dialectic of alienation." The fundamental premise, like the terminology of "dialectic" and "alienation," derives from Hegel's conception of the relation of subject and object. Man has the task of "creating" himself through the process of "objectifying," in which subjectivity is exteriorized and mediated through the world. Subjectivity is then reassimilated, enriched with its concretion in the objective, to become a new form of self-presence and self-fulfillment. Concretely, this process takes place in human knowledge, and also in all of man's external relations, especially in labor. Marx's argument, based on his analysis of the actual social conditions of his times, is easily summarized: human work should be a process of self-realization and self-creativity through the "subjectivizing" of the objects or products of man's activity. But, because of the existence of private property, the worker's product in fact never becomes subjectivized; rather, it becomes the property of another; it thus becomes alien to the worker, instead of self-fulfilling, and becomes the hostile force which is named "capital." The more man produces under such a system, the more the product becomes inimical to his/her selfhood.[53]

... the worker is related to the *product of his labor* as to an *alien* object.... The more the worker expends himself in work the more powerful becomes the world of objects which he creates in face of himself, the poorer he becomes in his inner life, and the less he belongs to himself.... The worker puts his life into the object, and his life then belongs no longer to himself but to the object. The greater his activity, therefore, the less he possesses.... The life he has given to the object sets itself up against him as an alien and hostile force.[54]

Expounding on the theme in greater detail, Marx explains how this basic and material alienation becomes the foundation for alienation on all levels of human being. The separation of the worker from the product of his/her work (because of the system of exploitation which is inherent in private property) leads to the disaffection of the worker from the activity of work itself, which has become not self-fulfillment, but self-denial. Work becomes merely the necessary condition for living; "it is not the satisfaction of a need, but only a *means* for satisfying other needs."[55] The worker is only at home (*bei sich*—with the Hegelian implication of freedom and satisfaction) after work, in leisure, while his/her creative activity is taken away: "... Man (the worker) feels himself to be freely active only in his animal functions ... while in his human functions he is reduced to an animal."[56] Because (again following the lines of the Hegelian dialectic) man becomes a self only in the process of objectification and appropriation of objects, i.e., in labor, the worker finally becomes alienated from his/her very self[57] and at the same time from others, since the self is only realized in society.[58]

This social alienation is the heart of the political problem. Because product (and therefore his/her selfhood) belongs to another, the worker becomes in effect the slave of another person. Human relations are reduced to the relations between things; people are used rather than treated as ends (cf. Kant's second statement of the "categorical imperative"). The supreme manifestation of this situation is the use and the worship of money: "*Money*, since it has the *property* of purchasing everything, of appropriating objects to itself, is therefore the *object par excellence*. The universal character of this *property* corresponds to the omnipotence of money, which is regarded as an omnipotent being.... "[59] Alienation in the social sphere produces in turn political alienation, for those who exploit the labor of others produce the bourgeois state, whose laws and institutions are intended to preserve property.

Finally, the material, social and political alienation of man inevitably produces alienation in consciousness, creating in philosophy metaphysics and above all religion, the ideological counterpart to the perverted world-order. The absence of real happiness constrains man to invent an illusory happiness in another world; the alienation of our true essence leads us to project a perfectly fulfilled being in God, the absolute Spirit. Religion is, therefore, an upside-down vision of the world, because the state and society that produce it are upside-down. At the same time, Marx's judgment of religion is not entirely negative; religion is also an expression of man's distress at this alienated condition, as well as a palliative, an opium or means of escape from it.[60]

Salvation from the whole process of alienation is to be achieved by tearing out the root of the problem, namely, private property.[61] Property is the negation of man; by the "negation of the negation," we can reattain man's lost essence and be returned from the status of a "thing" to true humanity. Mankind will thus not only be able to achieve self-realization in its products, but will also "redeem" nature, by bringing it into its proper relation to man. The agent of this redemption (Marx consciously uses Christian terminology) must be the proletarian class, which is, as it were, the personalized negativity of the alienating situation.[62] Communism, which is the uprooting of alienation, is therefore the solution to the problem of history, and is conscious of being such. It is by consciousness of the problem that man will be able to resolve it; for, according to Marx, man is not simply the product of material circumstances, but is able to produce and create the world.[63]

[The loose collection of insights, practical and philosophical, that typifies the early Marx has undeniably not only a certain truth value, but also a great appeal as a call to brotherhood, humanity, and social justice. Although Marx's analysis of the problem and its solution is undoubtedly naive, and is clearly tied to a social and economic system which even as he wrote was in the process of changing in ways that he did not foresee, he had the courage and insight to bring to the fore economic factors which had hitherto largely been overlooked, and of pointing out the importance of the unrecognized "hidden agenda" in the economic and social presuppositions of all philosophical thought. Whatever its drawbacks, the early Marx's philosophy rang out to many as an appeal to moral idealism, self-sacrifice, solidarity, human dignity—in short, to what is transcendent and personal in man; and it sounded a clear condemnation of the hypocrisy and inhumanity of social conditions of the times, as well as of the world of thought which either supported or ignored them. This ethical and visionary and at the same time simple and practical aspect of Marxism undoubtedly explains its appeal to critics of social and economic injustice, especially on the level of the "masses"; and it is this sort of "Marxism"—the praxis of social equality, rather than the later theory of dialectical materialism—which inspired, to a large degree, the development of socialism in Europe. Despite the metaphysicizing of Marxism by Engels and the later doctrinization (and according to many, the betrayal[64]) of Marxism by the orthodoxy of the Soviet Union, the ethical and humanistic dimension remains a powerful factor in some modern Marxist thought. The version of the Marxist heritage represented by the thought of Mao Zedong, for example, emphasizes (in theory, at least) the moral imperative: Maoism intends to teach man how to live, to struggle for a new and better type of society. It proclaims faith in man rather than in the laws of economics. Mao calls upon people to realize the ideal type of proletarian man, not by the automatic working of material forces, but by an internal transformation. The real revolution, according to Mao, is within man. The reader of Mao's works[65] cannot but be impressed with the continual references to the goal of fraternity, the value of poverty, self-sacrifice, and internal and moral attitudes as the foundation of the new order.

The pragmatic and ethical side of Marxist thought—which is more in accord with the young Marx than with the doctrines of Engels and of Soviet philosophy—has even attained a certain appeal to Christian reformers and revolutionaries, if not as an ideology, at least as a partner, not only in a theoretical dialogue, but in practical action. The atheism of Marx is seen as secondary to its practical revolutionary social goal of justice and equality; it may even be seen as "the unconscious search for the ultimate consequences of redemption."[66] In the Marxist revolutionary struggle for human values, some Christians see a genuine, although "anonymous," Christianity at work. Thus the Colombian priest-revolutionary Fr. Comilo Torres explained his collaboration with Marxist forces:

"I have said that I am a revolutionary as a Colombian, as a sociologist, as a Christian and as a priest. I regard the Communist Party as having authentically revolutionary elements and, therefore, I cannot be anti-communist as a Colombian, as a sociologist, as a Christian, or as a priest.

"I am not anti-communist as a Colombian, because anti-communism is oriented to persecute nonconformist compatriots, Communists or not, of whom the majority are poor people.

"I am not anti-communist as a sociologist, because in the Communist plans to combat poverty, hunger, illiteracy, the lack of housing, the lack of public services, we find effective and scientific solutions.

"I am not anti-communist as a Christian, because I believe that anti-communism carries with it a blanket condemnation of all that the Communists defend and, among that which they defend, there are both just and unjust things. By condemning them all together, we are exposed to condemning equally the just and the unjust, and this is anti-Christian.

"I am not anti-communist as a priest, because although the Communists themselves may not know it, among them there may be many who are authentic Christians. If they are of good faith, they can have sanctifying grace and if they have sanctifying grace and love their neighbor they will be saved. . . . "[67]

Perhaps above all the humanistic face of Marxism shows itself in philosophical neo-Marxism, outside the Soviet Union and China, which emphasizes less the doctrines of ontological materialism and more the implications of economics and social conditions for the fulfillment of man's true humanity. A Marxist social program is seen as a means to the attainment of a "new man," a call to full transcendence. Undoubtedly the most influential of this group, even to the extent of having greatly inspired the Christian "theology of hope" of recent decades, is the German Ernst Bloch. A sample of the spirit of his thinking may be gleaned from this passage at the end of his master work, *Das Prinzip Hoffnung (The Principle Hope):*

"Man is still living in pre-history—yes, each and all of us are living before the creation of the world—the real creation. *The real Genesis is not at the beginning but at the end;* it starts to come into being when society and existence become radical, that is, when they get down to the root. But the root of history is Man—the worker, creator, the one who transforms and reshapes the merely given. If man comes to himself and grounds what is his own in real democracy, without alienation or estrangement, there will come into the world something that appears only in childhood, and in which no one has yet existed: home."[68]]

The transformation of Marx's thought from a loose collection of practical, social, economic and philosophical reflections into an ontological system is due to the work of Marx's collaborator, Friedrich Engels, who deserves the title of "Father of dialectical materialism."[69] Engels names his system "materialist" in opposition to the idealism of Hegel (as understood—or misunderstood—by Engels).[70] According to Engels, philosophical idealism stands for two fundamental and related principles: (1) that matter is the product of Spirit (i.e. God); and (2) that the external world is the product and reflection of (human!) ideas. "Materialism," on the other hand, holds that (1) matter is the primal source from which all being emanates; and (2) concepts are the reflection of an independently existing real world. It should be noted that for Engels, just as "idealism" means both theism and the doctrine of the unreality of the phenomenal world, so "materialism" includes two ideas which are, in themselves, quite independent: the priority of matter over spirit, and epistemological realism.[71] (An epistemologically realist philosophy which nevertheless asserts the existence of spirit [God] as the source of reality—like "Thomism" of either the traditional or transcendental kind—is named by Soviet philosophy, following Engels, an "objective idealism.").

On the other hand, Engels is at pains to distinguish his position from a "vulgar" metaphysical materialism which would reduce all reality to matter and all of history to the unfolding of mechanistic laws.[72] Engels holds, on the contrary, that the nature of reality is "dialectical": that there are real grades of being, and that human consciousness—although it is merely the highest product of matter—is not reducible to matter; and that, therefore, human history is subject to higher laws than those of physics.[73]

[It is interesting to notice the degradation of the notion of "dialectic" as one proceeds from Hegel through Marx to Engels. For Hegel, dialectic is the scientific application of the laws of thought *("die wissenschaftliche Anwendung der in der Natur des Denkens liegende Gesetzmässigkeit"*—Encyclopedia, *1°)*. These laws form the famous triad of thesis-antithesis-synthesis, or affirmation, negation, sublation. Dialectic is therefore a movement of spirit or mind; it may be said to be found in nature, insofar as the world, for Hegel, is nothing other than Idea or Spirit "outside itself," negating itself. For the young Marx, the dialectic occurs between man and nature in work. Like the Hegelian dialectic, Marx's deals with the identity of subject and object, in this case realized in the relation of man to the world. The subject of the dialectic is still spirit (man). For Engels, however, dialectics becomes the general laws of the progress of *all reality,* prior to and apart from the existence of spirit at all. How a dialectic in the Hegelian sense, including a principle of negativity as its moving force, as is typical of consciousness, can exist without consciousness is one of the root difficulties of Engels' system.]

Engels "ontologizes" Marxism by applying the notion of dialectic, originally meaning the movement of mind, to the entirety of being, independent of the existence of any mind or spirit. He

distinguishes three fundamental "laws" of the materialist dialectic.[74] The first is called the law of the "transformation of quantity
into quality, and vice versa." Its purpose is to explain how there can
be a real evolution of superior forms of being from inferior ones; for,
as we have noted, "dialectical" materialism, in contrast to mechanistic systems, recognizes gradations in the ontological "values" of
beings. Such an evolution is possible (without a grounding creative
intellect) because of a spontaneous passage of quantitative changes
to eventual qualitative ones. In other words, there comes a point for
each individual thing where the addition (or subtraction) of matter
or energy (quantitative change) produces not merely more (or less)
of the same thing, but results in a leap to something new and
different (qualitative change). (The simple example given is the
heating of water; up to 100°C., the addition of heat energy merely
produces hotter water; but after the boiling point, a new "quality,"
steam, is produced.) This law applies not only to physics, but also to
biology, and in its most general form explains the possibility of all
progress to new forms of being.

The second law is that of "the interpenetration of opposites" (in
modern Soviet philosophy, "the law of the unity and struggle of
opposites"). Its purpose is to explain where motion or change comes
from. Engels, thinking to avoid both the dilemma of an infinite
regress and the postulation of a first cause, places the source of
motion in matter itself. All of reality is "dialectical"; no thing is
simply itself, but includes also its contradictory or opposite. The
interpenetration of opposites, i.e., the presence of a principle of
negativity or internal contradiction in things, is the source of their
dynamism. (Here we see clearly Engels' corruption of the Hegelian
dialectic, which holds that mind contains the principle of negativity.) Thus motion is self-caused, and there is no need for a "first
mover."

The third law is that of the "negation of the negation." Again
we have to do with the Hegelian view of "negativity" as the inner
dynamism of evolution. As in Hegel, so too in Engels the negativity
in question is not pure elimination or destruction, but "antithesis,"
which itself becomes negated in a final "synthesis" which sublates
(aufhebt, in Hegel's use of the term) everything positive in the
process. Thus the ascending evolution of the world is not a straight
line, but a kind of spiral.[75]

Engels' system and its three laws were canonized and further
developed especially by Lenin, who places more emphasis, however, on the uniqueness of man's place in the world. The law of the

passage of quantitative to qualitative changes has produced the qualitatively new phenomenon of consciousness, which, according to Lenin, can by no means be reduced to matter.[76] Although this had already been contained in Engels, Lenin now raises consciousness to the level of a fundamental principle: matter and consciousness are the *dual* foundation of dialectical materialism, in place of the single material basis of Engels. Lenin is thus able to soften Engels' historical determinism: social changes are not simply the result of the laws of dialectics, but depend also on man's intellect and will; we are called to participate in the evolutionary process. On this basis, Lenin justifies the supremacy of the Communist Party. The Party (and it alone) has attained the correct view of history and its meaning; it alone, therefore, can produce in the proletariat the proper class consciousness for the transformation of society. It is not historical destiny alone, but also the activity of the Communist Party which decides the fate of the movement of social evolution. Lenin thus rationalizes an uncritical and quasi-religious devotion to the Party; the dictatorship of the proletariat becomes the dictatorship of the Communist Party, whose pronouncements are absolute both in the sphere of practice and that of theory.

[This absolutizing tendency becomes even more pronounced under Stalin's regime. Soviet philosophy became purely dogmatic, based upon the absolute authority of the Party; the same was true of the sciences in general. Stalin's "contribution" to Soviet philosophy[77] was a distinction within the law of the passage of quantity to quality. As we have seen, qualitative changes, according to Engels, occur by "leaps." There is a kind of sudden "revolution" in the status of the thing. Stalin modifies this position by stating that once a certain stage has been reached in human social evolution—namely, the stage of Soviet society—the qualitative changes come only in steps dictated from above. That is, there can be no new revolutions, no new leaps, no new society. It also means that Soviet society—since it alone has "arrived"—must be the model of the whole communist movement: all communist parties must follow the Russian, which is infallible in all areas—not only politics and materialist doctrine, but also morals, science, art, history, etc.]

It would not be too much to say that dialectical materialism, in its Marxist-Leninist formulation, becomes a non-theistic religion. As the psychoanalyst Ignace Lepp, himself an atheist and communist in early life, points out, "it is communism itself that assumes the function of transcendence" in the psyche of the Marxist "believer."[78] Man is offered a vision of a meaningful and valuable life, striving for the perfect society for future generations, while on the emotional level class and Party represent a kind of mystical communion that anticipates and brings about humanity's final state.

In contrast with the individualist vision of meaninglessness and absurdity held out by existentialist atheism, or the spiritual solipsism of atheistic Hinduism or Buddhism, dialectical materialism seeks to offer man a reason for living in the world and a grounds for solidarity with one's fellow man. But does it really give a grounding for the transcendence in man that it attempts to affirm? As a philosophy of praxis, Marxism seems to stand condemned by its own principles: for wherever it has attained a position of undisputed power, it has not only failed to produce a conspicuously humanistic or transcendent quality to life, but has on the contrary been guilty of the most appalling crimes against humanity. As a system of thought, dialectical materialism is prey to multiple internal contradictions, stemming from its attempt to adapt the Hegelian dialectic of mind to unconscious material processes. It wishes to affirm the value of consciousness, yet at the same time the priority of matter; it assumes an idealist dialectic of negativity as the principle of evolution, while denying any spiritual subject to be its bearer; it proclaims an "eschatology" with no ultimate prospect of hope, since man and his society are eventually doomed to extinction. Above all, dialectical materialism fails to meet the ultimate question about transcendence: "Why?" What can be the ultimate meaning or justification of an existence which must end in annihilation—which is man's final fate, if materialism is correct? How can there be objective and binding values which justify self-sacrifice, if existence itself is merely the product of accidental physical causes? How can one make a claim for the "truth" of any system, if thought itself is finally only a determination of material processes? If man's life and the fact of human "transcendence" over the world have no ground except their own existence out of lower being, and no future but a return to the unconsciousness of matter, does not the affirmation of transcendence itself become an arbitrary decision and even an illusion?

IV. THE GROUNDING OF TRANSCENDENCE IN GOD—1

For God's anger is breaking forth from heaven against all the impiety and wickedness of the men who in their wickedness are suppressing the truth. For all that can be known of God is clearly before them; God has shown it to them. Ever since the creation of the world, his invisible nature—his eternal power and divine character—have been clearly perceptible through what he has made.

—Rom. 1:19–20

"Astounding!" cried their unbidden companion. Glancing furtively around and lowering his voice he said: "Forgive me for being so rude, but am I right in thinking that you do not believe in God either?" He gave a horrified look and said: "I swear not to tell anyone!"

"Yes, neither of us believes in God," answered Berlioz with a faint smile at the foreign tourist's apprehension. "But we can talk about it with absolute freedom."

The foreigner leaned against the backrest of the bench and asked, in a voice positively squeaking with curiosity:

"Are you . . . atheists?"

"Yes, we're atheists," replied Berlioz, smiling. . . .

"Oh, how delightful!" exclaimed the astonished foreigner and swivelled his head from side to side, staring at each of them in turn.

"In our country there's nothing surprising about atheism," said Berlioz with diplomatic politeness. "Most of us have long ago and quite consciously given up believing in all those fairy-tales about God."

At this the foreigner did an extraordinary thing—he stood up and shook the astonished editor by the hand, saying as he did so:

"Allow me to thank you with all my heart!". . . .

"But might I enquire," began the visitor from abroad after some worried reflection, "how you account for the proofs of the existence of God, of which there are, as you know, five?"

"Alas!" replied Berlioz regretfully. "Not one of these proofs is valid, and mankind has long since relegated them to the archives. You must agree that rationally there can be no proof of the existence of God."

"Bravo!" exclaimed the stranger. "Bravo! You have exactly repeated the views of the immortal Emmanuel on that subject. But here's the oddity of it: he completely demolished all five proofs and then, as though to deride his own efforts, he formulated a sixth proof of his own."

"Kant's proof," objected the learned editor with a thin smile, "is also unconvincing. Not for nothing did Schiller say that Kant's reasoning on this question would only satisfy slaves, and Strauss simply laughed at his proof."...

"Kant ought to be arrested and given three years in Solovki asylum for that 'proof' of his!" Ivan Nikolayich burst out completely unexpectedly.

"Ivan!" whispered Berlioz, embarrassed.

But the suggestion to pack Kant off to an asylum not only did not surprise the stranger but actually delighted him. "Exactly, exactly!" he cried and his green left eye, turned on Berlioz, glittered. "That's exactly the place for him! I said to him myself that morning at breakfast: 'If you'll forgive me, professor, your theory is no good. It may be clever but it's horribly incomprehensible. People will think you're mad.'"

Berlioz's eyes bulged. "At breakfast ... to Kant? What is he rambling about?" he thought.

"But," went on the foreigner, unperturbed by Berlioz's amazement and turning to the poet, "sending him to Solovki is out of the question, because for over a hundred years now he has been somewhere far away from Solovki and I assure you that it is totally impossible to bring him back."

Mikhail Bulgakov:
The Master and Margarita

THE PRESUMPTION OF MEANING

We began our attempt at the "correlation" of faith to our own situation by turning to subjectivity as our starting point. The examination of our consciousness of being in the world led to an awareness of "transcendence" as a fact of our experience, both of ourselves (primarily) and of the world around us. The existence of "transcendence"—in its basic sense of "going beyond" toward a receding and apparently infinite "horizon"—brought us to the question of *meaning:* What is the sense, the intelligibility, the value of existence?

This question regards the whole of existence, in every regard. We note in ourselves both immanent and "ecstatic" dimensions:[1] we live not only in a present moment of self-possession, but have a consciousness of a past and a future which are not "now," but are somehow outside us and yet "with" us. We have an ecstatic experience of the facticity of the world, of its independence of our subjectivity, its priority to our existence, its provenance from "outside" ourselves. Indeed, I find my own present self conditioned by the facticity of an absolute and unchangeable past (extending not only through my life, but to the ancestors whose lives brought mine about). The question of meaning asks about the explanation or intelligibility of this facticity: Where does the being of the world come from? Is there a source of existence? We experience an ecstatic dimension of consciousness also in an orientation toward the future: we anticipate, hope, purpose. Here again the question of meaning arises: Is there a purpose and goal to existence, and in particular to my own existence as one oriented to a "beyond," a "not yet"?

The double "ecstatic" dimension of conscious being is rooted and realized in our present existence, our being-now, which is not the simple being of things, but is being-there *(Dasein),* being self-present and caring about being. Here again we confront the problem of meaning: Is there a sense to man's caring? Is there a ground of intelligibility which founds my own need for sense and value in life?

The question of meaning, posed in its most radical and universal terms, implies the question of God—i.e., of the Absolute, the ultimately intelligible and valid, that which is the source, the ground, and the goal of transcendence. We have seen that the very existence of the word "God" guarantees and epitomizes man's capacity to ask the ultimate question; that is, the existence of this word is the condition for man's humanity, for having a horizon of infinity or ultimacy. At the same time, we noted that there exist currents of thought and belief, both philosophical and religious, which do not neglect man's ultimacy, or avoid the question, but which attempt to ground human transcendence without God. Our last chapter gave several brief examples of such attempts.

At this point, since our considerations have led us into widely diverse areas of thought, it would be well to remind ourselves of the basic purpose and premises of our investigations. As we stated at the beginning, our intent is to "give answer" for our faith by addressing the problems raised by modern man, and to do so in particular through the appropriation of our own subjectivity. This means that in the entire movement of our thought thus far, we have not been proceeding in a purely "objective," i.e., non-aligned and non-committed fashion, as though all options and all answers were equally possible and open for us. Such a procedure is first of all impossible; no person can abstract totally from the options he has already made in life and about life's meaning when he approaches the question of ultimate significance. Furthermore, to attempt to reach an "objective" conclusion by means of proceeding on the "principle of the empty head"[2]—that is, the abandonment of all presuppositions —would be in fact to make any conclusion impossible, for it would neglect the fundamental structure of human knowing, which can only take place through the commitment of our subjectivity, and which must have a starting point in the lived activity of knowing and deciding.[3] To attempt to discuss the question of the ultimate meaning and intelligibility of life without having any personal stance toward it would be to imitate Hegel's Gascon, who wished to learn to swim, but refused to go into the water.

We have entered our inquiry, then, with operative options and positions regarding the question of meaning and God—presumably with the presupposition of "faith." In asking the most radical questions about reality and its grounds, we are not abstracting from that faith, nor are we acting "as if" it were not present, or as though the question of the meaningfulness of existence were totally undecided for us. We have already taken a fundamental stance on the meaningfulness of life. Indeed, to admit *in all seriousness* the possibility that existence is really totally absurd, meaningless, unintelligible, would *a priori* exclude any further discussion.[4] The very effort to *look for* or *ask about* meaning or value already and of necessity includes a presupposition of the existence of some meaningfulness and value: at least the value of searching, the meaningfulness of asking. There is no point of view "outside" a stance on this matter. We exist as human subjects, and our every intellectual starting point is conditioned by our actual involvement in life, with the implicit personal stance which that involvement carries.

We have begun, then, with a certain *unavoidable presupposition of meaningfulness;* and, in the case of Christian believers, that presupposition is inextricably tied to commitment to an *ultimate* and grounding meaningfulness and value: i.e., to the affirmation of and the option for the Absolute or God. This does not mean, however, that we are not "serious" in asking the radical question about being, about meaning, and about God, or in entering conversation with other possible views.[5] Indeed, the attempts to "correlate" our initial faith to our "situation" as subjects necessarily includes a dialectical moment, in which conflicting interpretations of existence are considered, contrasted, and evaluated,[6] and in which our own presupposition of meaningfulness itself is open for evaluation, interpretation, correction, or even possible rejection. What makes our inquiry honest is that we recognize our presuppositions and admit them as such, and that we recognize, at the same time, that they are, in principle, *revisable.*[7]

It is for this reason that we have briefly considered the possibility of non-theistic responses to the question of human existence and transcendence.[8] Our primary purpose in this summary examination of alternative directions for grounding and explaining human experience—particularly that of transcendence—has been to see whether there is a convincing position which would lead us to revise, right at the outset, our own original presupposition in favor of the (ultimate) meaningfulness of existence. At this point, however, our "dialectical" considerations do not seem to warrant a revision of the presupposition that leads us to seek ultimate meaning; if anything, they seem to confirm us in our search. For the attempts to find a non-theistic grounding for existence seem either to end in an affirmation of absurdity which is self-contradictory and self-defeating, or to accept, at least implicitly, the validity of our presupposition, while giving partial solutions which leave the final question of meaning essentially unresolved. At the very least, the positive presumption of meaningfulness has not been convincingly refuted, and the theistic solution to its grounding is not *a priori* to be dismissed.[9]

What we have arrived at thus far, then, is simply a *negative* and *provisional* confirmation of our original and unavoidable presupposition: enough to say that we have no reason (at this point) to abandon it, and have, therefore, sufficient reason to go on asking the question that arises from it, the question of an ultimate meaning and ground for existence, summarized by the word "God." Our next step must be to ask positively whether this presupposition can be shown to be *valid:* Can it be supported, grounded, "verified," rationally borne out, or does it lead to blind alleys, contradictions, and unresolved questions?

The fact of human "transcendence"—which seems to be an undeniable datum (and which is admitted even in the non-theistic alternatives we have considered)—raises the question of a transcendence beyond the world, which gives a final and permanent sense to existence. If the affirmation of such a reality can be shown to be rationally justifiable and necessary, then our presupposition of meaningfulness will have been shown to be valid. At this point, therefore, we proceed to an examination of the question of the existence of God.

THE TRADITIONAL "WAYS" TO GOD BY REASON

We turn first to the traditional philosophical arguments regarding the existence of God within the thought realms of "common sense" and "theory,"[10] that is, to the now classical "demonstrations" of God's existence. These attempt to show that the recognition of the immanent intelligibility of the world and of man necessarily implies, as its explanation, the affirmation of an ultimate reality or supreme Being, God.

THE NOTION OF "PROOF"

[It has become common, at least in some traditions, to speak about these processes of reasoning as the "proofs" for the existence of God. Such a term is perhaps unfortunate and misleading in this context, for it may be taken to imply a clear and evident series of propositions which will infallibly carry conviction to anyone who grasps the meaning of the terms. The so-called "proofs" for the existence of God, however, are by their very nature not argumentations which can provide immediate evidence of God; and therefore they do not bear any guarantee of convincing everyone. Such was never their intent. St. Thomas Aquinas, although he does refer to his famous "ways" as "demonstrations," and does speak quite clearly of "proving" the existence of God,[11] insists that the human mind is incapable of reaching God's essence.[12] It is therefore impossible for God's being to be made "evident" to our minds.[13] (Since God's "essence" and his "existence" are identical,[14] God's very existence —his act of being—is something that surpasses the grasp of the human intellect; the "is" that is said of God is only analogous to the affirmation of being we make of those objects to which our mind is adequate.) The "proofs" for God adduced by Thomas and others are simply statements of the reasons which induce the mind to accept the proposition, "God exists."[15] These reasons, however, neither derive from nor arrive at any direct intuition of God's existence; rather, they proceed from the knowledge of the nature of the finite world,[16] which provides the only "evidence" available: "What our arguments render evident for us is not God Himself, but the testimony of Him contained in his vestiges, His signs or 'mirrors' here below. Our arguments do not give us evidence of the divine existence itself or of the act of existing which is in God and which is God Himself—as if one could have the evidence of His existence without having that of His essence. They give us only evidence of the fact that the divine existence must be affirmed, or of the truth of the attribution of the predicate to the subject in the assertion 'God exists.' "[17]

Furthermore, it is plain that no "proof" can work *"ex opere operato"*—i.e., independently of the subject hearing it. Any rational process which hopes to convince must presume the subject's good will, sincerity, personal probity, and dedication to truth, as well as the intellectual ability to grasp the argument. It also presupposes that the subject knows or can verify the premises upon which the argumentation is based. But unlike mathematical or scientific proofs, whose premises are based on universally available external experience, and whose truth is "objective" in the sense that it scarcely involves the subject personally at all, the reasoning about the reality of God regards the whole meaning and value of life. The object of this reasoning is not some *part* of experience, but rather something which by definition transcends and explains every part of experience. The being of God cannot be deduced as a consequence of any reality or process within the world, for God's being does not "derive" from anything; it is not explained by the world, but is the explanation of the world. There is nothing more "basic" or foundational than God, from which his existence could be deduced. It is clear, then, that the word "proof" in this context, because of the unique object of inquiry, has a much different sense from the ordinary usage.

God, because he is not an object in the world, cannot be shown to be real by any immediate evidence of a physical kind. The word "God," as we have seen, refers to the source and explanation of man's spiritual experience of consciousness, our drive to see value in existence. While the premises of empirical science are found in objective experience of the world, the "premises" for affirming God must be found in the spiritual reality of the subject as such. The question about God does not begin where inquiry about the nature or function of the world and its objects begins; it takes its origin in the experience proper to man *as person:* the irreducible experience we have named "transcendence," by which man is self-aware as a seeker of meaning and value. In order for the affirmation of God's existence to be meaningful to man, the experience it stems from must first of all be allowed to occur, i.e., to emerge in consciousness. As we have seen, however, its emergence (for every individual) is neither inevitable nor permanent; there are many obstacles to the fulfillment of human subjectivity, and many forces which conspire to retain man's life and consciousness at the lower levels of being. The emergence of transcendent subjectivity depends, then, upon many elements: health of mind and body, personal integration, sufficient experience and maturation, spiritual or intellectual ability, a certain moral concern for one's humanity on a level above the animal, etc. Moreover, once it emerges in consciousness, this experience of the transcendence of the person must also be adverted to—i.e., recognized and named. This process also encounters obstacles, and depends upon certain conditions: intellectual acumen, interest in the spiritual "dimension" of life, sufficient leisure to ask questions, possession of a language which allows some expression of the experience, etc. The "proofs" for the existence of God are in fact nothing other than the recognition and naming of the experience in its deepest implications. A major condition of this recognition, however, will be the degree to which the subject is willing to live out of a horizon of transcendence. In this question, in contrast with the purely "objective" realities of mathematics or science, the subject has an intimate personal stake in the conclusion; for he/she has invariably already made options in life which imply either a positive or a negative answer to the question of ultimate meaning. In other words, no matter what the validity or certainty of the reasoning process involved, no argument about God as the ground of personal existence can carry conviction unless the subject is existentially, personally moving toward that ground; because the discovery of God is inescapably linked with the discovery of one's own identity.[18] It is only with these reservations that we can speak of "proof" of God's existence.]

THE MIND'S WAY TO GOD IN UNDIFFERENTIATED CONSCIOUSNESS

The affirmation of God's existence does not, of course, begin with philosophy. Prior to its entry into the realm of "theory," with its systematic exigence, the mind operates in an undifferentiated way—reasoning, but for the most part unaware of its own processes. Within this undifferentiated sphere of consciousness, which is the normal state of the "common sense" relation to the world, we may discern a kind of "implicit" reasoning to the existence of God: what Jacques Maritain calls the "primordial" and pre-philosophic approach to God. Without elaborating an explicit metaphysics, the mind spontaneously proceeds by leaps of intuition and imagination to the need for an absolute. Maritain distinguishes two basic stages in this process. The first is the emergence of the consciousness of existence. Man at some point awakens to the experience of conscious being, a realization of the reality of one's own existence. One becomes existentially aware of "that formidable, sometimes elating, sometimes sickening or maddening fact *I exist*,"[19] and in this awareness is possessed by what Maritain calls the "intuition of being":

> Precisely speaking, this primordial intuition is both the intuition of *my* existence and of existence *of things*, but first and foremost of the existence of things. When it takes place, I suddenly realize that a given entity—man, mountain or tree—exists and exercises this sovereign activity *to be* in its own way, in an independence of *me* which is total, totally self-assertive and totally implacable. And at the same time I realize that *I* also exist, but as thrown back into my loneliness and frailty by this other existence by which things assert themselves and in which I have positively no part, to which I am exactly as naught. And no doubt, in face of my existence, others have the same feeling of being frail and threatened. As for me, confronted with others, it is my own existence that I feel to be fragile and menaced, exposed to destruction and death. Thus the primordial intuition of being is the intuition of the solidity and inexorability of existence; and, second, of the death and nothingness to which *my* existence is liable. And third, in the same flash of intuition, which is but my becoming aware of the intelligible value of being, I realize that this solid and inexorable existence, perceived in anything whatsoever, implies—I do not yet know in what form, perhaps in the things themselves, perhaps separately from them—some absolute, irrefragable existence, completely free from nothingness and death.[20]

Let us note that this enlightening experience is, according to Maritain, nothing other than "my becoming aware of the intelligible value of being," which is mediated by my own subjectivity. It is, in other words, an awakening to the intelligible self-awareness which is identical with conscious existence, *Dasein*, being-for-self. It is the intuition of our own spiritual reality (transcendence), bearing with it the always present unthematic co-knowledge of its unlimited "horizon." The consciousness of our being-toward-death and our relation to nothingness carries with it "intimations of immortality," since we intuitively perceive absolute being as the condition of our own relativity; being-with-nothingness implies, in order that it be at all, a being-without-nothingness. The concrete experience which "triggers" this intuition may be any life-situation in which the dimension of real humanity, i.e., subjectivity, comes to manifestation—that is, every act in which human being is raised above the level of biological purposefulness and implicitly acts within the horizon of transcendence.

[The revelation of the absolute horizon may occur, for example, in the awakening to human intersubjectivity or personal encounter: the finding of sense and value in life in dialogue with another, in self-giving love. The experience of interpersonal love reveals the incompleteness of the subject and at the same time an essential openness to finding selfhood in the other, the beyond-self. This dialogical self-fulfillment in self-gift itself manifests an incompleteness, insofar as it stands under the threat of failure, rejection, infidelity, and finally death; yet there is in the experience of loving an intuitive grasp of something of eternal validity in the act: the fact that love "is as strong as death." The "inexorability of existence" of which Maritain speaks is here experienced as the self-justifying value of being-for or loving, which implies that the negation to which human love is subject is not the last word, but that in the interpersonal encounter we touch upon and unveil the absolute. The trust involved in the gift of self to the other, even in the face of finitude and death, is only finally possible because of a basic trust in reality itself as confirming and grounding the act of love. It is this horizon of the absolute which enables the transformation of human community and human sexuality from mere biological-social instruments to a sign of the transcendent.

Maritain's "intuition of being" may also take its start as the intuition of the good, in man's moral sense, in the absoluteness of the "ought," in the inquietude about being which stems from the desire to be well. Again, it is manifest in aesthetic experience, in which we know the "feeling" of the greater, and are transported, so to speak, out of the world into a realm of beauty and goodness which transcends both the mere usefulness and the futility of life (it is because of this attainment of a sense of the transcendent whole in his art that Karl Barth calls Mozart one of the great theologians); or in the sense of humor, in which the irony and inconsistency or even the tragedy of existence is somehow able to be accepted because of a more ultimate vision of reconciliation and harmony. In short, the intuition may occur wherever human transcendence knows itself, not clearly and conceptually, but in the intersubjective and shared meanings which do not necessarily have the capacity for self-analysis.]

The second stage in the process is a spontaneous, immediate and wordless reasoning which springs from the primal intuition. One recoginzes, if only implicitly, in the very intuition of existence, the necessity of some absolute, some being-without-nothingness. One knows that one's self is not such a being. Furthermore, our own being-with-nothingness is a part of the universal whole of nature. By this very fact, the whole of which we are a part cannot be that which is without nothingness. There must, therefore, exist a being, an absolute Existent, apart from nothingness and also apart from the totality of nature; transcendent, self-sufficient, and unknown in itself, it is the final source of the absoluteness and inexorability of being.[21] And with this insight the mind has, without being aware of the structure of its own procedure, made its way by the leaps of intuition to the existence of God.

THE WAYS TO GOD IN THE REALM OF THEORY

As we have indicated, the primordial approach to God takes place in the context of an implicit and, as it were, intuitive reasoning. As we enter the realm of differentiated consciousness, there is a need to become aware of and to explicitate clearly the logical structure of the mind's affirmation of God. Spirit must "give answer" to itself for its hope in an ultimate sense to existence. The attempt to do so constitutes the classical formal demonstrations of God's existence.

From the Idea of God

We consider first the attempt to show God's existence from the very idea of God in man's mind. The classical form of this argument was proposed by St. Anselm of Canterbury in the eleventh century. He attempts to show that God's existence is evident from the very content or meaning of the word "God" once it is correctly understood. (The title of the "ontological argument," by which Anselm's reasoning has become universally known, stems from his critic Emmanuel Kant.)

Anselm begins by postulating that what is meant by "God" is "that than which no greater can be thought" (*id quo maius cogitari nequit*). If we meditate closely on this definition, however (and Anselm's "argument" in its original form is within the context of a meditative prayer), we find it revealed to us that such a being must necessarily exist; for otherwise it would not be that which it is by definition. That is, the denial of God's existence would be self-contradictory. What we think of when we think of God—i.e., that than which no greater can be thought—must exist in reality; for otherwise it would not *be* that than which no greater can be thought:

> It is certain that "that than which no greater can be thought" cannot exist only in the intellect. For if it is only in the understanding, it can be thought to have existence also in fact (*in re*), which is greater. If, therefore, that than which no greater can be thought is only in the understanding, then that very being than which no greater can be thought is something than which a greater indeed can be thought; but, of course, this is impossible. Without any doubt, therefore, something than which no greater can be thought exists, both in the understanding and in fact.[22]

Later, Anselm adds what may be considered another note to this reasoning:

> Now, we can think of the existence of something which cannot be thought not to be; and this is greater than anything which can be thought not to be. . . . That than which no greater can be thought, therefore, exists in such a way that it cannot even be thought not to exist; and you are this thing, Lord our God. So truly are you, Lord, my God, that you cannot even be thought not to be . . . and yet everything else, besides you alone, can be thought not to be. . . . [23]

Here Anselm comes to a more explicit recognition of the unique character of God's existence as *necessary*. God (if he exists at all) cannot not exist; he is by definition the one being that *must be*. His being, unlike that of any other existent, cannot be merely factual, i.e., a being which happens to be, but could also not be, under other circumstances. This means also that the *concept* of God has a unique logical property, according to Anselm. Logically, God is either *necessary* or *impossible;* what is meant by God cannot be within the realm of the "possible," that is, what can either be or not-be. This means that the concept of God is absolutely unique among all concepts, in that it alone signifies an existence which is absolute; if it is thought at all, it must be thought of as really existing. No other concept includes existence in reality as a part of its very meaning (Kant: "existence is no predicate"), but the concept or idea of God does.

There are many complications in determining more exactly what the force of this "argument" was in St. Anselm's mind. Is it to be conceived as a purely philosophical demonstration, or is it actually theological? Is it really based simply upon the *concept* of God, or does Anselm really refer to an irrefutable *experience* of God, in faith? The battle over the argument's validity has raged since Anselm's own day, and has not yet ended.[24] It has been taken up and defended, although in various forms, by St. Bonaventure, Descartes, Leibniz, Spinoza, Hegel, Gioberti, Rosmini, Tillich, Barth, and Hartshorne. It has been opposed—although on various grounds—by most Western philosophers, both atheists and theists, and including St. Thomas Aquinas and Emmanuel Kant, whose refutations have become classic.

Whatever else may be said of the "ontological" argument, it undoubtedly raises the central philosophical problem in the consideration of theism, that is, the problem of the identity of being and spirit (consciousness).[25] (To this we shall return in our consideration of transcendental method.) Anselm's considerations bring to the fore the mysterious and challenging nature of the word "God" itself and its centrality to the significance of human existence. Nevertheless, as a *heuristic* approach to the existence of God—as an "argument" to discover his existence—Anselm's reasoning fails, for it remains logically only on the level of thought, and argues from conception to existence, while maintaining that this is the unique case in which such a process is valid. But this is exactly what needs to be "proved." Aquinas' comments (we shall see Kant's later) are worth repetition:

> Perhaps not everyone who hears the name "God" understands it to signify "that than which no greater can be thought"; for some people have thought of God as being a body. Even granting, however, that everyone should understand the word "God" to mean "that than which no greater can be thought," it still does not follow that he must understand that what the word signifies actually exists in reality, but only that it exists in the mind. Nor can one argue that it must (also) exist in reality, unless one first grants that there actually exists something than which no greater can be thought; which is exactly what those deny who do not accept the existence of God.[26]

It should be noted that Aquinas does not disagree with Anselm's fundamental insight into the necessary character of God's existence.

God is, in fact, that which must be and cannot not be, the absolute being; but this fact is not known to us simply from the word or concept of God. If we were able to grasp the essence of God, his existence would be self-evident, for God's essence *is* his very existence. But, as we have seen, Aquinas insists that God so transcends the human mind that no concept of ours contains or grasps his essence. Therefore, "because we do not know God's essence (*nos non scimus de Deo, quid est*) his existence *is not self-evident (per se nota) to us, but needs to be demonstrated* through those things which are more known to us (although less intelligible in themselves), namely, God's created effects."[27]

It is possible, of course, to define the word "God" in such a way that he is thought of as the "necessary existent." To deny his actual existence, then, would be to say that what necessarily exists does not exist; it would be a contradiction in terms. But only *in terms;* for the denial of God's existence would simply state that the term "necessary existent" has no correlate in reality. In other words, conceptions, by their very nature, yield only analytic propositions; but from an analytic proposition, no conclusion about existence can be reached, for there is no evidence in the concept alone that the concept occurs (also) in a concrete judgment of fact. It is only judgments of fact, in the Thomistic view, which can reach existence. That is, every affirmation of existence must, for Thomas, be based on experience, whether immediate or mediated. A concept, in itself, does not yield experience of the reality it signifies, and therefore cannot found a judgment of existence.[28]

There is, however, yet another line of thought from the idea of God to his existence—this time based not directly upon the content of the idea alone, but rather upon its provenance. This reasoning is found again in St. Anselm, and also in Bonaventure and Descartes. Perhaps its simplest and most forceful expression is found in Tolstoy's *War and Peace*, in the words of the aging Mason to the self-styled atheist Pierre:

> "If God did not exist," he said quietly, "We would not be speaking about him, my dear sir. Of whom, of what were we speaking? Who is it that you deny?" he suddenly exclaimed with enthusiastic austerity and authority in his voice. "Who invented him, if he does not exist? How did there arise in you the conception that there is such an incomprehensible being? How is it that you and the whole world have formed an idea of such an inconceivable

being, an all-powerful being, eternal and infinite in all his qualities?. . ."[29]

In other words, where does the idea of God *come from?* How can
man—a finite and imperfect being—even conceive of a perfect
being? How can he think of a being which is literally unthinkable?
How can he have a concept whose very content is inconceivable?
Obviously such an idea cannot stem from us; it can only come from
such a being himself. Note that this argument does not apply simply
to the idea of "deity" as such, but refers specifically to God as
Absolute, as the inconceivable and utterly transcendent. The question is not how man comes up with an idea of a god or gods, who
might be the projection of human qualities, but how man arrives at
the idea of God, who is beyond not only every human quality, but
also every human thought.

This form of the argument opens up a very powerful line of
thought, for it restates the basic question about human transcendence, the question which is posed (as we saw earlier) by the very
existence of the word "God": Where does the *infinite* horizon of the
human spirit come from, what is its intelligibility, unless it is
grounded in an ultimate source of meaning, an absolute? We may
say that this argument is another way of synthesizing the "primordial" approach to God, contrasting our intuition of the need of an
absolute with our inherent knowledge of our own finitude. Unlike
the first statement of the "ontological" argument, this form does not
claim that God's existence is known through the very content of the
idea; it rather adumbrates the argument from causality, since it
begins with the fact of the *existence* of this idea, and asks about its
provenance. We shall see that this form of thinking has something in
common with the "transcendental" approach to God's existence as
formulated by Karl Rahner.

Arguments from Creation—The "Five Ways"

We have seen that for Aquinas the "way" of the mind to God
cannot begin with God himself, for his deepest being, his essence, is
unknown to us and transcends our every conception. We must
instead begin with what is closer and more knowable to our finite
minds, namely, the world of our experience. It is from it that we
receive testimony of the existence of its author. The affirmation of
God is based not upon direct experience of his essence, but upon a
mediated experience which depends first of all upon a grasp of the

intelligibility of the finite world. We shall here take Aquinas' "five ways" as a classic statement of the arguments for God from creation.

1) From change or motion:

The first and clearest way is from motion. For it is certain, and apparent to our senses, that there is movement (change) in this world; but everything that moves is moved by another. For nothing can be moved, except insofar as it is in potency toward that toward which it is moved; while that which performs the motion does so insofar as it is in act. For movement or change is nothing but the reduction of potency to act. But nothing can be brought from potency to act except by the agency of something that is already in act.... It is impossible that a thing be both mover and moved in the same regard and in the same way; that is, it is impossible for anything to move or change itself. Therefore anything that moves is moved by something else. Now, if that thing by which it is moved is itself moved, it also must be moved by another; and that other by yet another. But this cannot go on to infinity, because then there would be no first mover, and consequently no motion at all; for the secondary causes of motion only move insofar as they are themselves moved by the first mover.... Therefore, it is necessary to arrive at a first mover of some kind, which is not moved by any other; and this is what everyone understands by God.[30]

2) From efficient causality:

The second way is from the nature of efficient causality. We find that there is in the sensible world an order of efficient causes. We do not find (and it is not possible) that any thing is the efficient cause of itself; for in order to be so, it would have to be prior to itself, which is impossible. Now, it is not possible to have an infinite series of efficient causes: for in every series of efficient causes, the first is the cause of the intermediate cause, and the intermediate is the cause of the last cause, whether the intermediate be a plurality of causes or a single one. If, however, one takes away the cause, one removes the effect as well. Therefore, if there were no first cause among efficient causes, neither would there be an intermediate or a last. But if there were an infinite procession of efficient causes, there would be no first efficient cause; and thus there would be no ultimate effect, nor any intermediate causes. But this is plainly false. Therefore, it is necessary to posit some first efficient cause: which is what all men call God.

3) From possibility and necessity:

The third way is taken from the possible and the necessary, and it states the following: we encounter among things some which have the possibility of being or of not being; for things are found to be generated and to be corrupted, and therefore it is possible for them to be or not to be. But it is impossible for such things always to exist; for if it is possible for something not to be, then at some time it is not. It follows then that if everything had the possibility of not being, there would have been a time when nothing existed at all. But if this were so, then there would still be nothing in existence; for what does not exist can only come into being by means of something already existing. Therefore, if at one time there was nothing at all, it would have been impossible for anything to come into being; and thus there would now be nothing in existence. But this is plainly false. Therefore not all beings are merely possible; there must be something whose existence is necessary. But every necessary being either has its necessity caused by another, or does not. It is not possible, however, to proceed to infinity in necessary things that have their necessity caused by another, just as it is not possible to have an infinite procession of efficient causes, as we have shown. Therefore it is necessary to posit some being which is necessary in and of itself, and which does not have the cause of its necessity from another, but is rather the cause of the necessity of other things. And this is what all call God.

4) From the degrees in things:

The fourth way is taken from the degrees which are found in things. For we find among things some which are more or which are less good, true, noble, and so forth. But "more" and "less" signify that things to different degrees approach something which is the maximum; so, for example, something is "more hot" when it more greatly approaches the hottest. There exists, therefore, something which is the truest, and the best, and the most noble, and, consequently, something which is most in being; for those things which are most true, are the greatest in being (as is said in *Metaphys. ii*). Now, the greatest in any genus is the cause of all others which are of the same genus; just as fire, which is the maximum of heat, is the cause of all other things which are hot (as is stated in the same book). Therefore there exists something which is for all things the cause of their being, and goodness, and of every perfection; and this is what we call God.

5) From teleology:

The fifth way is taken from the ordering of things. For we see that certain things which lack knowledge, such as natural bodies, act for an end; and this is clear from the fact that they always (or at least nearly always) act in the same way, so as to obtain the best result; and this shows that they attain their end not by accident, but by intention. But things which have no faculty of knowledge cannot move toward an end unless they are directed by some intelligent and knowing being—as an arrow is directed by an archer. Therefore there exists some intelligent being, by whom all natural objects are directed to their end; and this being we call God.]

It is clear that the central and guiding principle of thought is the same in all of Thomas' "ways": the need of a cause of the finite world of our experience. The world as it were "cries out" that it is insufficient to explain its own existence, that it is radically dependent upon Another. Thomas' "proofs" are the theoretical exposition of the quasi-intuitive way to God seen in Augustine: "When you consider all the beauties of this world, does not that beautiful order itself, as though with a single voice, reply to you, saying: 'I did not make myself, but God did'?"[31] "Ask the whole world . . . ask all things, and see if they do not respond to you, in their own manner, 'God made us.' "[32] Every aspect of the world, by its very finitude, reveals the need of a source outside itself; the world as a whole manifests the necessity of a cause of the whole, a cause which subsists in itself and by itself, without need of another. This intuition of the insufficiency of the world and its need of an ultimate explanation is the single unifying principle of all the theoretical "demonstrations" of God's existence from creation. Nevertheless, one may begin by "asking" of the world its origin in different ways; that is, one's "way" to God may begin with different data of experience, and thus, despite the unity of the underlying principle (causality), there are different "proofs."

Aquinas considers the phenomenon of motion (in the wide sense of the word) the most obvious indication of the need for a first cause. "Behold the sun and the moon; they cry out that they are made: for they change and vary" (Augustine).[33] Motion or change implies having something in oneself that was not there before,[34] i.e., it means becoming what one was not. How is this possible? How can what is merely potential become an actuality? Only through the agency of something which is already in motion, or in act. Actuality, that is, is prior to potency; the realization of potency—and hence its reality, even as potential—depends upon what is actually in existence or in "motion" (in the respect in question). But agents themselves change or move—that is, they proceed from potency to act—and thus they also are dependent upon others for their being. Hence one is led to the idea of a first agent, not moved by any other, but entirely "actual" in itself, and the first cause of the actuality and motion in all others. Without such a "first mover," there would never exist the possibility of the motion of anything at all.

[In the *Summa Contra Gentiles* Aquinas dwells at greater length on this reasoning, which is taken from Aristotle.[35] Aristotle holds that everything that moves is moved by another. This other is itself either moved or unmoved. If it is moved, then either one proceeds to infinity in seeking the source of motion, or one arrives at a first mover which is itself immobile. But it is impossible to proceed to infinity in the causation of motion; therefore, there exists an unmoved (God). Two things in this reasoning must be demonstrated; first, that everything that moves is in fact moved by another; and second, that it is impossible to proceed to infinity in the series of causes of motion. The first principle may be proved in several ways. By induction, we can see that anything which moves in the finite world does not have that motion as a part of its very essence; for all motion is caused by nature, or by force, or by the agency of some being. All such motion, then, is "accidental" to the being of the thing moved. It is obvious, therefore, that no being which moves "per accidens" can be self-moved; thus, it must be moved by another. One can also proceed by deduction. Whatever moves itself (were there such a thing) would have to be both first mover and first moved. If any part of this being were at rest, the whole would have to be at rest; otherwise, this being would not be the "first moved," but rather some part of it. That is, the first-mover and first-moved must act as a whole. But if the non-motion of the whole depends upon the non-motion of its parts, then the state of non-motion of this being depends upon another (i.e., the parts). But if non-motion depends upon another, so must motion; and thus there can be no (finite) being which moves itself. Stated more simply: if something were to move itself as first-moved, it would not be because of its parts or in its parts, but as a whole, indivisible. But every finite being is divisible, and depends upon its parts for its motion, as indeed for its very existence. Therefore no finite (i.e., divisible or "composed") being can move itself. Furthermore, nothing can be both in potency and in act in the same respect at the same time. But everything that is moved is in potency, insofar as it is moved (i.e., receives the act of moving), and in act insofar as it moves. If a being were to be self-moved, the moving and being-moved would coincide; and thus it would be in potency and in act in the same respect and at the same time. Since this is impossible, it is clear that no finite being can be self-moved, but must be moved by another.[36] (It should be manifest that this whole argumentation rests upon Aristotle's analysis of the finite world as being "composed" of potency and act; once this is admitted, it is an easy step to the recognition that no composed being can be self-sufficient or self-explaining, but requires a cause.)

The impossibility of infinite regress in causation is also shown in several ways. If there were such an infinite process, then there would have to exist an infinite number of bodies moving and being moved; for everything that is moved is divisible and (hence) bodily (again, presupposing the Aristotelian analysis of potency and act). In an infinite regression of causes of motion, every body that moves something would simultaneously be moved by another. Thus there would be an infinity of bodies being moved simultaneously. But it is impossible for an infinite number of bodies to be moved at once, in finite time. Furthermore, if one conceives of a series of causes of motion, not acting all at once, then there must be a first in the series; for without a first, there would be no initiation, and hence no motion at all, which contradicts the facts. Moreover, everything that moves "instrumentally," i.e., which is not itself the prime mover, but receives motion and passes it on, depends upon some first mover. On the hypothesis of an infinite regress in causality, there would be an infinite series of instrumental movers, with no prime mover. But without a first mover, there could be no instrumental motion, and hence no motion at all. Therefore there must be a prime mover.[37]]

It should be noted that Aquinas' reasoning here does not reach God as the first cause in a series of which he is a member. Rather, God or the first mover is different in kind from every other cause of motion, in that he is (in Aristotle's terminology) "unmoved" and "unmoving" (unchanging). He is therefore of a different sort altogether from "movable" (changing) beings which are composed of potency and act. The point of the demonstration comes down to the fact that finite, changing being cannot explain itself; it must ultimately have its reason for being in an unchanging and totally actual source.

St. Thomas' second "way" repeats the reasoning of the first, but this time begins with causes, rather than with effects (motion or change). Clearly, there are many causes which work together to effect the existence of any individual thing. These causes complement each other, and are caused by each other and by further causes. It is impossible, however, to project an infinity of causes; for without a first (and hence uncaused) cause, none of the others could exist, since they would not have been caused. Again, the crux of the argument lies in the contention that every (finite) being needs a cause (just as all motion presupposes a mover), and in the Arsistotelian principle, ἀνάγκη στῆναι, it is necessary to come to a starting point, a first cause, for an infinity of causes is impossible. With regard to this principle, it is important to note that Aquinas is thinking not of physical causes, but of metaphysical causality. Because he begins with physical reality, it is easy to assume that the "first cause" or "first mover" is the first in a series. Aristotle's principle would then come down to saying that every series must have a beginning, a starting point in time. In fact, however, Aquinas explicitly holds[38] that the principle on which he bases his argument does not mean that the world must have had a beginning in time. As far as physical causes go, an infinite series *is* possible. But such a series would still demand a "first" cause in the order of *explanation,* that is, on a metaphysical level. An infinitely extended process of causality would not be self-intelligible. Even an eternally existent world, therefore, would necessarily be a *created* or caused world. The impossibility of infinite regress refers not primarily to the succession of causes in time, but rather to the levels of causality, the line of reasons for being or intelligibility; and on this level, it is necessary to posit a primary being or intelligibility which is of a different metaphysical quality from any caused existent; and this is what is meant by "God."

The third way makes this distinction clearer. The being which is posited as the ultimate ground of all beings is necessary being—that which cannot not-be. In our world, there is clearly an element of chance or contingency. Everything in our experience can either be, or not be. But it is not possible that the totality of reality be contingent; for that which is not necessary cannot have been always; at some time, given infinite extension, there would have been a point when nothing was in existence (unless, of course, it was caused, *ex aliunde*). The existence of things which are of their nature potential, which can not-be, implies the existence of something which is absolutely necessary and self-explanatory. The *Summa Contra Gentiles*[39] makes explicit the relation of this reasoning to that of the first and second ways; since things can either be or not be, if they are, there must be a cause (i.e., a reason) for their existence; and this ultimately implies some being which is its own reason for existence, which is because it must be.

[The statement of the "third way" is similar to the proof of God's existence given by Avicenna: we know with certainty that there exists some being. But all being is either necessary, or merely possible. Likewise, the *totality* of beings is either necessary or possible. If it were necessary, then the necessary would be constituted or composed of what is merely possible, which is contradictory; if, on the other hand, the totality of beings is merely possible, then it needs some reason for being. This reason for the being of the totality can only be a Being which is extrinsic to the totality of beings, and necessary in itself; and this is God.[40]]

Aquinas' fourth way states that the different degrees of perfection in things implies a supreme degree in which all lower forms participate, and by which they are (exemplarily) caused. The argument from the gradation in being and goodness is characteristic of Augustine's thought, and is ultimately traced to Plato's ideal of ascending from earthly beauty and goodness to its source in the Divine Beauty:

> ... beauty absolute, separate, simple, and ever-lasting, which without diminution and without increase, or any change, is imparted to the ever-growing and perishing beauties of all other things. He who from these, ascending under the influence of true love, begins to perceive that beauty, is not far from the end. And the true order of going, or being led by another, to the things of love, is to begin from the beauties of earth and mount upwards for the sake of that other beauty, using these as steps only, and from one going on to two, and from two to all fair forms, and from fair forms to fair practices, and from fair practices to fair notions, until from fair notions he arrives at the notion of absolute beauty, and at last knows what the essence of beauty is.[41]

Aquinas' version of this "ascent" of the mind consists in recognizing that any value that we perceive in finite beings is not self-explanatory; that is, it is a "participation," an incomplete realization, of a supreme value; and this is manifest by the fact that there are degrees of perfection in the things of our experience, with no thing exhausting the fullness of value or goodness. If these degrees of value, beauty, etc., are real—that is, if they are not simply arbitrary and subjective designations of our minds—then what is the basis on which we are able to make comparative judgments of value? Ultimately, this implies the question: What is the source of ground of *value* (goodness, beauty, etc.) at all? Such a source cannot be found in finite things, for they are of their nature incomplete; they "participate" in ideal values, but do not exhaust them. They are not, therefore, the reason or explanation for their own goodness; no finite thing is fully good, good in itself, the ground of goodness as such. Their goodness or value—presuming, again, that it is real—demands an explanation outside themselves; they are "caused" in their goodness. This is to say that the degrees of value in things are unintelligible unless there is some fundamental value and intelligibility in existence itself. But a final value, goodness, intelligibility —like the final ground of being—must be "outside" the series of finite beings. It must be goodness, beauty, value, truth, etc., in the supreme degree, i.e., *in se;* and this is what is meant by God. In Avicenna's terminology, God is conceived as the "cause which gives [degrees of] perfection": he is that *for* which things exist, that which gives meaning to the values perceived in them. As such, he exists for and in himself, as the source and goal of all perfection.[42]

[Aquinas presumes in accord with ancient physics, that in the physical world as well there exists a "maximum" of any quality (e.g., heat), which is the "cause" of that quality wherever it exists. The argument, however, does not depend upon this physical theory. The existence of degrees of heat, or of any generic quality, does not in fact imply the existence of some supreme degree of heat, or heat "in se"; it only implies that there is an idea of heat, abstracted from hot things, which is the "norm" of comparison. Such ideas are abstractions, and not "realities" existing in themselves, as in some Platonic world of forms. Prescinding from the example taken from Aristotle's physics, the real scope of Aquinas' reasoning can be seen to be the realm of *transcendental* qualities or values, that is, those which are perfections of *being,* and are hence not generic, but analogical attributes. The argument then appears similar to the preceding "ways," except that it begins not with being or act, but with goodness, beauty, value, etc., which demand an ultimate metaphysical principle to explain their existence in the incomplete and non-self-explanatory finite world.]

The fifth way develops the argument of John Damascene:[43] contrary and dissonant tendencies can only come together to serve a common end of they are directed by some governing intelligence. But, in fact, we observe concord and harmony in a world composed of conflicting forces. Therefore, we infer the existence of a supreme governing intelligence, which is God. Aquinas explicitates: things in the world follow regular courses, and act for purposes, toward ends (that is, man observes intelligible and purposeful patterns in the world). But most things do not have the faculty of thinking or willing; therefore no intention of an "end" or purpose can come from them. Unless the finalities we observe are not real, but merely the product of our own minds, there must be some intelligent and willing being who directs the unconscious forces of the universe to their individual and common ends. This being is what is called God. (Note that Aquinas' reasoning does not imply that the order of the world is for the best of all possible realizations, but only that things "for the most part" tend toward a good which is relative.)[44] The argument may again be summed up in the words of Augustine: "Just as you know the existence of the soul, which you cannot see, from the movements and governance of the body, so from the governance and ordering of the whole world, and of souls themselves, you should acknowledge the existence of the Creator."[45]

THE NERVE OF THE PROOFS:
THE MIND AND INTELLIGIBILITY

"Man's mind, in making judgments about visible things, is able to recognize that it is itself of a higher order than all visible things. However, because of its own defects and its ability to progress in wisdom, the mind itself is revealed as incomplete and changeable, and finds above itself the existence of the changeless and perfect truth. By devoting itself to this truth, the mind is made happy, finding within itself the creator and lord not only of itself, but of all visible things as well. . . . From the beauty of those things which are external, we discover the maker, who is internal to us, and who creates beauty in a superior way in the soul, and then, in an inferior way, creates beauty in the body."[46]

The words of Augustine on the ascent of the mind to God from the world clearly indicate the critical position of the mind's intuition of itself in the process of coming to recognize the creator. The "external" world does not so much reveal God directly, as it points to the "internal" world of spirit itself, in which God is to be found. In Aquinas' ways, the "interiority" of the process is perhaps not so evident; nevertheless, the center or "nerve" of all the proofs is in fact the "implicit" presence of God to the human spirit, which recognizes and explicitates that presence in its reflection on the world.

As we have seen, for Aquinas the existence of God "in himself," which is identical with his essence, can by no means be "rendered evident," least of all in or by the material world. We know the fact of God's existence, without knowing the essence of God, by a process of inference *from* the existence of the world. The incompleteness of the world's existence on the level of intelligibility leads to the affirmation of God. This process is mediated by the mind's knowledge of the self-evident principles (like the principle of causality) which form the crucial argument of each proof. These principles, however, are nothing but the "principle" of intelligibility itself: the fact that the world is in basic accord with the human mind's desire to know. It is thus mind or spirit itself which reveals the "horizon" in which the world becomes understandable; that horizon is ultimately the Absolute, the ground of all meaning, which founds and supports the very fact of intelligibility and value. In this sense, Aquinas' "proofs" are an attempt to make explicit a knowledge of God which is implicit in every spiritual act, as the latter's horizon. Aquinas acknowledges this in the celebrated text of *De Veritate: "Omnia cognoscentia cognoscunt implicite Deum in quolibet cognito. Sicut enim nihil habet rationem appetibilis nisi per simultudinem primae bonitatis; ita nihil est cognoscibile nisi per simultudinem primae veritatis"* ("All knowers implicitly know God in every object of knowledge. For just as nothing can be desirable except insofar as it possesses a similitude to the first good [Good in itself], so nothing is knowable except insofar as it possesses a similitude to the first Truth").[47] That is, the intelligibility in things is nothing other than their "participation" in the intelligible nature of God, who is the condition for the existence of any intelligibility (or goodness, value) at all. The rational creature—man—can recognize this intelligibility because mind participates in the "light" of God's intelligible nature. It is this light which manifests itself as the self-evident principles on which man makes judgments; it is likewise what makes man "capax Dei,"[48] capable of the explicit knowledge and love of God. Thus the mind proceeds from the world to God through the mediation of the innate principles of intelligibility, which are ultimately identical with man's spiritual nature itself; they are nothing other than the presence of God to spirit as the ground and horizon of its being and dynamism.

The "interiority" of the ways of the mind of God—that is, the mediation of the presence of God by the mind's own intelligible nature—is even more explicitly manifest in the writings of Thomas' contemporary, St. Bonaventure. Indeed, for Bonaventure the "ways" from the external world are little more than reminders which serve to turn the mind to reflection on its own spiritual and intelligible nature, in which the existence of God is permanently and implicitly .present.[49] Although we can know God from his "vestiges" in the world, for Bonaventure the more immediate and higher way is from the mind's capacity to make judgments, i.e., to discern intelligibility in being.[50] According to Bonaventure, *every* positive affirmation whatever implies the existence of God; for every affirmation posits something as true; every such positing posits truth itself; and the positing of truth implies the existence of the Truth which is the cause of all that is true.[51] The existential judgment, that is, would be impossible if there were not present to the mind, implicitly, in every affirmation, the absolute *norm* of being (also goodness, beauty, etc.), which is God himself:

> Judgment takes place through our reason abstracting from place, time and mutability, and thus from dimension, succession and change, through reason which is unchangeable, unlimited and endless. But nothing is absolutely unchangeable, unlimited and endless unless it is eternal. Everything that is eternal is either God or in God. If, therefore, everything which we judge with certainty we judge by such a reason, then it is clear that he himself is the reason of all things and the infallible rule and light of truth, in which all things shine forth infallibly, indelibly, indubitably, irrefutably, indisputably, unchangeably, boundlessly, endlessly, indivisibly and intellectually. Therefore those laws by which we judge with certainty about all sensible things that come under our consideration—since they are infallible and cannot be doubted by the intellect of the one who apprehends them, since they are as if ever present and cannot be erased from the memory of the one who recalls them, since they cannot be refuted or judged by the intellect of the one who judges because, as Augustine says, "no one passes judgment on them, but by them"—these laws must be unchangeable and incorruptible since they are necessary; boundless since they are without limits; and endless since they are eternal—and for this reason they must be indivisible since they are intellectual and incorporeal, not made, but uncreated, existing eternally in the Eternal Art, by which, through which and according to which all beautiful things are formed. Therefore we cannot judge with certainty except in view of the Eternal Art which is the form that not only produces all things but also conserves and distinguishes all things, as the being which sustains the form in all things and the rule which directs all things. Through it our mind judges all things that enter it through the senses.[52]

True judgments, then, are possible because of the self-evident and indubitable first principles of knowledge, the changeless truths which are the basis for all judgments. These are nothing other than the "remembrance" of the eternal light of God, the ultimate intelligibility, shining in our intellects. Thus, the implicit knowledge of absolute being (intelligibility, goodness, beauty), *per se,* is the condition *sine qua non* for our knowing any particular being whatsoever, as well as for our ability to know the limitations of finite being. For, asks Bonaventure, "how could our intellect know that this being is defective and incomplete, unless it had a knowledge of a being without any defect?"[53] Since our mind knows also *itself* as finite, the light or intelligibility which founds all judgments whatever can only be the absolute being, God, enlightening our minds by the participation in his eternal truth: "Our mind itself is formed immediately by Truth itself."[54]

KANT AND THE CRISIS OF INTELLIGIBILITY

The classical arguments for God's existence, as we have seen, are grounded in a serene assurance of the power of the human mind to know *reality:* not only to know the objective world in its particularity, but also to perceive in it a real intelligibility corresponding to the mind's own spiritual "light," its orientation to an ultimate meaning, goal, and source of truth. As long as the confidence in the mind's ability to know the real, on the basis of its "first principles" of intelligibility, remained unshaken, the arguments for God appeared to rest on solid and indeed indisputable grounds. But the decline of high Scholasticism and its replacement with the schools of nominalism and voluntarism, with the consequent loss of the epistemological principles of Thomist realism, combined with the rise of modern empirical science, produced first a shift in the criteria for scientific knowledge, and then a new questioning about the very bases upon which philosophical theology had been based. Man's confidence in mind's ability to know anything beyond the sensible was slowly eroded, and finally profoundly disturbed, and with it the possibility of a rational assurance of an ultimate intelligibility to the world. The culmination of this long process, and its crucial moment for the philosophy of God, occurred in the philosophical "revolution" of Immanuel Kant. Kant's critique attacked the "proofs" for God's existence at their very root: the capacity of reason to attain to an objectively real intelligibility and ground of existence.

THE CRITIQUE OF METAPHYSICS

[Kant (1724–1804) appears in the history of philosophy at the moment of the juncture of the movements of continental rationalism—represented by Descartes, Spinoza, Leibniz and Wolff—and English empiricism, stemming from Francis Bacon and finding expression in the philosophies of Locke, Berkeley, and Hume. Kant was himself trained in the rationalist tradition, especially in the philosophy of Wolff; but he was also immersed in empirical science, and he awoke from the "dogmatic slumber" of rationalism largely because of his contact with the philosophy of Hume, which forms much of the background to his own.

Hume had accepted a theory of phenomenalism, according to which the immediate objects of consciousness are not the things of the objective world, but rather *impressions* of things, or internal sensations. These impressions are conceived by Hume elementaristically, as individual and unrelated facts; they become related to each other by the mind that perceives them. On a second level, the mind also develops *ideas*, which are derived from sense impressions by memory and imagination. The only certain knowledge, according to Hume, is that of logical relations of the conceptual order, like the invariable relations of mathematics. All other "knowledge" is in fact a form of "belief," and can only achieve at best a certain degree of probability, never certitude. This is especially true of all causal reasoning, which attempts to link the atomistic elements of perception.

Hume's elementarist perceptionism leaves no room for the direct knowledge of "substances," of causality, of God, or even of the self. These all transcend the possibility of direct experience, and are ideas which arise from a kind of extrapolation beyond the multiplicity of perceptions linked by memory because of similarity. (Thus, the "self," for example, is never experienced directly; it is rather an idea extrapolated from the many discrete but similar experiences of receiving sensations. Memory links these together to form the notion of a permanent "receiver," or self. Likewise, clusters of similar experiences or perceptions give rise to the idea of "things" existing continually in an external world, although we never directly experience such "things" or such a "world," but only individual perceptions.)]

Kant was profoundly influenced by the philosophy of Hume; but the latter's reduction of causality to psychological association disturbed him, because it seemed to undermine the very basis of scientific knowledge. Kant, however, was convinced of the validity of science (that is, the mathematical and Newtonian science of his day, with its universal and absolute physical laws). Kant's philosophical question therefore became: How is scientific knowledge epistemologically possible? That is, how can we attain knowledge that is at once *synthetic* (containing new information, as opposed to merely analytic knowledge, in which the predicate is implied in the definition of the subject) and also *a priori* (i.e., universal and necessary, like scientific laws, and anterior to experience, which—according to Hume—can only produce an accumulation of probabilities)? Kant resolved the problem by means of his famous "Copernican revolution" in philosophy, by which he shifted the center of the epistemological world from the object of knowledge to what is brought to the act of knowing by the subject. This signified a movement away from both Hume's phenomenalist skepticism and from the dogmatic "slumber" of rationalism. But more significantly, it marked an overturning of the naive and common-sense type of realism which assumes that knowing is simply a matter of "taking a look" at "what is out there,"[55] and focused attention on a critical study of the *a priori* conditions of knowing within the subject.

Kant's solution to the problem of the synthetic *a priori* (and hence the possibility of science) rests upon a distinction between the "phenomenal" and "noumenal" (mental or ideal) orders. According to Kant (and following Hume), our real immediate knowledge is limited to intuition, which takes place only within the range of sense experience. But even by sense intuition, we do not know objects, but merely *phenomena;* things "in themselves" remain unknown and unknowable. Nevertheless, according to Kant, we can make true synthetic and *a priori* statements about the world, because the mind contributes the elements which give order to sensible data: namely, the sensible *a prioris* of space and time, which give physical order and direction to our sense perceptions, and the "categories" (including causality) which impose an intelligible ordering or understanding on the multiplicity of perceptions. The function of human understanding is to synthesize sense data by means of the *a priori* categories; the function of judgment is to link them together. In such a system the empirical and mathematical sciences, which are concerned with what Kant calls "understanding" *(Verstand)*, the informing and ordering of the data of sense experience, are saved; but the valid functioning of "reason" *(Vernunft)*, the "transcendental" faculty, is limited to a purely logical, "regulative" role. For "reason" has as its object not any data of empirical experience, but rather the understanding itself;[56] it gives a further intelligible dimension to the categories by giving them an ideal and final unity, in the notions of the self, the world, and God.[57] This "regulatory" function of reason is legitimate, according to Kant, but only as long as it yields merely ideal and logical constructs of the mind. To attribute to these real existence would be to go beyond the limits of experience, and would be an illicit and illusory use of reason. Thus the metaphysical or transcendental use of reason is limited to the *a priori* elements of the subject's own mind; any attempt to reach reality via metaphysical intelligibility is a "transcendental illusion." The categories of the understanding are themselves mere "forms" of thought, and must be referred to the sensible if they are to represent objective reality. But "ideas"—such as the self, the world, God—are still further removed from objective reality, because they cannot meet with any phenomenon whatsoever in which they can be found concretely.[58] Thus the idea of God, "like all speculative ideas, means no more than that reason requires us to deal with all the connections in the world according to principles of a systematic unity, and therefore *as if* the whole had derived from a single all-encompassing Being as the highest and all-sufficient Cause."[59] Thus for Kant any approach of the mind of God from the intelligibility of the world is undercut by the conviction that this intelligibility is *imposed* upon the world by the mind itself.

[The concept of God for Kant is necessarily an idea or ideal of "pure reason." But such an idea cannot produce any evidence of its own real existence, beyond the need of reason to complete the synthetic unity of the world by means of this type of intelligible construct.[60] "The ideal of the Supreme Being is, according to these considerations, nothing other than a *regulative principle* of reason."[61] It is parallel to the concept of "space," which is not a real object, but only a category for unifying the material objects of experience.[62] Synthetical principles, which give knowledge of existence, are applicable only within the sphere or empirical experience; in order to arrive at the knowledge of a supreme Being, they would have to be used transcendentally—which is illegitimate.[63] Transcendental questions, on the other hand, can produce only transcendental answers: i.e., concerning only *a priori* concepts, with no empirical content. "Synthetic a priori" knowledge—science and mathematics—is possible only on the basis of possible experience; a metaphysical knowledge of existence, such as would be required for God, has no such basis, and is therefore impossible.[64] Reason may, indeed, reach the *concept* of God; but the *existence* of such a being is beyond its reach. For the existence of an object cannot be derived simply by analysis of its concept, since the knowledge of existence means that it is given outside our thoughts; but it is totally impossible to reach beyond our thoughts except by empirical connections, which are not given in the case of the ideas of pure reason.[65] "It is clear that in admitting a conception (*Vorstellung*) of the grounding idea of a Supreme Author, I do not accept as fundamental the existence and the knowledge of such a being, but only the idea of it; and that I do not really derive anything from that being, but only from the idea."[66]

Thus the idea of God derives, for Kant, from a hypostatization of the legitimate "regulatory" ideal of reason. Every determination of a finite being (as Spinoza had already declared) is a negation; being "this" means being "not-that." But we cannot think a negation without its opposite affirmation. Reason, however, postulates a transcendental substratum for *all* determinations, that is, an affirmative being which is the opposite of all the negations. This substratum cannot be other than the sum total of reality, the "All," which is the condition for recognizing the limitation or determination of every individual being. This unlimited "All" is the "transcendental Ideal."[67] When this ideal is hypostasized, we arrive at the concept of God, as the possessor of all positive perfections, the opposite of the negative limitations in determinate things.[68] This hypostasized use of the transcendental ideal, however, is illegitimate. For reason uses the ideals merely as the *concept* of the totality of reality, in order to give a mental grounding for the complete determination of all things. This does not imply that the substratum signified in the concept itself exists objectively, and constitutes a thing.[69] The notion of God arises when the idea of a "most real," which is originally only a "representation" (*Vorstellung*), is first reified, or made an object, then hypostasized, and then personified,[70] and becomes regarded not as the concept of the sum total of things, but as their cause.[71]

Reason "urgently desires" to presuppose some foundation for the complete determination of the concepts of the understanding; it wishes to find an unconditioned source and explanation for the conditioned given. Such a final halting point in the regress of reason from conditioned to condition could only be infinite being: "the immovable rock of the Absolutely Necessary." Such a being itself could be no foundation; it would "hang in empty space," unless it filled everything, leaving no room for a further "why?"; it must, in short, be the final, complete, absolute and infinite Reality.[72]

However, this final source and condition of reality which reason wishes to presuppose, is a mere creation of *thought;* it is purely ideal and "fictitious." We cannot admit this creation of the mind as a real being—unless we were forced to do so by some circumstance outside pure speculative reason.[73]]

CRITIQUE OF THE TRADITIONAL PROOFS FOR GOD

According to Kant, there are only three kinds of proof for the existence of God from speculative reason. He names these the "physico-theological," the cosmological, and the ontological.[74] Kant's epistemological position, however, leads him ultimately to reduce all the proofs to the last; for "God" can only be a concept of pure reason, a transcendental ideal, and hence purely *a priori*. This being so, it is impossible to draw any legitimate rational inference of his real existence: "It is easy to see . . . that the idea of an absolutely necessary Being is a concept of pure reason, that is, a mere idea, whose objective reality is not at all demonstrated by the fact that reason has need of it. . . . "[75]

It is of course possible to give a verbal definition of the concept of an absolutely necessary Being in which its necessary existence is included; this is the procedure of the "ontological argument," as Kant sees it. "But this process does not make us any the wiser concerning the conditions that make a thing's non-existence absolutely inconceivable; and these conditions are precisely what we wish to know: i.e., whether by means of this concept we are genuinely thinking something, or are really thinking nothing at all."[76] In other words, one can define the Absolute God, as necessarily existing, or as that being whose non-existence is impossible; but this is merely an analytic proposition, while every proposition involving real existence must be synthetic. This is expressed in Kant's famous dictum that "being is no real 'predicate,' that is, a concept of something that can be added on to the concept of a thing."[77] What is lacking to the concept of God, the necessary Being, is an *a posteriori* knowledge of the real possibility of his existence.[78] This knowledge is, however, impossible because of the very nature of the ideas of pure reason, which occur entirely within the *a priori* realm of the subject's mind:

> For objects of pure thought there is no means whatsoever of knowing their existence, for it would have to be known entirely *a priori;* but our consciousness of all existence (whether through immediate perception, or by conclusions which connect something with perception) belongs entirely to the unity of experience; and thus any existence outside that field, although it cannot simply be pronounced impossible, is a presupposition which we cannot in any way justify.[79]

The second type of proof from pure reason is the "cosmological," from the contingency of the world. Kant derives his idea of this argument from Leibniz. Formulated syllogistically, it reasons as follows: "If anything at all exists, then there must exist also an absolutely necessary Being. But I, at least, exist. Therefore, there exists an absolutely necessary Being. The minor contains an experience; the major draws the conclusion from experience in general to the existence of the Necessary."[80] Kant explains in a note that the syllogism "rests on the apparently transcendental natural law of causality: that everything *contingent* has its cause, which, if it is likewise contingent, likewise requires a cause, until the series of subordinate causes must end in an absolutely necessary cause, without which the whole series would have no completion."[81] Ostensibly, this proof appeals to experience; but, according to Kant, this appeal is in reality superfluous, since the argument inevitably ends up in a hidden use of the "ontological" argument. For the transcendental principle which argues from the contigent to a cause really only has meaning within the world of sense experience, and outside that world it does not even have a meaning. "For the purely intellectual concept of the contingent cannot produce a synthetic proposition, like that of causality; and thus the principle of causality has no meaning at all, and no criterion for its use, except within the world of sensation."[82] The appeal to the experience of causality within the world can, indeed, lead to a concept of an absolutely necessary condition; but in order to identify this concept with any definite object, the mind must abandon experience and turn to pure concepts, to find one which contains the conditions of possibility of an absolutely necessary Being. But reason can recognize as absolutely necessary only that which is necessary by its very concept.[83] Such a concept is found in the *ens realissimum,* whose notion carries the note of absolute necessity. To make this identification, however, is again to rely upon pure *a priori* ideas of reason, which is the substance of the ontological argument.[84]

[For Kant the cosmological proof, like every transcendental attempt to arrive at the existence of a necessary being, rests upon a "dialectical illusion." It may be necessary to think of something necessary as the condition for existing things in general; but I am not therefore obliged to think of any particular thing as being necessary in itself. For "necessity" and "contingency" according to Kant do not concern "things themselves"; they are rather merely subjective principles of reason. The Absolutely Necessary Being is nothing other than the principle of the greatest unity (in the mind) of all phenomena; but to affirm the actual existence of such a being is an illegitimate leap.[85]]

Much in accord with his temperament as a follower of Newtonian science, Kant accords his maximum respect to the proof from order, which he calls "physico-theological."[86] While the ontological argument begins from the concept of things in general, and the cosmological from existence in general, the physico-theological begins from our definite experience of the world.[87] It rests on the fact that "the present world offers us so immeasurable a stage of variety, order, purposefulness, and beauty:

> Everywhere we see a chain of effects and causes, of ends and means, of orderly regularity in coming to be and departing; and, since nothing has entered by itself into the state in which it is found, so everything points to some other thing as its cause; but this cause makes necessary precisely the same further seeking, so that in this way the whole universe would sink in the abyss of nothingness, unless we admitted something which existed by itself, self-subsistent and independent, outside this chain of endless contingencies and supporting it, both as the cause of its origin and as the guarantee of its continued existence.[88]

The world, that is, shows marvelous order and finality: an intentional arrangement, carried out with great wisdom. But the purposefulness of the ordering of the things of the world belongs to them contingently; they cannot themselves create their ordering and unity, nor can it be an accident. There must exist, then, a final, unique, sublime and wise Cause, who orders all things with wisdom and freedom.[89] The mind, then, beginning with the wonders of nature and the beauty of the cosmos, is led from the conditioned to its conditions, and finally to the supreme and unconditioned Author of all.[90] This reasoning, according to Kant, suffices to give the mind rest and comfort, and embodies a "faith" which does not demand unconditional submission.[91] Nevertheless, the physico-theological proof cannot by itself actually establish the existence of the Supreme Being; at most, it can reach an Architect of the world, not a Creator. That is, the physico-theological reasoning cannot reach, from experience, the *concept* of the highest cause; to do so, it must leave empirical proof behind, and argue on the basis of *contingency*. But in doing so, it becomes identical with the cosmological proof, which is, as we have seen, nothing but the ontological proof in disguise; for one cannot demonstrate the contingency of the world without recourse to "transcendental" argumentation, which involves hypostasizing the regulative ideas of pure reason.[92]

Thus for Kant any conclusion—like the existence of God —which leads beyond the sphere of possible experience, is fallacious and groundless. Human reason has, unfortunately, a natural inclination to overstep its limits, and, once it has legitimately conceived the transcendental ideals, it is prone to seek the security and comfort of illegitimately admitting their existence in an extra-mental world. They are, nevertheless, simply an "irresistible illusion," and the mind can only be defended from them by the vigilance of the philosophical critique.[93]

At the same time, Kant insists that although the existence of God (and the other transcendental ideas) cannot be demonstrated by reason, neither can it be *disproved*.[94] "The unconditioned necessity of the existence of a being simply cannot be comprehended by us, and therefore *subjectively* every speculative proof of a necessary supreme Being is rightly excluded; but this does not legitimately militate against the existence of such a grounding Being *in itself*."[95] Kant adheres strictly to his conception of the limitations of the mind; simply because our reason cannot speculatively reach the existence of God, we have no cause to say that he does not in fact exist; and indeed the *concept* of God—like those of the self and the world—retains a necessary and regulative function, even when the possibility of affirming his existence has been rejected.[96]

THE "MORAL ARGUMENT"

Kant does not, however, leave man finally in a simple state of agnosticism because of the limitations of speculative reason. For there is also a *practical* function of reason, regarding the determination of man's freedom and action in life. It is true that the transcendental ideals comprehended by speculative reason—which are expanded by Kant to include not only the existence of God, but also freedom of the will and the immortality of the soul[97]—have no use as far as *knowledge* is concerned. They have, however, an important *practical* use: they are crucial to our determination of *what ought to be done*.[98] Man has within himself an undeniable and absolute moral imperative, an "ought." The basis of that imperative, imposed by reason, cannot be derived from any empirical content, but is inseparably connected with the suppositions of the existence of God and of a future life (of reward or punishment).[99] Without God and immortality, states Kant, morality would lose its grounds; [100] the only cause which could give binding force to the moral law of our being is a supreme Will of God.[101]

The existence of God, therefore, which Kant has excluded from the knowledge of speculative reason, is reintroduced as a "postulate" of "practical reason" (i.e., reason insofar as it regards man's free action, or "will"). The relationship of the mind to the reality of God Kant now names "belief," which is different from speculative knowledge:

> The word "belief" refers to only the guidance which an idea gives me, and to the subjective influence it has on the conduct of my reasonable actions; these make me hold fast to it, even though I may not be capable of justifying the idea from a speculative point of view.[102]

A purely "doctrinal" belief, says Kant, is always beset with difficulties; but with moral belief the situation is different:

> Here it is absolutely necessary that something be done: namely, that I obey the moral law on every point. The goal is here unalterably established, and in all my insight, there is only one single condition possible, which can bring that end into agreement with all other ends, and thus give it practical validity: that condition is, namely, the existence of God and of a future world.[103]

Thus we must end in admitting the existence of God despite the limits of pure reason, because of the overwhelming character of the moral imperative:

> I shall inevitably believe in the existence of God and in a future life, and I am sure that nothing can shake this belief, because with it would be overthrown my very moral principles themselves; and I cannot give them up without becoming detestable in my own eyes.[104]

Moral obligation or the universal law is, for Kant, undeniable. But obligation would be unreasonable and without motivation were it not for God. Therefore we are after all obliged to follow, in our practical lives, concepts which are "objectively" insufficient for knowledge, but which are practically preponderant and more probable than any other solution.[105]

Kant ends up, in his own phrase, doing away with knowledge (of God) in order to make room for belief. But does that belief itself have any real grounds? Is the imperative of "practical reason," the moral law, so undeniable as Kant felt it? Or does this reduce the existence of God simply to the postulate of a certain highly rigid and moralistic temperament, without objective grounding? Is Kant's argument, as Schiller put it, only fit for slaves? Again, why is the will's moral need for grounding in God more compelling than the urgent need of intellect? Can the "practical" reason indeed be separated in the Kantian manner from the speculative?

Once the conviction of the mind's ability to reach the real intelligibility of existence has been shaken, can the obligation of the moral imperative last for long? "Without God," declares Dostoievski in *The Brothers Karamazov,* "everything is lawful." If God's existence becomes simply an appendage of the law itself, has the law any basis to uphold it? Can a "postulate" of reason really give a ground to man's decisions about ultimate meaning and responsibility, or would it be merely an "opiate," as Marx would claim, an "illusion," as Freud insisted, a failure to face the truth of man's own responsibility to create our own morality, as Sartre claimed?

V. THE GROUNDING OF TRANSCENDENCE IN GOD — 2

... Then the king will say to those at his right, "Come, you whom my Father has blessed, take possession of the kingdom which has been destined for you from the creation of the world. For when I was hungry, you gave me food, when I was thirsty, you gave me something to drink, when I was a stranger, you invited me to your homes, when I had no clothes, you gave me clothes, when I was sick, you looked after me, when I was in prison, you came to see me." The upright will answer, "Lord, when did we see you hungry and give you food, or thirsty, and give you something to drink? ..."

—(Mt. 25:34ff)

When we wish to understand a person, the life of a person, we seek first of all to find out what are his ideas. ... But our idea of reality is not our reality. Our reality consists in everything that we in fact count on in living. ... It seems to me of exceptional importance for clarifying human existence to inject this distinction between thinking *something and* counting on *something. ... The greatest influence on our behavior rests in the hidden implications of our intellectual activity: in the things we* count on, *and not in what we* think. ...

—José Ortega y Gasset, *Ideas y Creencias*

THE POST-KANTIAN QUESTION

The turn to the experience of subjectivity, or of conscious, personal being, poses the question of God in its most urgent form. If the presumption of meaningfulness, intelligibility and value in life is to be rationally justified, we must seek their grounding outside ourselves and our mortal existence. For this reason we have exam-

109

ined the notion of God and the traditional ways to the affirmation of his existence. Those ways, as we have seen, explicitated and drew the consequences of the mind's apprehension of intelligibility. Their validity, however, was challenged by the erosion of confidence in the mind's ability to reach reality beyond itself. Is the human presumption of meaning, of value, of ultimate intelligibility to the world—in short, of all that leads to the notion of God—*nothing but* a presumption, a postulate which makes life livable, but which is incapable of being verified as reality? This is the question left to challenge metaphysics and theology by the critique of Kant. Can the ways of mind to reality and to God, built, as it seems, on the once-solid ground of *objective* theoretical intelligibility in the world, find a path through the inner space of "interiority," in which the mind becomes critically conscious of its own mode of knowing?

We have already accepted in principle the legitimacy—indeed, the necessity—of this question, in directing our correlation of faith to human experience to the "turn to the subject." We have now arrived at a point where we may further specify the method which our project calls for. Kant's critique had the benefit of destroying dogmatic rationalism. Any approach to transcendence must henceforth take its stand on the vital experience of the subject. The position left to metaphysics in the Kantian system—that of a postulate of practical living—is in itself, as Gómez Caffarena remarks, no mean status.[1] The problem is that it leaves man's morality and faith disassociated from our drive for intelligibility. If metaphysics is to be validated within the realm of interiority, we must close this gap between vital experience and reason; we must formulate, in Ortega's felicitous phrase, a "ratio-vitalism" which can show that the absolute of metaphysics, far from being divorced from human experience, is at its core. A modern justification of faith must, in short, take its stand on a appeal to the subject's *metaphysical experience.*[2] Only on this basis can we invite mankind to see in the affirmation of God a basis for constructing truly human life and for meeting the dilemma of the world.

THE CRITIQUE OF KANT'S CRITIQUE

[Seen from the perspective of the turn to the subject, Kant's critique is itself revealed as incomplete and limited, both in its presuppositions and in its performance. Without embarking on a full critical examination, we may remark the following:

1. Kant's turn to subjectivity was incomplete insofar as he was

not liberated from the classical object-dominated mentality which ruled in the physical science of Newton. He overlooks the existential subject *as such*, in its act, reducing it merely to either a "phenomenon" or an impersonal *a priori* form (the "transcendental unity of appreception"). He is therefore concerned exclusively with the formal structures of knowing; the content of the act, for Kant, comes from without, from the unknowable, and the performing subject is overlooked. He is left, then, with the empty form of knowledge.

2. Kant is limited likewise by the phenomenalism and elementarism he inherited from Hume; he presumes, that is, that the subject never encounters being, but only representations of being, and that these are perceived as atomistic items which must be related by mind (assuming a classical, as opposed to a *Gestalt* psychology.)

3. The elementaristic cast of thought is manifest again in Kant's failure to integrate the different "faculties" of the human spirit. Not only is there a gap between "practical" and "speculative" reason, but within the speculative function there is a gap between categorical understanding (*Verstand*) and "reason" (*Vernunft*).

4. As Kant's immediate successors already recognized, the fundamental Kantian distinction between phenomenon and noumenon, with the identification of phenomenon with experience, and of noumenon with "reality in itself," is highly questionable, if not actually involved in antinomy (as Hegel intimates).

Kant's critiques were powerful in their analysis; but, in the last resort, Kant's method was rather like that of the biologist who dissects an animal: he gets an excellent view of each individual part, but he loses the living organism.]

TRANSCENDENTAL METHOD

The procedure which attempts to legitimate the affirmation of transcendent being within the realm of interiority by appealing to the subject's own metaphysical experience has become known by the name "transcendental method." (The name derives from Kant himself, who wrote: "I call all knowledge *transcendental* which is occupied not so much with objects *as with our manner of knowing objects, so far as this is meant to be possible* a priori."[3]) Although the development of a "ratio-vitalist" philosophy of man and his/her relation to the Absolute owes much to other philosophers—in particular one must mention Maurice Blondel and his philosophy of action—it was especially the work of Joseph Maréchal which provided the foundations for a metaphysics of interiority expressly addressing the problematic raised by Kant.[4]

Maréchal's masterful work, *Le Point de Départ de la Métaphysique*,[5] opened a fruitful dialogue between Thomist realist metaphysics and the philosophy of Kant. Accepting the Kantian problematic and hence the starting point of "interiority," Maréchal corrects Kant's theory of knowledge (still limited by its rationalist inheritance) by means of a new appreciation of the subject *in action*. Maréchal considers Kant correct in holding that judgment or affirmation is the central moment in the knowing process: "intuition" is limited to sensation; true knowledge takes place only in the act of judging. Kant's conception of judgment, however, was too static: being fundamentally interested only in the *object*, he reaches only an incomplete understanding of judgment, namely as the synthesis of sense data. For Maréchal this synthesizing function, which occurs on the level of concepts, is only the first phase of judging. Its more crucial role, however, is in the *assertive* function overlooked by Kant. This dimension of judgment is revealed not on the conceptual level, but in the *performance* of judgment. In every assertion that "S *is* P," there is not only a unifying of the concepts of subject and predicate, but also an existential affirmation, i.e., an affirmation of *existence*. The conceptions are referred to reality, to being. Maréchal thus goes beyond the Kantian use of transcendental method by focusing upon the dynamic between the richness of the implicit, lived *act* and the relative poverty of the *concept*. It is the *activity* of judging or affirming, as distinguished from its mere content, which reveals the transcendent horizon of consciousness. For Maréchal, therefore, transcendental method attempts to make *explicit* what is present at least *implicitly* in every act of knowing and loving, thus revealing the *a priori* conditions of those acts.

Maréchal's philosophy opened the way to a verification of metaphysics by an appeal to the personal performance of the subject in act—to our "metaphysical experience." This direction was subsequently taken up by a new generation of thinkers, including (to name a few) Emerich Coreth, J.-B. Lotz, Karl Rahner and (in a different way) Bernard Lonergan. All of these have attempted to formulate a new approach to metaphysics and to God, based upon critical realism and using the conditions of consciousness as a starting point.

Transcendental method (used, of course, with different nuances and emphases by its various practitioners) attempts to give a foundation to philosophy by examining the conscious operations of the existing human subject, and by setting forth the necessary conditions and implications of those operations. There is always more "known" in our consciousness than is made explicit in any content (concept); this implicit dimension can be made explicit by reflection. Transcendental method is therefore concerned with the "dialectic between concept and act, between *pensée pensée* and *pensée pensante,* between the conceptualized, explicit, thematic content of our knowledge and the unthematic, pre-reflexive, implicit knowledge that is co-affirmed with the act of knowing itself."[6] It is of greatest importance to realize that the method is based upon the conscious *activity* of the subject in knowing and willing. It does not begin with ideas or concepts or decisions, the "content" of knowing and loving, but with the acts of knowing and deciding. Transcendental method as conceived in this "movement" is concerned to uncover the usually hidden implications of our intelligent spiritual activity. To borrow again Ortega's phrase, it is concerned with what we in fact *count on* as real, rather than with what we *think* about, or our "ideas" of reality. The knowledge that we "count on"—what Coreth calls "lived knowledge" or "exercised knowledge"—is immediate and undeniable, but non-thematic.[7] It is made thematic and explicit through reflection—although here again the content of reflection will never exhaust the act.[8]

Transcendental method, then, as we conceive it, aims at a "self-appropriation" of the subject's consciousness.[9] We seek to bring to our reflective attention those elements of conscious activity on which we always rely in thinking and willing, without normally being explicitly aware of them. Since transcendental method relies on the revelation of our conscious activity, it is clear that *each subject must practice it for* him/herself; each person must observe his/her own conscious performance, to verify that the facts referred to in a transcendental theory of cognition or metaphysics are actually contained in experience. The descriptions and analyses of the philosophers can only be "signposts"[10] to point to the subject's own metaphysical experience. Transcendental method is, in this sense, a most radical turn to the subject. It demands not merely learning of concepts and their interrelations, but a personal turn to the data, which are found only in each person's consciousness, insofar as he/she is actively performing the operations in question.

[This demand for personal involvement is, of course, not new.[11] Indeed, it exists wherever learning ceases to be an imposition from without and becomes real—when philosophy is no longer a "subject," but the "love of wisdom." The appeal to the subject, however, is usually implicit; in classical philosophy, for example, the metaphysical experience of the subject is presupposed as the foundation of the "self-evidence" of the so-called "first principles." What distinguishes transcendental method is its effort to take nothing for granted: to find an absolute starting point and to explicitate the necessary and implicit performance of the subject as the basis for metaphysics and the affirmation of the Absolute.]

THE QUESTION AS STARTING POINT ·

Transcendental method attempts to systematize reflectively the profoundest implications of what we do all the time, and thus to justify the validity of our knowledge, especially in its metaphysical aspect. As set forth by Emerich Coreth (whom we shall take in this section as the representative of the German-speaking transcendental Thomists), this process has two major phases: transcendental *reduction* starts from an act of the mind and proceeds to inquire about the necessary prior conditions which make it possible. The subject uncovers thematically what is implied in his acts of knowing, by returning from the thematically known to the unthematic co-known or pre-known. The second stage, transcendental *deduction,* then proceeds from the conditions uncovered to the essential structures of the experience.[12]

Is there a fundamental and undeniable starting point for this transcendental reflection? We have already indicated that the starting point cannot be any particular content of consciousness, but must be in the subject's performance. But what act of performance? Coreth finds the undeniable starting point in the act of *questioning:* "The question itself cannot be challenged or questioned, it presupposes nothing, it takes nothing for granted. Should we nevertheless question it, then the question by which we challenge it will be the starting point. If we wonder about the very possibility of questioning, we will do so by questioning."[13]

The act of questioning itself (as opposed to any particular content of a question) is indubitable, since even in order to doubt we must question. The problem then becomes: How is the question possible?[14] It is clear that every question involves a kind of mixture of knowledge and ignorance. "We can question only when we do not yet know that which the question is about, otherwise there is no need for a question. On the other hand, we can ask questions only if we know something already about the object of the inquiry. Otherwise, we do not know what question to ask."[15] There is, then, a certain "pre-knowledge" which is presupposed by the question. It is not explicit or thematized, but is presupposed by the very act; it is the "horizon" of the question.[16] When we ask not about some particular question but about questioning as such, we may say that there is always, as condition of asking, an "anticipation" of the yet unknown. This pure anticipation or pre-knowledge, the *a priori* condition of any question whatever, Coreth calls the *Vorgriff* ("pre-grasp").[17] What is this *Vorgriff* an anticipation *of*? That is, what is the horizon of the question as such? Clearly, it is the full range of the questionable—the anticipation of every answer. But the questionable as such is without limits. Were we to set limits, we could in turn question them. The object of the pure question, then, is simply everything—not, of course, every particular thing, but everything at once, in unity. This unity of all things is simply *being*. Every question asks about what *is*. "Hence being as such is the ultimate aim, the unlimited horizon of every question. This totality of being is not the sum of all previously known beings, but the anticipation of the totality and the unity of all beings, present to the human mind as the unthematic pre-knowledge of every question."[18]

For Coreth, then, in sharp contrast to Kant, transcendental method, far from destroying the bases for metaphysics, lands us in the middle of it.[19] Man questions because he is a metaphysical animal; being is not only the object of our intellect, but is so because we are a living awareness of being, in our selfhood, even prior to any explicit question: "When we inquire whether anything really is, we are aware that our act of inquiring and that we, the inquirer, really *are*."[20]

Furthermore, it is being "in itself" which is intellect's horizon—not merely "being-for-us." What we seek to know by questioning is reality, what or how things really are. Indeed, "we can speak of 'validity for me' only because we contrast it with 'validity in itself.' "[21] Absolute validity or reality is the horizon of inquiry and affirmation. Thus there is a latent antinomy in all forms of relativism and idealism, including Kant's assertion that we know only "phenomena"; for the *content* of the relativist affirmation is contradicted by the very *act* of affirming. That is, the very affirmation that we know only "phenomena" or "things for us" implicitly contains the co-affirmation that *this* affirmation, at least, *is really so*. The relativist "affirms that it is absolutely valid to say that human knowledge is only relatively valid, and thus he contradicts himself."[22]

The horizon of our questioning being is thus revealed as unconditioned, or absolute. "It is the unconditioned which is expressed in the word IS. Because and inasmuch as it is, that which we inquire about is unconditioned. Hence being appears as the unconditioned, the absolute; it is the unconditioned condition of all questioning, it is the absolutely necessary."[23] This horizon is unlimited, for there is no going beyond it: "If the horizon of our knowing were limited, our knowledge would not be absolute. We could then occupy other points of view, with other horizons, where things might look different to us. Within a limited horizon we would not even be able to ask about the ultimate, absolute, unconditioned point of view."[24] But we do in fact ask about the unconditioned, about what is; and therefore the horizon of our questioning is *being,* the unconditioned reality of things, that which includes and affects everything about everything, both intensively and extensively.[25]

THE TRANSCENDENTAL WAYS TO GOD — I

Paul stood up in the Areopagus and delivered this address: "Men of Athens, I note that in every respect you are scrupulously religious. As I walked around looking at your shrines, I even discovered an altar inscribed, 'To a God Unknown.' Now, what you are thus worshiping in ignorance I intend to make known to you. For the God who made the world and all that is in it, the Lord of heaven and earth, does not dwell in sanctuaries made by human hands, nor does he receive man's service as if he were in need of it. Rather, it is he who gives to all life and breath and everything else. From one stock he made every nation of mankind to dwell on the face of the earth. It is he who set limits to their epochs and fixed the boundaries of their regions. They were to seek God, yes to grope for him and perhaps eventually find him—through he is not really far from any one of us. 'In him we live and move and have our being,' as some of your own poets have put it, 'for we too are his offspring.' "

Acts 17:22–28

"Thou hast made us for Thyself, O Lord, and our hearts are restless until they rest in Thee."

Augustine: *Confessions*

The recognition of the unconditioned and ultimate nature of the act of being (*esse*) does not yet vindicate the affirmation of the existence of God;[26] for "being" here refers to what the Scholastics called "common being" (*esse commune*), and does not distinguish between finite and infinite. Nevertheless, the necessity of being is the starting point for the recognition of God's existence.

Coreth develops first of all the notion of necessity in being, which has already been uncovered in the transcendental examination of the question. Every being, insofar as it *is*, is necessarily, and cannot not-be or be other than itself. This fact, implicitly co-affirmed in every question and in all knowledge, finds thematic expression as the "principles" of identity and of non-contradiction.[27] Being is necessarily being; it cannot not-be. "It follows at once that in our every act of thinking there is co-posited and presupposed the primordial realization of the necessity of absolute being."[28] The beings of our experience, however, are multiple and changing, and are therefore revealed to be *conditioned;* they *are* unconditionally, but only *if* they are posited in being.[29] But being or the real in itself must be completely unconditioned. Being is absolute. "The mind's dynamism can reach the existent in its unconditioned validity only if it always anticipates the simply unconditioned."[30] That is, we must have as the horizon of our judgments the unconditioned or absolute, in order to recognize things as conditioned or relative. This horizon cannot be other than being itself, the absolute and necessary. "Only an unlimited horizon can give rise to absolute validity."[31] But all the beings which we experience within this horizon are finite and non-necessary, i.e., they are conditioned. Likewise the *totality* of these beings is still finite; it is only a potential, not an actual infinity; it is not necessary. Because the absolute, the actual infinity which is the horizon for all knowledge of being, is not any finite being, nor the totality of them, there must be a reality *beyond* (or *above* or *before*) the finite: an infinite being, which we call God.[32]

Man has, therefore, a kind of "immediate" knowledge of God; it is, however, unthematic and implicit in the unthematic knowledge and co-affirmation of the necessity of being. *Explicit* knowledge of God—as infinite being, distinguished from the world and from "common being"—requires the mediation of the world. Nevertheless, "the knowledge of God does not really represent a passage of our mind to something hitherto unknown, but only an explicitation and development of our knowledge of the necessity of being."[33] The "proofs" for God's existence are nothing but the process of explicitation. The basic (although not exclusive) ways for Coreth correspond to the three ontological principles of identity, causality, and finality. The considerations we have outlined constitute the first demonstration: "The principle of identity, which underlies our every act of thinking as a condition of its possibility, presupposes the primordial affirmation of the necessity of being,"[34] and this in turn presupposes the Necessary Being in existence, God. The demonstrations from causality and finality are implicitly contained in this.

Causality, for Coreth, is a principle which is immediately evident, but which can only be critically established through the transcendental reduction.[35] The dynamism of the intellect irresistibly urges us to "look beyond every being to the ground or cause of its being."[36] Every being, insofar as it is, necessarily is. The intellect seeks a *sufficient reason* for the contingent necessity of finite beings. It does so because the horizon of the intellect is the unconditioned. Since conditioned beings are not absolute or ultimate, and since our thinking "irresistibly strives toward the ultimate and the unconditioned," we necessarily go beyond every being to its intelligible ground or reason for being. Because each being is conditioned, it cannot be its own ground. Hence another ground is needed; and this ground is called the "cause." "Thus we have formulated the *principle of causality:* contingent being is brought about by a cause."[37] This is nothing but an application of the "principle of sufficient reason," or of *intelligibility,* which is co-affirmed unavoidably in the very act of inquiry or of knowing. Thus for Coreth the principle of causality is shown to be the necessary and unavoidable explicitation of the primary and lived knowledge of the intelligibility of being. It is not merely a "category" imposed on the world in order to make it intelligible; it is rather *lived* in the mind in its own grasp of being. It is justified not by deduction, but ultimately by the lived and unavoidable experience of the subject. It is verified negatively by the fact that its denial ends in antinomy and self-contradiction.

Once the principle of causality is transcendentally justified, the "way" to the existence of God is similar to that of the traditional proofs. Our experience of the beings of the world—beginning with ourselves—is one of *contingency.* Things may be or not be. Beings are multiple, relative, and finite; they stand in the flux of becoming; they are temporal. The contingency of beings, their non-absoluteness, shows that they require a cause. The cause of any particular being may be finite; and indeed we may suppose an infinite series of finite causes of beings in the world. However, such a series of contingent causes, even if indefinitely extended, remains itself contingent, and hence incapable of explaining itself or the beings which it produces.[38] Furthermore, no contingent (or "secondary") causes can produce being *as being,* however much they may determine the characteristics of beings.[39] "To produce beings as beings supposes a cause whose formal object is being as being, which is therefore capable of producing absolutely all beings, of realizing all the possibilities of being."[40] Finite beings therefore require a first cause, which can only be Absolute and Infinite Being itself.

The third principle, that of finality, is known to us first of all in our own spiritual activity. Whenever we inquire, we do so for a purpose: in order to know. But intellect is not satisfied merely with the knowledge of contingent beings, for, as we have seen, these are posited only within the horizon of being itself; and we have not grasped fully any being until we have known it in its ultimate ground. Hence the mind always unthematically intends absolute being; it is the "final cause" of our spiritual activity, co-affirmed in every act.[41] (What is true of inquiry, moreover, is true of all our spiritual activity. Whenever a finite being acts, it actuates itself in a new manner; it transcends its present being, at the same time realizing and becoming itself. This new being is the purpose or goal of the action.)[42] The goal which is the *a priori* condition of possibility of the undeniable dynamism of spirit is the unity of the unconditioned. This goal—i.e., an act in which spirit reaches absolute and infinite being—must be possible; otherwise the actual experience of the striving of spirit would be impossible and contradictory. But if an act of union with infinite being is possible, absolute being itself must be possible. Yet absolute being cannot be *merely* possible; since its essence is "to be," being itself, it would not really be possible if it were merely possible. If absolute being is really possible—not just logically possible—it must actually be.

[Coreth here formulates a line of thought which has a strong similarity to some forms of the "ontological argument," particularly that which argues not from the content of the concept of God, but from the provenance of that concept.[43] Coreth insists, however, that "we do not conclude from a conceivable, non-contradictory *concept* of God to his reality. This would be an invalid conclusion. But we start from the real activity of the spirit, which is possible only if it aims at a really possible end, the absolute being. And the latter is possible only as *being itself* . . . whose essence it is to be . . . which by its very essence cannot not be. . . . Since its essence is to be, it would no longer be possible if it were merely possible and not real."[44]]

Put more simply, Coreth's proof from finality states that the question presupposes the possibility of an answer. But our questioning—in the fundamental sense of the dynamism of spirit—is unlimited; it aims at all that is knowable. But no finite being, nor the totality of finite beings, can supply an infinite answer; further questioning is always possible. Therefore the act of inquiring presupposes the possibility of an infinite and absolute answer—an end to all questions. It implies and presupposes, that is, an infinite being which, as knowable, is the infinite Answer.[45] Such an absolute being must be real, actual, not merely possible, in order to ground the real and actual dynamism of the intellect; for the absolute is by nature necessary, and the necessary cannot be merely possible. The *a priori* condition of the question is not an *idea* of absolute being, but is the existence of the absolutely necessary itself; and if the act of questioning is real—as experience shows—then its condition is also real.

Coreth explicitly states what we have said is implicit in the Scholastic proofs for God's existence:[46] that every demonstration is ultimately based on the transcendence of the spirit. Every proof (of which there can be many, beyond those given) must begin from some aspect of reality as given in experience and show that it presupposes, as the condition of its possibility, the absolute being of God, and that it is intelligible only under that condition.[47] This means that every "demonstration" of God's existence is really a rendering thematic of the actual but implicit horizon of human spirit: its essential relation to the absolute and unconditioned. "Whenever through reflection we make explicit the metaphysically transcendent nature of the human spirit, we have a proof of God's existence."[48]

All of the foregoing contains an important implication for our thinking about God. It is clear that the absolute being is never encountered or known by us *as an object*, but always as the *horizon* within which all objects are grasped,[49] the necessary goal and condition of our spiritual activity. This means that every *concept* of God will always and necessarily be inadequate, although through them we dynamically *intend* the reality of the Absolute in itself.[50] Again, the act of knowing (or loving) is more than the content of the act; God is what is co-known in all knowledge as the True itself, co-willed in all love as the Good.[51]

Coreth's approach to the existence of God is similar, in its general lines, to that which had been set forth earlier by Karl Rahner in his now classic work, *Hörer des Wortes* (*Hearers of the Word*).[52]

[The epistemological groundwork for this study had already been provided by Rahner in his *Geist in Welt (Spirit in the World)*,[53] subtitled, "toward a metaphysics of finite knowledge in Thomas Aquinas." In this work Rahner, following in the line of Rousselot and Maréchal, attempts to "recover" the Thomist theory of knowledge in dialogue with modern philosophy, and especially the Kantian problematic. In doing so, he establishes by the use of transcendental method what Rahner considers the central point of the Thomist metaphysics of knowledge: that man is *spirit*, i.e., a power which reaches out beyond the world to the transcendent, and at the same time *in the world*, i.e., knowing everything which is metaphysical and transcendent only in and from the world (Thomas' doctrine of the "return to the phantasm").[54] Rahner's transcendental reflection upon the fact of human knowledge as completed in judgment shows that knowledge can be receptive and sentient, and at the same time objective and universal, only on the condition of an *"excessus,"*[55] a dynamism of the mind which is the pre-apprehension (*Vorgriff*) of absolute being (*esse*).[56] He thus arrives at the critical realism which, while acknowledging the place of the *a priori* structures of the mind in knowing, sees these as thoroughly determined by the transcendental *a priori* of being.]

Rahner's first concern in *Hearers of the Word* is to establish the transcendental "openness" of being and of man. He begins by placing metaphysics immediately within the anthropological context, the "turn to the subject." Metaphysics is concerned with the question about the being of beings; it is the explicitation of man's necessary question about being in general,[57] the fundamental and implicit question which is the condition for all knowledge of individual beings. The question about being, however, is also inextricably the question about the being who asks; our own being is the primary instance of the being we are questioning about. Hence metaphysics is also necessarily an analysis of man.[58]

The examination of being in our own existence shows that the essence of being is a certain "luminosity" or self-presence.[59] That is, "knowing" and being are one; to be, and to be an object of knowledge (at least possible knowledge) are the same.

[Rahner demonstrates this by means of an analysis of the very question which is the starting point of the investigation—a process we have already seen in Coreth. Man's questioning is unlimited in scope; it extends to all being. But the question includes a pre-apprehension (*Vorgriff*) of the answer. Therefore, all being is contained within the pre-apprehension. Although not necessarily everything is knowable *by us,* a *purely* unknowable is impossible, from the very fact that all being is already "known" being in the question itself,[60] that is, in the *Vorgriff* of being.]

Knowing is nothing other than being coming "to itself"; it is being "for itself" *(für sich)*; it is the capacity which being has to reflect upon itself (the Thomist *"reditio in seipsum"*), or, in short, subjectivity.[61] Because he begins with the concrete being of the questioner, the subject, Rahner sees being, properly speaking, as *conscious* being, enlightened being, being-for-itself, or "spirit."[62]

Our experience of the world shows, however, that not all being is (self-) conscious. Nevertheless, even here the identity of being and knowing remains. The being of things (as opposed to subjects) is the lowest form of being, in which being is identical with knowing not in the thing itself, but *in another.* That is, purely material being does not know, but can *be known:* it comes to subjectivity, but by means of the other, the subject. This capacity to become conscious by being the object of another's knowledge is precisely what constitutes the essence of "matter." We can therefore say that a being "has" being to the degree to which it is a subject, or is capable of consciousness.[63]

This qualification removes Rahner's identification of knowing and being from an idealistic (or pantheistic) framework. Being is *analogous.* Being is knowing *to the extent* that a being "has" being.[64] On the basis of the analogy of being (which is also the analogy of subjectivity), we are able to conceive a Being which is the absolute case of "having" being. Only this being would be "pure" being, the identity of being with spirit or self-presence; only here is the meaning of "being" simply and completely verified. This being would be pure knowledge and consciousness, complete subjectivity, unalloyed spirit. In this case alone there is no problematic of being; for the Being who "has" being absolutely is the identity of knowing and being, and already possesses in pure luminosity all that can be known, and thus all that can be questioned: being in general. This being is therefore the νόησις νοήσεως (Aristotle's "thought of thought"), Absolute Spirit: God.

Our question about being, however, shows that man is both able to question and must question. For us, being is not only the intelligible, but also the problematic. Man, therefore, is not pure being or spirit, not the Absolute Consciousness, but is *finite* spirit· spirit which is indeed open to the complete intelligibility of being, but must seek that intelligibility through questioning.[65] In the activity of judging, man experiences selfhood—not the complete unity of being, but a finite transcendental consciousness, a subject who exists opposed to objects which exist independently of the self.[66]

From this arises the transcendental question: What is the *a priori* condition of possibility of being a finite subject? How is a being or consciousness possible which is not the full identity of being and knowing, but which knows things *objectively:* i.e., a subject who intentionally becomes identical with the other (for knowing and being are identical), while at the same time remaining a "self"?[67]

The ability to know objectively as a subject resides in man's judgment. This faculty in turn depends upon the capacity for abstraction, thanks to which man is not lost in the sense knowledge of mere particulars, but can know the universal (being) in the individual.[68] (This capacity, Rahner notes, is what Thomas calls the *intellectus agens*.)[69] The question now becomes: What is the transcendental condition of possibility of abstraction? Rahner finds this condition in the pre-apprehension (*Vorgriff*) of being as such, which includes all possible objects. Because consciousness grasps its individual objects within the pre-apprehension of being, it always extends beyond every individual known being and grasps each not merely in its individual and unrelated "thisness," but rather sees each thing with a recognition of its limitation and its relation to all other possible objects.[70] The pre-apprehension of being is the horizon which allows us to know the limitation or finitude of beings. (To know a being *as limited* is to contrast it, implicitly, with the fullness of being.) This renders possible the process of abstraction, by which we recognize that the "whatness" of a being is not limited to the "thisness" of a particular object.[71] This is, in turn, the condition for knowing sensible objects *as* objects, and of thus differentiating them from our own being as subjects.

The *Vorgriff* or pre-apprehension of being is thus an *a priori*, given with the dynamism of spirit toward the absolute horizon of all possible objects. Only by means of this implicit horizon of unlimited being can man recognize individual beings as limited. The *Vorgriff* is the conscious (although unthematic) horizon within which all individual objects are known, and is an integral part of man's being.[72]

Finally, Rahner concludes that "with the same necessity with which we posit this *Vorgriff*, we also co-affirm the existence of God as the absolute 'possessor' of being."[73] The *Vorgriff* does not immediately present God as an object to the mind; for the pre-apprehension of being is only the *condition* for objective knowledge, and is not itself an object of knowledge. Nevertheless, within the *Vorgriff*, the unavoidably present condition for all human spiritual activity, we necessarily and non-thematically co-affirm the existence of a being who absolutely *is*. For with and in the *Vorgriff* we must also co-affirm the ground of its own possibility. That is, only if there exists a being in which being and knowing are completely identical, one who "has" being absolutely, is it possible to explain the incomplete identity of knowing and being that we find in ourselves. Our own knowledge of finite being is real, and we really know it *as* finite; therefore the condition of this knowledge, a knowledge of Absolute Being, must also be real, and unthematically implied in every spiritual act. Thus the *Vorgriff* leads to or points to God.[74]

[It must be noted that the reality of the *Vorgriff* would not be intelligibly grounded in a mere *idea* of an absolute possessor of being. As Rahner explains in *Spirit in the World*, the *Vorgriff* would then really pre-apprehend "nothing": the mere *possibility* of what must be apprehended as *reality*. If the *Vorgriff merely* revealed the finitude of things, in the sense of showing their intrinsic limitation, it would be possible that it would in itself pre-apprehend a merely privative infinity—really nothing existent. But the *Vorgriff* reveals finitude in the pre-apprehension of *being*—something really "more" than what is known as finite. The affirmation that the *Vorgriff* anticipates what is really "nothing" is implicitly contradicted by the very action of affirming, which presupposes an anticipation of being, and not of nothing.[75]]

Rahner insists that his process of thinking is no purely *a priori* or "ontological" proof for God. For the *Vorgriff* and its universal extension are only known and affirmed as the condition for our *a posteriori* knowledge of real being. The process begins, then, with factual empirical knowledge, and proceeds to its necessary conditions. Rahner's proof is simply a "translation" of the traditional proofs into the field of interiority, or of critical metaphysics. "Instead of saying, the finite being *factually* affirmed as real demands as the condition of its existence the existence of the infinite being of God, we simply say (meaning the same thing): the *affirmation* of the real finitude of a being demands, as the condition of its possibility, the affirmation of the existence of an absolute Being; and this affirmation already takes place in the pre-apprehension (*Vorgriff*) of common being, through which the limitation of finite being is first known as such."[76] Rahner's proof is thus an extended explanation of

St. Thomas' dictum that *omnia cognoscentia cognoscunt implicite Deum in quolibet cognito.*[77]

[The same general process of thought that we have encountered in Coreth and Rahner is repeated, from a slightly different perspective, in the works of J.-B. Lotz. Beginning with the fact of knowledge, Lotz proceeds to a recognition of Heidegger's "ontological difference"[78] and to the identity of consciousness, or spirit, with being. An analysis of judgment leads to the notion of an absolute: being as such. For Lotz, the transcendental condition of the possibility of affirming the real world—saying "is," in its existential sense— is absolute being: *esse simpliciter.*[79] From this arises the further question: Does being-as-such suffice to explain the identity of spirit and being (i.e., the fact of knowledge and subjectivity)? Lotz notes that the absolute, being, is a *purely formal* reality; being-as-such does not exist in itself, but is found only in individual beings. As such, it exists nowhere; nor is any individual being identical with it, for each only participates in it.[80] To this extent, then, the absolute, being, is marked with non-being, non-identity with spirit. Because this is so, purely formal being does not suffice to explain the absoluteness of the judgment, which presupposes a being which is not connected with non-being. The absolute which is presupposed by judgments of reality must be different from the being of beings.[81] The absolute quality of judgment, which results in the existing identity of spirit and being in ourselves, can only be ultimately explained as a participation in an existing absolute—i.e., a *subsistent Being,* which is co-affirmed in the *Vorgriff* of common (formal) being, but is not identical with it.[82] Lotz calls this being, "doubly absolute Being" or subsistent Being, because it is not the being of beings, but is being in and of itself.[83]

In short, for Lotz the identity of spirit and being demands, as its condition of possibility, an absolute and subsistent identity of spirit and being, or an Absolute Spirit.[84] The progression to the affirmation of God, subsistent Being, arises from the question: How can man, who is not pure being, but only a limited being with a limited actuality, advance in knowing to reach being itself? Indeed, how can we live as an identity of spirit with being—which is what is meant by consciousness? How, in short, is finite spirit possible—an identity of spirit with being, which is at the same time not a pure identity? Lotz's answer is that human spirit's identity with individual beings (i.e., intentional becoming, or knowing) finds its transcendental condition of possibility in the identity of spirit with the absolute being. But the condition of possibility of absolute being is a *subsistent* absolute, which is present in a co-affirmed manner in all human judgment. Ultimately, therefore, human spirit is possible only as a *participation* in the life of God, the absolute identity of spirit and being.]

THE TRANSCENDENTAL WAYS TO GOD—II

For all they were by nature foolish who were in ignorance of God, and who from the good things seen did not succeed in knowing him who is, and from studying the works did not discern the artisan; but either fire, or wind, or the swift air, or the circuit of the stars, or the mighty water, or the luminaries of heaven, the governors of the world, they considered gods. Now if out of joy in their beauty they thought them gods, let them know how far more excellent is the Lord than these; for the original source of beauty fashioned them. Or if they were struck by their might and energy, let them from these things realize how much more powerful is he who made them. For from the greatness and the beauty of created things their original author, by analogy, is seen. But yet, for these the blame is less; for they indeed have gone astray perhaps, though they seek God and wish to find him. For they search busily among his works, but are distracted by what they see, because the things seen are fair. . . .

Wis. 13:1–7

It is not when I am going to meet him, but when I am just turning away and leaving him alone, that I discover that God is. I say, God. I am not sure that that is the name. You will know what I mean.

Henry David Thoreau

The exposure of the dialectic between concept and performance, or the process of getting beyond "ideas" to what the subject "counts on," namely the actual conditions of his spiritual activity, is also the foundation of the metaphysics of Bernard Lonergan, although Lonergan's use of transcendental method arises from a context different from that of its continental practitioners.[85]

[While Lonergan clearly may be classified as a part of the "transcendental movement" within modern Thomist philosophy, it would be well to recall that this "movement," despite the name, is no directed and consistent approach, but a convenient and somewhat artificial grouping of thinkers who have more or less independently resolved on an examination of the *a priori* conditions of human subjectivity as the foundation for epistemology, metaphysics, or fundamental theology. Within the grouping we may distinguish different purposes and emphases: in Maréchal, a concern for the role of judgment; in Rahner, the importance of the return to the sensible in the stage of reflection preceding judgment ("return to the phantasm"); in Coreth, the question as the indubitable starting point.[86] In Lonergan's work, we find a search for the patterns or structures of human activity as spirit. There is a general agreement that transcendental method implies that all ontological concepts can be validated only by reference to corresponding concepts of cognitional theory; that every "ontic" statement can be translated into an onto-logical one.[87] But there is a wide divergence in the practice of the method. Thus, while Rahner begins his transcendental anthropology with the "luminosity" of being, we find it typical of Lonergan to ask first about operations and activities, to determine their structures and relations, and only later to ask why these activities constitute knowing, and how knowledge is identified with being.[88]

Thus Lonergan's use of transcendental method is largely occupied with the preliminary steps of discerning and describing patterns of activity: patterns, because human knowing is found in fact to take place not casually, but according to definite and discernable unchanging steps; activity, because knowing can only be grasped in the very act itself. For Lonergan the transcendental approach becomes identical with the finding of the "basic method"—the heuristic structure which underpins all inquiry: an a priori, necessary series of acts which, once discerned, can be applied to absolutely every reach of human knowing. "Thoroughly understand what it is to understand, and not only will you understand the broad lines of all there is to be understood but also you will possess a fixed base, an invariant pattern, opening upon all further developments of understanding."[89] Lonergan attempts to attain, then, a kind of universal point of view which, because grounded in the self-knowledge of the knowing subject, would have a universal validity and would provide a heuristic anticipation not only of all truth but also of every deviation from true knowledge.

Lonergan's method, like Rahner's, implies an "anthropological turn," in which the understanding of being is mediated by man's understanding of self.[90] Lonergan therefore constantly opposes any "essentialist" or "conceptualist" metaphysics in which the activity of the human intellect is overlooked, and he insists that the grounding of the meaningfulness and validity of the truths of philosophy, as well as those of faith, depends upon the attainment of the basic "positions" on human knowing.[91]

From Lonergan's transcendental derivation of the basic method issues his use of dialectic. The fundamental dialectic in transcendental method, as we have already seen, is that of performance vs. content; that is, every content of thought can be examined in the light of the *activity* of thinking through which it came to be; comparison will reveal whether the content is in accord with the basic structures of knowing, or conflicts with them, whether explicitly or in its implicit suppositions. The "fixed base" of cognitional theory (whose own validity is established by showing the impossibility of doubting the fundamental experience of the operations of knowing[92]) thus becomes a norm of judgment for the myriad opinions and theories one is faced with. Lonergan's dialectic, then, is not based simply on conflict of opinions or of concepts; it is based on his claim to have reached a basic, indisputable, and personally verifiable method to all human thought: the irreversible structure of mind itself. That structure is brought to light and expressed in the process of "self-appropriation" of the subject. Assertions which are in accord with the basic "positions" revealed in self-appropriation invite further development. Assertions which contain or imply a denial of what is inevitably and unthematically contained in the very act of knowing constitute "counterpositions," which, by their reversal, advance the process of knowledge. Hence the cardinal principle for Lonergan's method is to affirm the basic structures of knowing, develop the "positions" wherever they are found, and reverse the "counterpositions."

This rule implies that no system of thought or of concepts— even one based on correct cognitional theory, epistemology, and metaphysics—is ever complete: it is always open to further and new questions which necessitate the breaking of new ground. The transcendental method thus grounds the technique which is central to Lonergan's works: the "moving viewpoint." A cognitional "move" is implied by the very recognition of the disproportion between every cognitional content and the performance by which it comes about. This dialectic leads to the resolution of conflicts by moving to new levels of understanding, or "higher viewpoints." The fixed base from which every such move to wider horizons takes place is nothing other than the appropriation of the structure of the subject's own grasp of the intelligible.]

The most significant point of difference in Lonergan's use of transcendental method regards the treatment of being. For Coreth, for example, being is primary; it is both mediated and immediate, and knowledge must eventually be described in terms of it. "Being," in other words, is the most fundamental notion possible. For Lonergan, on the other hand, metaphysics, or the doctrine of being, is not the total and most basic horizon; prior to it is a transcendental doctrine which reveals the total horizon of which metaphysics is simply the objective pole. Concretely, this means that for Lonergan it is being which must be described in terms of knowing, not vice versa. Lonergan's most fundamental categories are cognitional, and these cognitional terms are derived from the subject's self-appropriation of the operations by which one knows and loves.

Lonergan expounds his transcendental examination of the subject in *Insight*, his study of human understanding. As we have seen,[93] his presentation addresses three major questions: "What am I doing when I am knowing?"—this is the question of cognitional theory; "Why is doing that, knowing?"—this is the epistemological question; and, "What do I know when I do it?"—the question whose answer constitutes metaphysics.[94]

To answer the first question, the subject must actually perform the operations of knowing, and appropriate his/her own activity. Lonergan begins, therefore, with the experience of immanence in man, and the operations or performances that take place within the field of that immanence. What is meant by immanence is defined by the experience of one's own conscious self-presence. It is an irreducible experience, and one which is presupposed by any attempt to thematize man phenomenologically. Within this immanence there occurs the fact of knowing. There is for Lonergan no doubt *whether* knowing happens; the question is: What exactly is going on when it does? The answer comes from the examination of interiority, or immanence, itself.

Lonergan starts with the experience of attaining understanding, or what he names "insight." The example of Archimedes and his cry of "eureka!" provides a dramatic instance of its occurrence; but every person can recall his/her own experience of its happening. Insight is the act which comes as a release to the tension of inquiry; it comes suddenly, although its coming is also prepared; it is a function of inner rather than outer conditions; it pivots between the concrete and the abstract; and it passes into the habitual structure of the mind.[95] Insight emerges from the empirical and founds the formation of concepts,[96] hypotheses, implications; it is a grasp of unity, Aristotle's "understanding of indivisibles" in empirical multiplicity.[97] Like seeing or hearing, insight is a non-describable, irreducible experience; each person must refer to his/her own immanent awareness of its occurrence. Hence, to understand insight, one must proceed by a method which begins in the subject's self.

From the fact of insight Lonergan proceeds to its source. That source is ultimately found in the question, that psychological impulse or tension that finds its release in the joy of discovery: "It is that tension, that drive, that desire to understand, that constitutes the primordial 'Why?' Name it what you please, alertness of mind, intellectual curiosity, the spirit of inquiry, active intelligence, the desire to know. Under any name it remains the same. . . ."[98] Lonergan calls this primordial drive the "pure" question, for it is a fact of human consciousness prior to any formulations: "It is prior to any insights, any concepts, any words, for insights, concepts, words have to do with answers; and before we look for answers, we want them; such wanting is the pure question."[99] The pure question is identical with the "wonder" which Aristotle placed at the beginning of all science and philosophy. It presupposes images and experiences, for it must be about something—namely, the concretely given or imagined.

The question reveals the fundamental dynamism of human intellect. It stands between ignorance and knowledge; it is both the desire to know and, in some sense, the already known. Inquiry is less than knowledge, for otherwise there would be no need to inquire; yet it is more than sheer ignorance, for it makes ignorance manifest and strives for understanding. In the question, then, we find an initial sense of self-transcendence, for inquiry reveals the fact of heuristic anticipation. Lonergan notes that man is not limited to simply waiting for answers to inquiries to turn up; the success of empirical science shows that insight may be attained by method, the ordering of means to attain an end. "But how can means be ordered to an end when the end is knowledge and the knowledge is not yet acquired?" The answer lies in "heuristic structures": "Name the unknown. Work out its properties. Use the properties to direct, order, guide the inquiry."[100]

[This process is "heuristic" because it anticipates insights; it is a structure because, although commonly operative, it is not known explicitly except in a correct cognitional theory—that is, one in which insight is recognized and given its proper place.[101] The possibility of heuristic structures is, of course, based in the very nature of the question as a "*Vorwissen*," an anticipation of knowledge. Since knowledge, as the "answer," must correspond to the question, the inquiry itself provides a kind of immanent norm for self-transcendence; the unknown, transcendent element is not so foreign that it is not already in some way present in immanence.]

The pure question takes its origin in the experienced given, and can renew the process of inquiry indefinitely until it reaches satisfaction. The dynamism of the question, however, always reveals a residue of material not explicable by a particular insight or cluster of insights. There is, therefore, a need for the inquirer to advance to a new and more comprehensive stage of explanation, or, as Lonergan calls it, a "higher viewpoint."[102] The persistence of inquiry leads to a need for successive and ever more inclusive higher viewpoints; for the dynamism of the question ultimately aims at *complete intelligibility;* there is no theoretical limit to inquiry's drive, for there is always a further question that can be raised beyond any particular answer. Man's conscious being is thus defined by an "unrestricted desire to know."

Lonergan divides the operations which respond to this desire into four levels: experience, understanding, judgment, and decision. (These "levels," however, are not to be thought of as discrete and independent; experience—which includes both sensation and the internal experience of consciousness—leads to questioning; questioning to the function of imagination; images to the formation of hypotheses; hypotheses to understanding. Understanding in turn includes the further process of formulation, which can lead to systematizing, etc. Furthermore, the higher levels lead us back again to the earlier ones, for understanding makes possible more systematic questions and the directing of experiences, etc.)

The completion of the act of knowing takes place on the level of judgment. (To the final level, that of decision, we shall return in the next stage of our study.) A given proposition may be for us merely an object of consideration, or we may be called upon to agree or disagree with it. In the latter case, we are involved with judgment, in which a proposition becomes the object of our affirming or denying. The judgment is the answer to a question for "reflection," a question which demands a "yes" or "no."

[Lonergan here follows the general outline of his study of the Thomist analysis of intellect, in which there are basically two levels of activity. Direct intellectual activity concerns insights into phantasms and the consequent definitions, concepts, etc. Reflective activity knows the results of direct activity as hypothetical, and poses them as questions which are resolved by appeal to the data. "Thus return to sources terminates in a reflective act of understanding, which is a grasp of necessary connection between the sources and the hypothetical synthesis; from this grasp there proceeds its self-expression which is the *compositio vel divisio,* the judgment, the assent."[103]]

The judgment is not merely an automatic act; it involves personal commitment, for it is possible to suspend judgment and await more evidence. In taking a stand, the subject involves him/herself; he/she assumes responsibility for his/her answer.[104] Reflective understanding is the attainment of an insight which justifies the subject's commitment; it grasps the sufficiency of the evidence for a proposed judgment. But to grasp evidence as sufficient is, in Lonergan's terminology, "to grasp the prospective judgment as virtually unconditioned."[105]

In the "virtually unconditioned" we have one of Lonergan's central categories, and the key to man's openness in judgment to the absolute. For the virtually unconditioned is defined by comparison with the formally unconditioned, i.e., that which has no conditions at all. By contrast, the virtually unconditioned has conditions, but they are fulfilled. Thus the virtually unconditioned involves: (1) a conditioned; (2) a link between the conditioned and its conditions; (3) the fulfillment of the conditions. A prospective judgment is then virtually unconditioned if: it is the conditioned (which is so by the very fact that a question for reflection is posed), its conditions are known, and its conditions are fulfilled. The function of reflective understanding is to transform the conditioned (a proposition which asserts that something *is*, *if* certain conditions are present) to a virtually unconditioned (a grasp that the conditions are present).[106]

In the idea of the "unconditioned" Lonergan implicitly introduces into his cognitional theory the notion of the *absolute*. For the "formally unconditioned" has no conditions whatsoever; that is, it is completely independent of anything else. Even the "virtually unconditioned" enjoys a kind of absoluteness, in that *if* its conditions are fulfilled, it necessarily *is* so. It is the formally unconditioned which has priority; the virtually unconditioned, or that which happens to exist, is a dependent notion which is formulated by contrast to that which *is* unconditionally.[107] Note that Lonergan has not introduced here any implicit "ontological" argument; for he has not yet affirmed that any subsistent absolute *exists* in fact. He has, however, pointed out that the notion of the absolute (an implicit horizon of unconditioned "is-ness") is the necessary condition and the *a priori* norm of the activity of judgment.

The judgment is the end and the motive for all previous cognitional operations: we conceive, define, think, consider, form suppositions, hypotheses, and theories—in order to judge.[108] It is by judgment that the value of all the other acts is ascertained. This is to say that the dynamism of the intellect, which is expressed in the continually recurrent question, is toward the true, toward real reach of the unconditioned, not merely toward conception or possibility. In fact, judgment not only regularly occurs, but is demanded by the drive of our minds. We are not satisfied with what may be, or with mere ideas; the reflective question "Is it so?" is unavoidable and, although it may be put off temporarily, it inevitably recurs.

The analysis of judgment provides the link with the epistemological question proper. Up to this point, Lonergan has considered knowing simply as operation; he has not dealt with the question of the objectivity of those operations, but merely with their occurrence. (Note that in this way Lonergan avoids asking Kant's question—What are the necessary conditions for knowing objectively?—until after he has already brought to light the structures and conditions of the *fact* of knowledge. He will thus be able to base his epistemology on the *performance* of the subject, already verified by the subject himself.) Judgment shows that man has the dynamism toward what really *is*. But do the operations of knowing actually bring us to what is? Are we capable of making true judgments?

This question is answered by the self-affirmation of the knower. To answer the question of whether a true judgment can take place, I must make one. If I can judge correctly that I am a knower, then there is at least one judgment which is true, certain, and invulnerable; and since that judgment will concretely be about myself *as a knower*, it will found the possibility of further judgments about what is.

To make the judgment that I am a knower, I must first know what the conditions are which would make the affirmation true. But these conditions are known from the cognitional theory which has preceded. I am a knower if I am a concrete and intelligible, united, identical whole, characterized by performances like sensing, perceiving, imagining, inquiring, understanding, formulating, reflecting, grasping the unconditioned, and affirming.[109]

I must next verify whether these conditions are met; and in order to do so, I must turn to the data. In this case, the data consist not in a sensible given, but in consciousness.

The structure of the judgment of self-affirmation as a knower is clear: the conditioned is the proposition, "I am a knower"; the link between the conditioned and its conditions is the proposition, "I am a knower if I am a unity performing certain acts"; the fulfillment of the conditions in consciousness is verified by reverting from our formulations of conscious acts to the experience of the acts themselves.[110]

Of course, every person must decide for him/herself whether he/she is a knower. Only the individual subject can perform the necessary act of verification in consciousness. But anyone who asks the question is rationally conscious, for "Am I a knower?" is a question for reflection; and if one asks it seriously, then the very asking means entering into the mind's demand for affirmation. If one knows what the question means, then one is intelligently conscious, or has understanding. Consciousness itself supplies the other conditions. If a person can affirm that, at least in this single case, he/she senses, understands, formulates, reflects, grasps the unconditioned—then that person is prepared to affirm him/herself as a knower. The actual answer depends upon the asker. "But the fact of the asking and the possibility of the answering are themselves the sufficient reason for the affirmative answer."[111]

Self-affirmation as a knower appears, then, as an immanent law. To deny that one is a knower, or to claim ignorance of the fact, is to involve oneself in blatant self-contradiction. The *fact* of being a knower is what any intelligent and reasonable person cannot avoid; and this fact is reached not by any *a priori* deduction of the necessity of knowing, but by actual performance: by actually doing it, a person knows that he/she is a knower.[112]

We can now recognize that the self-affirmation of the knower is transcendentally implied by any judgment of fact whatsoever; that is, the content of the judgment of self-affirmation is what is presupposed as the condition of possibility of every other judgment. If there is any judgment of fact, no matter what its content, there must also be the self performing the operations that constitute knowing.

The self-affirmation of the knower provides the necessary background for the epistemological question proper: the question of the objectivity of the human knowing achieved by the operations which have been affirmed.

[In Lonergan's system, the question of the objective value of these operatively self-transcending acts could not be raised until the concrete judgment of self-knowledge had taken place. As Rousselot had stated, "To be able consciously to discriminate between self and non-self one must be capable of judging one's own perception and also of self-reflection. *Omne intelligens est rediens ad essentiam suam reditione completa.* By definition it is necessary to know oneself in order to know truth as such."[113]]

Now that the self and its operations have been affirmed as the condition of possibility of every judgment, it is possible to ask: "Why does the performance of experiencing, understanding, judging, make me a knower?" Or, "Is there a common objective to all knowledge?" Or, "Why is knowing what it is?" Lonergan's answer to all these questions lies in the knowledge of the transcendent, *being*.

Being, in Lonergan's operative definition, is the objective of the pure desire to know. This desire is "the dynamic orientation manifested by questions for intelligence and reflection."[114] It is not the utterance or formulation of any question, or any particular insight, concept, or judgment; it is rather "the prior and enveloping drive that carries cognitional process from sense and imagination to understanding, from understanding to judgment, from judgment to the complete context of correct judgments that is named knowledge."[115] It is identical with the critical inquiring spirit that prevents contentment with the animal level of pure experience, that demands adequate and accurate understanding, that excludes inertia by raising further questions, and that the subject has appropriated for him/herself in self-affirmation. Each person must experience it by allowing intelligent and rational consciousness to function.[116]

[This desire is directed toward knowing. As "pure" desire, as "cool, disinterested, detached," it is not aimed toward cognitional acts and the satisfaction their performance brings, but toward cognitional contents: what is to be known. Initially, the pure desire is an orientation toward a totally unknown; as cognition proceeds, its object becomes more known. This objective always includes all that is known, as well as all that remains to be known; "for it is the goal of the immanent dynamism of cognitional process, and that dynamism both underlies actual attainment and heads beyond it with ever further questions."[117]]

Since "being" is the objective of the pure desire to know, it follows that being is all that is known and all that remains to be known; and since knowledge is complete only in judgment, being is what is "to be known by the totality of true judgments," "the complete set of answers to the complete set of questions." This definition of being is "heuristic": it does not determine directly what being means, but only how that meaning is to be determined: "It asserts that if you know, then you know being . . . if you wish to know, then you wish to know being; but it does not settle whether you know or what you know, whether your wish will be fulfilled or what you will know when it is fulfilled."[118]

Being is all including, since the desire to know is unrestricted. Apart from being, there is nothing. Likewise, being must be both completely concrete and completely universal; the first, because beyond the being of any thing, there remains nothing more; the second, because apart from being, there is simply nothing.[119]

[By defining being as the object of the pure desire to know, Lonergan implicitly makes present the antinomy of human intellect: that is, the contrast between its "proper" and "formal" objects.[120] The entire first part of *Insight* shows that human intelligence knows the intelligible-in-the-sensible. This object is "proper" to man in the sense that man in this life understands no intelligible except as a derivative of that object; and also that no pure spirit has the sensible as part of its proper object. The "proper" object thus belongs to intellect precisely as human. The "formal" object—being, or everything—belongs, on the other hand, to intellect as intellect.[121] In speaking of human intellect in terms of a pure desire to know being, Lonergan is considering it not simply in terms of what it actually achieves, but in reference to its ultimate desire.[122] That is, Lonergan is *implicitly* already defining man's intellect in terms of its capacity for God—the "natural desire to see God."[123] There is already present, although in a way that becomes explicit only in the unfolding of the moving viewpoint, the idea that the intellect is the faculty of the divine; that its power to know the contingent derives from its capacity for the Absolute. As Rousselot put it, "mind is θεός πῶς before being πάντα πῶς."[124]]

Lonergan distinguishes between the spontaneously operative and unrestricted *notion* of being, and theoretical accounts of its origin and contents.[125] The spontaneous notion is invariant and common to all; it functions in the same way, no matter how one explains it. Theories of being, on the other hand, vary with philosophical contexts.

The notion of being is an anticipation of understanding; it expresses knowing in its questioning phase. To have a "notion," in Lonergan's sense, is to be in a state of wonder or inquiry. To have a notion of being is to know being immediately, and yet not understand it.[126] In Lonergan's account of the spontaneously operative notion of being, being is unrestricted: it extends beyond the known to everything not known yet. It is prior to each instance of knowing being. It is nothing but "the immanent, dynamic orientation of cognitional process ... the detached and unrestricted desire to know as operative in cognitional process."[127] It is a "notion" rather than merely an orientation, because that desire to know, the heading toward being, is *conscious,* intellectually and rationally; the notion of being is identical with inquiring intelligence and reflecting reasonableness.[128] It is the supreme heuristic notion, for it penetrates and underlies all contents of the mind.

[Lonergan insists that the notion of being must not be confused with any "concept." Because it is represented by the name "being" and the verb "to be" it seems to resemble concepts; but it is unique. Concepts result from insight: into the use of names, or into things-for-us, or into things-themselves. But the notion of being generates all concepts. It cannot result from insight into being, for this would mean understanding everything about everything, which we manifestly do not have. Concepts in general, furthermore, mean understanding of essences, and prescind from existence; but the notion of being does not result from the understanding of being, nor does it prescind from existence, since it moves conception to the level of judgment.[129] Since the notion of being is unique and regards one unrestricted objective (the concrete universe), and thus underpins all cognitional contents, it may be called univocal. Insofar as it penetrates all contents, and thus has a variable meaning, it may be called analogous. This underpinning and penetration is what is frequently meant by the "analogy of being."[130]]

It is clear from Lonergan's treatment of the notion of being that intelligibility—that is, what is known by understanding—is intrinsic to being, since being for Lonergan is defined by its intelligibility. It is in this context, then, that Lonergan is able to conceive the "objectivity" of knowing. Objectivity is simply a patterned context of judgments. It exists if there are distinct beings, some of which both know themselves and know others as others.[131] The subject's knowledge of self has already been established. The concrete judgments of fact that decide the actual plurality of subjects and objects are made in metaphysics. The epistemological basis for those judgments is the philosophical position that "the real" is the concrete universe of being, intelligently grasped and reasonably affirmed. "The real is what is; and 'what is' is known in the rational act, judgment."[132] It is in reaching the *unconditioned* in judgment that the self-transcendence of human knowing reaches its term in affirming an object which "is" in the sense that its reality does not depend on our cognitional activity.[133] Thus knowing is objective, if the appropriate set of judgments can be made. Lonergan thus avoids defining self-transcendence in terms of the Kantian problem, as a going beyond a known-known to an unknown object-in-itself; rather, cognitional transcendence is our heading toward being; and within the field of being, the intelligible, we can make judgments which differentiate the subject from the object.[134]

Lonergan's answer to the epistemological question is: being. Performing the operations described in cognitional theory is knowing, because by them we know being—the "is-ness" of things. Once the notion of being is established, Lonergan turns to the metaphysical question: What do I know when I perform the operations of knowing being?

The first object of metaphysical knowledge is the world of proportionate being: that is, beings which are known through sensation, intelligence, and judgment: the beings of the world. Lonergan goes through the process of making the concrete judgments which distinguish objects from the subject, then proceeds to the metaphysical composition of the beings of experience, and finally passes to the specific metaphysics of the subject *in se*. This leads to an examination of the level of freedom or decision (to which we shall return), and to the fields of ethics and beliefs. Finally, man can ask whether our metaphysical knowledge is confined to the universe of proportionate being (i.e., being known through the starting point of sensation), or whether it goes beyond, to a transcendent domain of being.[135]

[The posing of this question itself is the unavoidable result of the operation of the immanent source of human transcendence: the detached, disinterested desire to know, the dynamism of intellect (and, as we shall see, of freedom). Lonergan notes that this unrestricted desire does not, of itself, imply unrestricted attainment; there are, obviously, other conditions to the accomplishment of knowledge besides simply desiring to know.[136] Desire in no way means exigence. The unrestricted desire simply excludes all narrowness; it insists that every question be admitted critically and intelligently. Its object, as we have seen, is being, the unrestricted— that apart from which there is nothing.[137]]

The question whether human knowledge extends beyond the proportionate world ultimately can only be answered by a judgment of fact. In order to know whether such judgment is possible, we must make one. The possibility of knowledge of transcendent being—being which is beyond the range of human experience, whether inner or outer—is the possibility of grasping intelligently and reasonably affirming that such being exists; and the proof of the possibility is in the fact that such a grasp and affirmation actually occur.[138]

[The kind of knowledge of transcendent being with which Lonergan is concerned here is a heuristic structure: what we can and do know about transcendent being prior to attaining an act of understanding which comprehends it. The possibility of transcendent knowledge, therefore, is not by any means the possibility of *experiencing* a transcendent being, but only "the possibility of intentionally anticipating, intelligently grasping, and reasonably affirming its existence."[139]]

Lonergan distinguishes four different answers to the question of the meaning of being:

1. The pure notion of being is the desire to know, man's conscious heading toward knowledge.

2. Since this pure notion unfolds through understanding and judgment, it is possible to formulate a "heuristic notion" of being, namely the notion of "whatever is to be grasped intelligently and affirmed reasonably."[140] (The "heuristic" notion of being is thematic, while the pure notion is implicit.)

3. There are restricted acts of understanding, conceiving, and affirming being: the answers to particular questions in particular domains of being. None of these, however, answers the question, "What is being?"

4. The answer to this question is the "idea of being": an unrestricted act of understanding which knows being completely, is completely universal and completely concrete, and for which there are no further questions.[141]

If one works out the implications of the concept of an unrestricted act of understanding, the "idea of being," it becomes manifest that this "Idea" is what is meant by "God."[142] This being would be the primary intelligible, understanding itself and all being in a single unrestricted act. It would be self-explanatory, for otherwise its intelligibility would be incomplete; it would be unconditional, for if dependent upon another, it would not be self-explanatory. It would be personal, or rationally self-conscious, for it would be identical with an unrestricted act of consciousness; it would be in perfection what man is only as an unrestricted desire.[143]

The question about being leads Lonergan to the formulation of the idea of being, God, an unrestricted act of understanding. The conception of God, however, does not in itself answer the question whether he exists. In order to know this, we must proceed to the notion of causality.

Causality is simply "the objective and real counterpart of the questions and further questions raised by the detached, disinterested, and unrestricted desire to know."[144] It is, in short, an extension of the basic principle of the intelligibility of being. If what is apart from being is nothing, then what is apart from intelligibility is nothing. This means that there cannot be mere matters of fact without explanation, for they would then be apart from intelligibility, and thus apart from being.[145] This leads to the conclusion that human knowledge cannot be confined to proportionate being; for it would then be reduced to mere matters of fact without explanation. This is true because judgment is based on the grasp of the virtually unconditioned. But the virtually unconditioned is simply a matter of fact; it is a condition that happens to have its conditions fulfilled; and thus it leaves a further question for explanation. That explanation—which is ultimately the explanation of the very existence of proportionate being—cannot come from conditioned being itself, simply because it is, in every aspect, conditioned.[146] It follows immediately that if proportionate being exists, and being is intelligible, then we cannot exclude knowledge of transcendent being as the ultimate explanation of all we know. To say that conditioned beings require a cause is to say that their intelligibility is incomplete, while the very fact of judgment rests upon the anticipation of complete intelligibility, the formally unconditioned.

With this background, we may proceed to Lonergan's argument for the existence of God. (Note that here, as throughout, Lonergan's procedure presupposes the performance of the subject. He does not claim that he can prove to you that God exists, but rather that, if you are intelligent and rational, and can affirm yourself as such, then you can yourself arrive at the conclusion that in order to *be* rational and intelligent, you must affirm the existence of God. The "argument" is only a series of "signposts" to the subject's

own appropriation of his/her rational self-consciousness and its implications.)

Lonergan believes that every valid argument for the existence
of God is included in a single general form: ".If the real is completely
intelligible, God exists. But the real is completely intelligible. Therefore, God exists."[147]

The crux of the argument is complete intelligibility. Lonergan
does not claim that we know complete intelligibility; we do not
know the answer, but in asking questions, we *intend* complete
intelligibility; and, "since intending is just another name for meaning, it follows that complete intelligibility, so far from being meaningless to us, is in fact at the root of all our attempts to mean
anything at all."[148]

The minor premise of the argument, that the real is completely
intelligible, is the fruit of the entire process of self-appropriation
which is Lonergan's goal in *Insight*. It means rejecting the counterpositions and accepting the position that being is completely intelligible, that is, that being is what is known by the totality of correct
judgments; and that the "real" is being, and not simply the object of
sense knowledge.

The major premise is demonstrated in a series of steps. If the
real is completely intelligible, then complete intelligibility must
exist:

> For just as the real could not be intelligible, if intelligibility were
> non-existent, so the real could not be completely intelligible, if
> complete intelligibility were non-existent. In other words, to af-
> firm the complete intelligibility of the real is to affirm the com-
> plete intelligibility of all that is to be affirmed. But one cannot
> affirm the complete intelligibility of all that is to be affirmed
> without affirming complete intelligibility. And to affirm complete
> intelligibility is to know its existence.[149]

If complete intelligibility exists, then the idea of being exists. This
amounts to a restatement, in Lonergan's cognitional terms, of the
principle of causality. Intelligibility (the identity of spirit and being)
is either material, spiritual, or abstract. Material intelligibility (what
exists in the objects of empirical science) is necessarily incomplete,
for it is contingent. Abstract intelligibility is also necessarily incomplete, for it only arises in the self-expression of spiritual intelligibility. And spiritual intelligibility is incomplete as long as it can still
inquire. "It follows that the only possibility of complete intelligibil-

ity lies in a spiritual intelligibility that cannot inquire because it understands everything about everything. And such unrestricted understanding is the idea of being."[150] Finally, if the idea of being exists, then God exists: for God is what is meant by the primary component of the idea of being (a being which understands itself, and in itself all other things).

[There are two principal moments in Lonergan's argument, and they correspond to the two operations in grasping the virtually unconditioned: affirming a link between the conditioned (the proposition, "God exists") and its conditions of verification (namely, that anything contingent and intelligible exists at all); and affirming the fulfillment of the conditions. The second step takes place simply by the affirmation of some reality. In *Insight*, it begins with the self-affirmation of the knower, and is extended to the whole universe of proportionate being.

The first step involves a more complex process. It must identify the real with being, being with complete intelligibility, complete intelligibility with an unrestricted act of understanding that possesses the properties of God and accounts for everything in the universe. This is the equivalent of establishing that the contingent world demands a cause. In Lonergan's opinion, it is the identification of the real with being which is crucial in this process, for the rest follows easily from this. It is for this reason that cognitional theory and the epistemological question occupy such a preponderant place in his account.[151]]

Lonergan concludes that because cognitional theory is difficult, it is hard for us to know what knowing is; and it is therefore difficult to know what our knowledge of God is. The grasp of the "proof" for God's existence is difficult, for it involves an arduous process of self-appropriation. *If* the real is completely intelligible, then God exists. Lonergan insists that there is evidence of the complete intelligibility of the real; but each person must find that evidence in him/herself; it cannot be done for us. Nevertheless, just as knowing is prior to and easier than the analysis of knowing, so the knowledge of God is earlier and easier than our attempts to express it formally. For even without any formulation of the notion of being, we always and invariably *operate* through it; and thus we *implicitly* acknowledge the existence of God whenever we inquire, understand, reflect, and judge. God, the absolutely transcendent, is present to us as the condition of every level of self-transcendence, even when we are not conceptually aware of his existence, or perhaps even conceptually deny it.[152]

Lonergan claims that his formulation of the mind's itinerary to God gives a general statement, of which other proofs—like Aquinas' five ways—are particular cases. In fact, there are as many proofs for God as there are aspects of incomplete intelligibility in the universe of proportionate being—for God is always the answer to the demand of intellect's drive for complete intelligibility, which cannot be had from finite beings.[153]

THE UNITY OF THE APPROACHES TO GOD

As we have already stated, the affirmation of God stems from and expresses an *option* in favor of the meaningfulness and intelligibility of existence. The "proofs" of God's existence are meant to show that this option is not "blind" or irresponsible, but is rational, responsible and necessary. The crux of all the arguments is intelligibility. To affirm the existence of God is to affirm that human spirit, which demands meaning and explanation, is not an accident or a quirk in an absurd and meaningless world, but is responding to the very nature of being.

As Joseph Ratzinger points out, the affirmation of God means a decision in favor of *Logos*, meaning or intelligence, over mere matter. The existence of God means that idea, freedom, love, intelligence—all that we mean by "spirit"—stand not only at the end of history, as a by-product of evolution, but also at its beginning, as the originating power behind all being.[154] Thought, meaning, and love are not the chance accidental production of being; rather, all being is the product of these spiritual realities. The subject or person is primary over the "objective" world—not only in our experience, but really and metaphysically. The "objective mind" or intelligibility which we find in things is not the invention of our minds, but is found by us and affirmed by us because it really is the expression of a Subjectivity which produces it. The structure of being that we meditate on is the expression of a creative pre-meditation; our thinking is in reality a grasping and re-thinking of the creative thought from which the world proceeds.[155] It is because there is an "Idea of Being" that our ideas are able to grasp reality.

Man, as spirit in the world, experiences two kinds of reality: matter, or what "is," but does not understand itself; and "spirit" or mind, being which is in itself and for-itself, which knows and understands itself. Which of these is ultimate and grounding reality? The materialist holds that the ground and beginning of all being, including spirit, is that being which does not understand itself. Understanding, mind, arises as an accident in a finally absurd world; its drive for meaning has no grounding outside of itself. The affirmation of Spirit as the grounding reality means recognizing that matter itself is not ultimate; that it is, in fact, "objectivized thought," or "objective spirit"; it is intelligible, and therefore it cannot be ultimate: before it comes thought. For the theist, the unity of all being is in its being thought by one supreme Consciousness.[156] (In distinction to idealism, however, realist theism recognizes that the world is not only thought, but is "created"—given independent existence through freedom.[157]) "To be" and "to be thought" are the same; not, indeed, to be thought by any human mind, but by that spirit which is identical with being itself.

All of the approaches to the existence of God begin, at least implicitly, with man's experience of the self as spiritual being. We seek for a complete meaningfulness, an infinite fullness, in a limited world. Whether the starting point is the subject's own existence, or the confrontation of that existence with the world, and whether we consider ourselves and the world in their positive moments of fulfillment and beauty, or in their negative moments of poverty and evil, we find that our existence cries out for an "other" who can explain the "graceful" quality of being and meet its neediness. Our experience of subjectivity is incomplete without an other; yet every finite other, every "thou," is unfulfilling except in the perspective of a final and absolute "Thou" who gives meaning to all. Since the thematic search for God begins with the dual experience of an anticipated fullness of being and the present limitation of finite existence, the "demonstration" of God can take place from any point where these two factors are experienced: that is, from any experience in which we know ourselves as subjects and confront our finitude. On the level of "common sense," there is an intuitive grasp of the need for God as existence-without-nothingness as the condition for the awe-inspiring and terrifying fact of our contingent existence-with-nothingness. On the level of theory, the recognition of the principle of causality leads to the conclusion that finite being must be caused by another, which must be infinite. On the level of interiority, the subject seeks in him/herself the source of the "principles" of intelligibility, and finds that the finite cannot be affirmed as real without an implicit reference to an already present and co-affirmed horizon of the Absolute.

Every "proof" of God's existence manifests the fact that all being "refers" to God's being, because all being *participates* in the divine being, in that which is absolutely and without which nothing else is. This is especially evident in the case of self-reflective or conscious being. We cannot avoid reference to God, because consciousness itself, being at the level of spirit, is a conscious, although mysterious and perhaps obscure, participation in the divine "light": that self-luminosity in which being and being-for are identical. It is perhaps in the realm of transcendence, in mystical experience, that the "ontological" argument has its place—not as a "proof" of God's existence, but as showing the structure of the experience of union with or participation in the absolute and self-evident being of God.

VI. THE FREE HEARER AND THE FREE REVEALER

So, brothers, we are under obligations, but not to the physical nature, to live under its control; for if you live under the control of the physical you will die, but if, by means of the Spirit, you put to death the body's doings, you will live. For all who are guided by God's Spirit are God's sons. It is not a consciousness of servitude that has been imparted to you, to fill you with fear again, but the consciousness of adoption as sons, which makes us cry, "Abba!" that is, Father.

Rom. 8:12–15

To understand, to observe, to draw conclusions, a man must first of all be conscious of himself as living. A man knows himself as living, not otherwise than as willing, that is, he is conscious of his free will. Man is conscious of his will as constituting the essence of his life, and he cannot be conscious of it except as free.

Leo Tolstoi, *War and Peace*

THE SEEKER FOR GOD'S WORD

The examination of the subject in his/her performance has revealed man as a spiritual being—that is, a being in whom the world comes to being-for-itself, being-as-awareness. In Rahner's terminology, man is spirit because we are open to the horizon of being itself; we are finite transcendence toward the horizon of Absolute Being. This openness to the absolute is the non-thematic, non-objective condition of possibility of man's interaction with the world, self-actuation, and thematic self-consciousness.

Furthermore, we have seen in the philosophy of transcendental method that this *Vorgriff* or "pure notion" of being implicitly includes or implies the affirmation of an absolutely subsistent Being or Intelligence, who is the source of the intelligibility of the world, and the ultimate goal of man's transcendent dynamism to know and understand. The non-objective, non-thematic co-affirmation of the Absolute can be made thematic and explicit in the process of coming to the rational knowledge of the existence of God. This process is in reality nothing else than the unfolding and explicitation of the dynamism toward God that man *is* by man's very being. Thus the whole of transcendental philosophy is an explanation of Augustine's idea of God as the *"interior intimo meo"*—the One we necessarily seek in all our knowing and loving activity.

FREEDOM AND LOVE

We have from the beginning been aware of the dimension of option, decision, self-determination in the being of the subject. We have now arrived at the point where we must explicitly reflect upon this dimension of spirit, and relate it to the results of our transcendental reduction-deduction of human consciousness.

Transcendental Consciousness of Freedom

We have seen in transcendental reflection that there is a dialectic in man between our implicit and transcendental consciousness, and our reflexive awareness of self. Man does not "have" being all at once, but must become him/herself; we must, through the mediation of being in the world, reflexively objectify our selfhood and affirm ourselves. Man is, as the existentialists proclaim, a "project" in the world. Because of our need to become selves, to realize our spirituality through being in the world, man questions about the world. The presupposition of these questions is the question about being itself—the question which man is, in the very depths.[1] When we recognize the anticipation of being as constituting our own spirituality, we affirm the "luminosity" of being, found in our own experience of transcendence. The experience of luminous being confronts man at once and inseparably with the absoluteness of being, and the contingency of man's own being. We have already seen how the implications of the experience of absoluteness-in-contingency lead to the affirmation of God; we shall now see how the same experience is the root of the transcendental consciousness of freedom.

This transcendental consciousness of freedom, as Karl Rahner points out,[2] is implicit already in the very experience of questioning itself. By the fact that man must question, human being is revealed as contingent—that is, as not completely intelligible in itself, but deriving its intelligibility (and therefore its being) from another. At the same time, each person finds his/her own existence in some sense "absolute"; despite its contingency, it imposes itself as somehow self-standing and independent. *Within* contingency, a kind of absoluteness is revealed. Man's existence, even though it is finite and radically dependent, absolutely excludes—for each individual— the possibility of its own negation. Man's being is contingent; but we find it necessary to be contingent. We must affirm ourselves, and precisely as finite. We necessarily place ourselves in an absolute relation to our own contingent existence; we affirm ourselves, we are "with" ourselves. This necessary and conscious relation with the contingent and non-necessary character of our own being manifests man's existence in its ontological difference from the being of things. Human being is conscious being, which means not only an "awareness," but a positing of one's own being, an affirming of one's existence, despite its contingent nature.

But in positing something contingent (our own being) necessarily, and with a kind of absoluteness, man is conscious of performing an act of *freedom*. For the act of positing one's self (an act which occurs, implicitly, in every act of being a conscious self) cannot be a purely "intellectual" intuition. Insight and judgment find their sufficient reason (Lonergan's "reaching the virtually unconditioned") in the *object* of judgment itself. But a contingent being does not contain in its essence a reason to be posited absolutely; if it is correctly and necessarily judged *to be,* its being is nevertheless recognized as merely factual, and the absoluteness of the judgment is hypothetical: *if* something is, it necessarily and absolutely is. The absoluteness with which I posit my own being, however, is of a different order. It cannot find sufficient grounds in my being as objective; it is grounded rather in my subjectivity, in the very action of positing itself. The ground for positing my own being absolutely is freedom; for only as the effect of freedom can the absolute positing of a contingent being be intelligible. But such an act of positing is always taking place in man, implicitly, as the ground and precondition of every conscious action. Therefore, we may say that man is, in the depths of personal being, freedom.[3]

Freedom (or "will"[4]) is thus primarily a transcendental experience of man, given in the very act of conscious being itself. It is nothing other than being, on a certain level: being as spirit, as self-aware and self-positing. In its primary instance, then, freedom or responsibility is not an empirical datum, but an *a priori* condition for man's experience of objects; it is identical with man's self-possession or conscious being. Insofar as I experience myself as a subject, as person, I experience myself as free: not in the sense that I may choose this or that, but in the more fundamental sense of being responsible for my own subjectivity, being able to choose my own being, positing myself.[5] The basic mode of freedom, then, is the transcendental experience which is identical with spirit, or subjectivity: the faculty of "illuminating" being, including my self.

The reflection on the idea of freedom allows us further to determine the nature of the "luminous" experience of subjectivity. We can now say that the ultimate essence of being and of knowing is none other than *love*[6]—the free and conscious positing of the good. That is, being—in its primal case, which is not the being of things, but *Dasein*—is not merely intelligible, but is personal, free, and responsible. Being is not only that which is "transparent" to itself, but that which *cares* (cf. Heidegger's notion of *Sorge*).[7] Conscious being is in itself apprehension of value or goodness. Knowledge and love are revealed, then, as interior moments of being as being. "Meaning" and "value" ultimately are the same. This is what is expressed in the Scholastic maxim, *ens-verum-bonum convertuntur:* Being, the True, and the Good are interchangeable. If human existence, then, is defined in terms of a "notion" or *Vorgriff* of being, it is at the same time a "notion" or preapprehension of the good.

[If knowledge and love coincide on the transcendental level, as the essence of conscious being, they are meant also to coincide on the level of categorical operation. Love is knowledge in its full state. This implies that the truest form of knowledge is not the "objective," in the sense of uninvolved, impersonal, uncommited apprehension of realities, but is rather "subjective," in the sense of involving the *disposition* of the free person. It is therefore personal knowledge, rather than the knowledge of things, which most truly shows the essential nature of knowing. It is personal knowledge, in which knowing is identical with freedom or love, which more truly realizes (knows) *being*, what is.[8]

If we have spoken of man as "question," or in Lonergan's terminology, as an "unrestricted desire to know,"[9] this is not to be taken as a reduction of man to pure "intellect," conceived in abstraction from freedom and love. Indeed, we have insisted that we are dealing not with concepts, but with the performance of the living subject; and anyone who has appropriated his/her own intellectual life in its full reality knows it, not as an "abstract" and lifeless immersion in ideas or concepts, but as a vital dynamism which is finally identical with love, and which demands the commitment and decision of the whole person. To speak of man as an "unrestricted desire to know" does not mean that we conceive man as being merely eternally "curious," as desiring an infinitely extended range of objective information. The "question" which is identical with man's being is *existentielle;* it involves us totally. The unrestricted desire to know is an unrestricted desire to be—not merely to have objective existence, like things, but to be consciously, freely, caringly—in short, to be *well,* to be in love. The "question" which man is, the "unrestricted desire to know," is the positive expression of man's rebellion against death as the extinction of consciousness or annihilation.]

The Categorical Realization of Freedom

On a second level, the freedom which is transcendentally experienced is the ground for freedom as thematic operation: those activities which are the operations of deliberating, deciding, choosing, "willing."[10] We have already spoken of the activity of judgment as the culmination of all prior intentional acts of man. But man's unrestricted drive to know, to be, to be well, to be "for" self, seeks a yet higher integration than that of mere thought: it must include man's action as a former of him/herself and of the world. The action of man is "free"—although within limitations—precisely because of the transcendental experience of freedom, which makes man a "notion" of the good. Because the good-as-such, identical with being and the true, surpasses any finite good, and because man's necessary drive is toward the transcendental good, we find ourselves with the possibility of choice when faced with particular goods. That is, man's dynamism is unnecessitated by anything less than *the* Good; since no finite and concrete reality is identical with that Good, one finds oneself—in principle—free before them. Transcendental freedom, therefore, is the basis and condition of possibility of freedom of choice, or the level of decision.

In rationally choosing his/her own life, man reaches the highest level of operation as a subject in the world. To seek for the good is the culminating moment of rationality. While on prior levels of evolution the successive integration of lower manifolds into higher syntheses takes place unconsciously, through chance and the finality of natural selection, in man the synthesis of the elements of life takes place through rational decision. As Lonergan explains, in continuity with the Thomist tradition, the capacity for this rational decision is the "appetite" which draws spirit toward the objects presented by intellect.[11] The objects of intellect, however, include not only the facts of the world, but also its practical possibilities, including the changing and the determination both of the environment and of man's own subjectivity. By willing particular goods, man is able to introduce a higher meaning or intelligibility into the world and man's own existence.[12]

The operation of decision is parallel to the operation of judgment, from which it flows; but the object of its actuation is not simply what "is," but rather what is *to be*, or to be done. It depends, therefore, upon a judgment of value. Like judgment, decision reaches a "virtually unconditioned"; but while judgment reaches a virtually unconditioned truth, decision reaches a virtually unconditioned good: that is, a conditioned value (this act is morally good, rational, and obligatory, *if* . . .) whose conditions are in fact fulfilled.

Since decision or willing is nothing other than the highest integration of human knowing, there must be a principle of correspondence between these two levels: that is, there is an exigence for consistency between man's knowing and doing. The act of love, the choice of value, is eminently intelligent and reasonable; it is the decision for the order of the world, for being as meaningful. Although the "good" may be perceived on many levels, from that of mere sensation to that of reflection,[13] the good in itself is what is reached in the judgment of value: not what is pleasant for me, but what corresponds to the intelligible and affirmable good. Every particular good choice, therefore, implicitly affirms the intelligible and valuable as such: that is, the whole order of the world as meaningful. As we have seen, the transcendental condition of possibility of free choice of the good is a "notion" of *Vorgriff* of the good-in-se. To the extent that I really will or choose any particular good, in its entire reality, I must will it in its relation to the whole—for this relation constitutes its reality. Thus in choosing or loving any good, I implicitly choose and love the content of the *Vorgriff*. As every act of knowing implicitly affirms the existence of God, so every act of love implicitly chooses and loves him, as transcendental ground of all good.[14]

By virtue of freedom, man is the being in whom the process of transcendence reaches the point of responsibility for itself. In man, transcendence is not merely a fact, but also a duty: an achievement.[15] This achievement takes place within the context of an absolute horizon: the transcendental notion of the good. It must always be realized, however, in the finite world: in man's "situation," which is one of historicity and community.[16] Freedom on the categorical level is that dimension of consciousness by which intelligible and meaningful courses of action (internal or external) become actualized—not by virtue of necessity or chance, but by a spiritual act which determines both the subject's self and the contingent world around him/her. The notion of freedom, with its correlative notion of responsibility, transforms our vision of man from that of a locus of awareness of the universal drive toward being, to that of a self-determining and creative part of that drive, in which spirit not only knows being, but is response-able toward it, determinative of it by the immanent power of love.

THE FINALITY OF LOVE

God's love for us has been revealed in this way—that God has sent his only Son into the world, to let us have life through him. The love consists not in our having loved God, but in his loving us and sending his Son as an atoning sacrifice for our sins. Dear friends, if God has loved us so, we ought to love one another. No one has ever seen God; yet if we love one another, God keeps in union with us and love for him attains perfection in our hearts.

1 Jn. 4:9–12

"What then is Love?" I asked. "Is he mortal?" "No. . . . He is a great spirit, and like all spirits he is intermediate between the divine and the mortal. . . . For God mingles not with man; but through Love all the intercourse and converse of God with man is carried on. . . ."

"And who," I said, "was his father, and who his mother?" "The tale," she said, "will take time; nevertheless I will tell you. On the birthday of Aphrodite there was a feast of the gods, at which the god Poros, or Plenty . . . was one of the guests. When the feast was over, Penia, or Poverty, as the manner is on such occasions, came about the doors to beg. Now Plenty, who was the worse for nectar (there was no wine in those days), went into the garden of Zeus and fell into a heavy sleep; and Poverty, considering her own straitened circumstances, plotted to have a child by him, and accordingly she lay down at his side and conceived Love. . . . And as his parentage is, so also are his fortunes. In the first place he is always poor, and anything but tender and fair, as the many imagine him; and he is rough and squalid, and has no shoes, nor a house to dwell in; on the bare earth exposed he lies under the open heaven, in the streets, or at the doors of houses, taking his rest; and like his mother he is

always in distress. But like his father, whom he also partly resembles, he is always plotting against the fair and good; he is bold, enterprising, strong, a mighty hunter, always weaving some intrigue or other, keen in the pursuit of wisdom, fertile in resources; a philosopher at all times, terrible as an enchanter, sorcerer, sophist. He is by nature neither mortal nor immortal, but alive and flourishing at one moment when he is in plenty, and dead at another moment, and then alive again by reason of his father's nature. But that which is always flowing in is always flowing out, and so he is never in want and never in wealth. . . . And of this too his birth is the cause; for his father is wealthy and wise, and his mother poor and foolish. Such, my dear Socrates, is the nature of the spirit Love."

Plato: *Symposium*

Plato's myth of the parentage of Love expresses in symbolic form the paradox which man experiences in the fulfillment of his/her freedom. As the child of "Plenty," love is strong, outgoing, independent, generous. It is the act of man experiencing self as giver and creator. Unfettered by necessity, we choose a good outside ourselves to commit ourselves to. This is the height of the transcendent dimension in man; for by love man transcends the ego and wills the other for its own sake, as a good in itself. At the same time, love always reveals itself as the child of "Poverty"; for the choices of freedom, even at its most generous and outgoing moments, are always motivated by a kind of prior need or desire. Even in self-sacrifice, human love must be motivated by a drive to self-fulfillment:[17] for I cannot will anything unless I perceive that it is good for me to do so, and I can will nothing except as a good, that is, as corresponding to the "appetite" or hunger of spirit which we have named the *Vorgriff* or "notion" of the Good. Thus underpinning and supporting the unnecessitated character of freedom of choice is a deeper necessity which consists in the unavoidable transcendental orientation to the good-as-such.[18] Every act of love, as we have said, implicitly chooses and loves God. Only in God, as absolute ground of all value, can the paradox of love be resolved finally: for God as "Other" is at the same time the ground of selfhood ("*interior intimo meo*"). In a love which is immediate union with God himself, the good "for me" and the good "for itself" coincide.

But can this resolution be reached by man? Clearly, God is the "final cause" of all love, the source of the dynamism toward every good. But man is spirit *in the world:* our love toward absolute Good is mediated by created goods which never fulfill our deepest need nor exhaust our deepest capacity to give ourselves. Is man's destiny an "asymptotic" movement toward God as the ever-unreachable horizon behind every immediate good? In this case, there would simply be no absolute fulfillment of the infinite longing of man's spirit. Is human love then, in de Lubac's phrase, *"une finalité sans fin"*—a finality with no final point, no end?[19] Is man a dynamism and a question with no final attainment of an answer, but only an infinite progress? Or is there an end in which man finds this infinite longing satisfied? If indeed our hearts are made for God, and cannot rest except in him, then such an end could only be God in himself as the object of our love: God not as "horizon," but as the addressee, the "dialogue partner" of our love.

Again, love of its nature seeks eternity and permanence. Human consciousness rebels at the thought of its own annihilation or extinction;[20] and in particular man at the peak of human being-for-self, man in love, experiences within him/herself the desire and need for the eternal. The literature of love—sacred and profane—in every generation testifies to the preoccupation with love as a value which cannot pass away, that must be stronger than death.

[One example from literature may serve to illustrate the point. José Maria Gironella in his master work on the Spanish Civil War, *The Cypresses Believe in God,* observes how the working of love creates a psychological need for eternity in the character of Matías Alvear, the telegraph operator who is the father in the family of the book's protagonists: "He was a life-long republican, and was so anti-clerical that when he got married to Carmen Elgazu he hardly knew how to genuflect. But Carmen Elgazu had inherited from the North the type of faith that 'moves mountains'; and in this case the mountain that was moved was Matías Alvear. This telegraph operator loved his wife so much that suddenly the idea that everything should end with death horrified him. It seemed to him impossible that Carmen Elgazu was not eternal; and, for his part, he desired with all his heart to have all eternity to continue living joined to her. And after ten years of marriage, his desire had become conviction. . . ."[21]]

Yet man must die. Is there, in God, a basis for hope in a life that transcends death and so provides the fulfillment of love?

Moreover, as Karl Rahner insists, freedom as the desire for the eternal is the faculty of finality or definiteness. It is not the capacity to do or to become first one thing and then something else completely opposed; it is rather that by which we become a particular subject, putting aside certain possibilities in order to realize others. Rahner writes:

> Thus freedom is precisely *not* the faculty of performing acts that can always be changed later; it is rather man's sole capacity for the finally definitive, the capacity of subjectivity: for by this freedom the subject brings himself into being in a final and irrevocable way. In this sense and for this reason freedom is the capacity for the eternal. . . . Freedom does not exist so that everything can always be changed again, but so that by it something can really possess final and irrevocable validity.[22]

Freedom is the faculty of choosing or loving in such a way that we determine ourselves definitively; it is the faculty of absolute commitment. As Dante realized, a spirit which refuses definite commitment, the spirit of the "drifter," refuses being: it is in hell.[23] True freedom means deciding in a way that determines our selfhood finally. To progress in love, to become a self through loving or choosing the good, means becoming increasingly more definite, and thus more unique, more distinct from every other self. As C.S. Lewis remarks, "Good, as it ripens, becomes continually more different not only from evil but from every other good."[24]

At the same time it is clear that, in another sense, love progresses toward both unity and universality. As the self becomes more definite, more unique, it also becomes more universal, more extended to the other. In the perspective of universal love, with Plotinus we may say: "There is no point at which we may fix our own limits, so as to say: 'Thus far, it is I'. . . ."[25] The act of love is by its nature a union with the other, whether its goal is a person, a course of action, or an object. Each such act determines the subject and closes off possibilities, but it does so by placing the subject in relation to the other; and every truly loving encounter with an other in its reality implicitly affirms the love of all, of the whole,[26] and directs the subject further outward. Love as the child of "Plenty" seeks definitiveness, finality, permanence in whole-hearted commitment; as the child of "Poverty" it seeks ever to press on, beyond every limit, to the universal.

Human subjectivity is *inter*-subjectivity: man is a dialogical being, and love creates a communion in which the self attains a greater wholeness than it can encompass in its individual being. But even if extended beyond death, the dialogue and communion among human subjects could never suffice to reconcile the drive to universality with the goal of freedom as an irrevocable and definitive validity. Only in dialogue with the one "Thou" who contains, as ground and source, all good could spirit become through love both a definitive and final self and, at the same time, a part of the whole good in all its extension.

The dynamism of love, therefore, moves us from the consideration of God as the "horizon" of human spirit, to the notion of God as the "addressee" of man's dynamism: the final "Thou," the dialogue partner of man's subjectivity. The question which man is in the depths of his/her being—the question about God—has now become the question *to* God. What is the ultimate destiny and meaning of human spirit, with its longing for the Absolute? Only from God himself could a word of answer come. Humanity is by its very spiritual constitution the "capacity" or "potency" for such a word from the Absolute, for we are the unlimited question about and to Being. If such a word were to come to man in the condition of spirit in the world, it would have to come within the conditions of human subjectivity: i.e., within history and community. Thus man is and must be, by very nature, in Rahner's phrase, a "listener" for God's word in history: a seeker for a revelation from God.[27] Moreover, whether God should "speak" to man or not, a kind of revelation will take place: for God's silence would be significant for man even as would be his speech.[28] Yet, as our considerations above have indicated, man is also a *free* listener for an historical word from God: it is insofar as man opens him/herself to realizing the dynamism of love that he/she will encounter within the self the desire for the infinite "Thou" and open him/herself to Him.

THE FREE REVEALER

For my thoughts are not your thoughts, neither are your ways my ways, says the Lord. For as the heavens are higher than the earth, so are my ways higher than your ways and my thoughts than your thoughts.

Is. 55:8–9

What can a person say, when he speaks of Thee? And yet, woe to those who are silent concerning Thee, when even those who speak are like the dumb!

St. Augustine

Our reflections on freedom and love have brought us to the point of recognizing in man a capacity and a desire for dialogue with God. But "dialogue" must be mutual. Is such dialogue possible from God's part? What, indeed, can man know about the Absolute toward whom our being is directed?

SPEAKING ABOUT GOD

The first problem we must face is that of making any positive statements about God at all. Transcendental method, as we have seen, expands the notion of "verification"[29] and of "experience" to the realm of the immediate and irreducible data of consciousness. The existence of God is affirmed as the necessary condition of my personal experience of conscious being. By this very method it is revealed at the same time that God enters human experience not as an object, but as the pre-condition of all experience: the non-objective horizon of consciousness. God is therefore by definition beyond the sphere of finite and "proportionate" being.[30] But this is precisely the realm where language arises and to which it refers. Hence there occurs the problem of language about God. God appears beyond the reach of ordinary language, because he is beyond the realm of "proportionate" being. Nevertheless, as the object of the "unrestricted desire" which defines being for man, God cannot be said to be beyond the realm of "being" altogether. The theoretical attempt to justify language about God on a metaphysical basis takes the form of the traditional doctrine of the "analogy of being."

The Thomist Notion of the Analogy of Being

On the subject of the "analogy of being" the great Protestant theologian Karl Barth remarks: "I regard the *analogia entis* as the invention of anti-Christ, and I consider it *the* reason why one cannot become a Catholic."[31] Barth's objection is a good place to start in the understanding of the analogy of being and its foundations; for

Barth's opposition to philosophical analogy, as Henri Bouillard has shown,[32] is based upon a misunderstanding of analogy which is shared by many of its proponents. Barth presumes that the analogy of being means that there is some supreme concept or "genus," "being," which applies both to God and to the creature. But such an idea detracts from the uniqueness, the absoluteness, and the transcendence of God: it makes him into *a being*—one of the existents within the most general horizon—rather than *above* every being, as the ultimate and absolute horizon itself.

This understanding of analogy, Bouillard insists, derives not from St. Thomas, but from the misunderstandings of his later interpreters, notably Cajetan and Suarez (who were trying to save the Thomist doctrine from the objections of Scotus). The crux of the misunderstanding is the idea that *concepts* are analogous—i.e., that there are certain ideas or contents of understanding which can be "stretched," so to speak, so that they apply both to creatures and to God. In this theory, which Bouillard calls the "popular" notion of analogy, "one tends to attribute to certain concepts the power of representing, although imperfectly, the essence of God."[33]

For St. Thomas, on the other hand, analogy is not a matter of concepts, but of *attribution:* the basis of analogy does not lie in the contents of insight, but in the act of judgment. Concepts for Thomas remain always inseparable from the sensible experience from which they are "abstracted." No manipulation can make them adequate to represent the divine and transcendent (i.e., totally intelligible) being; they are linked unavoidably to the world of "proportionate" being. "For St. Thomas it is not a question of discovering analogical concepts which would represent in a proportional or simply imperfect way the essence of God. It is a question of determining how, by means of concepts which by themselves are applied only to the creature, we can make affirmative propositions which are true of the incomprehensible God."[34]

For Thomas, no analogical statement (although it may be true) can grasp or contain the essence of God. What God is in himself remains completely unknown to us in this life; he always transcends every *content* of our thought about him. Thus Thomas states: "All that our intellect conceives of God fails to represent him." (That is, God cannot be re-presented—made present—by means of the contents of concepts, which always derive from sensible being. This is because God does not "occur" within the realm of the sensible. Every concept derives, in Thomas' cognitional theory, from images. But God is not imaginable, for the same reason that he is not visible:

not simply because we do not have powerful enough eyes, but because he does not exist in the sphere of perceivable objects at all. Similarly, God is inconceivable: not because we have not happened upon the right concepts, but because every concept whatever is founded upon an empirical basis.) Thomas continues: "Also, that which God is in himself remains hidden from us, and the highest knowledge we can have of him in this life is to know that he is above everything which we can conceive about him."[35] (Note, however, that this is a true knowledge of God; for to know that he transcends our concepts, we must know God *as transcending*.)

St. Thomas also affirms: "We cannot grasp what God is, but what he is not, and the relationship which everything else sustains with him."[36] It is this relationship which makes it possible for us to speak meaningfully of God. All of our knowledge of God is analogical because it is founded completely on the relationship of creatures to the creator. That is, we know God not "in himself," but in *our*selves: *in* finite beings, insofar as they are really related to the Absolute, we know that Absolute. Analogical knowledge and speech about God are therefore always mediated by our subjectivity, as related to him; and this subjectivity is an embodied, finite, sensible consciousness in-the-world.

This does not mean, however, that we are able to speak only of the relationship, and not of God himself. Our speech about God truly *refers* to God; but the way of speaking or of signifying is symbolic, not direct. The *mode* of our discourse is fitting only to creatures, even when the reality we are speaking of—e.g. goodness, or truth—is pre-eminently attributable to God.[37] St. Thomas explains that a word, when we apply it to a creature, in a way contains or circumscribes the quality we are signifying. But when we apply the same word to God, we cannot circumscribe what it refers to: its "content" eludes us, since it goes beyond any experience we have had of the quality in creatures. Thus when we say that God is "good," we do not have a direct insight into God's essence as goodness; yet we are truly saying something about God, since we are affirming that what we call "goodness" in creatures "pre-exists" in God in a superior way, and derives from him.[38]

The term that we analogously predicate of God and creatures is therefore not a sort of "common denominator" between them:

> From the divine goodness and human goodness we cannot, through abstraction, disengage a general concept of goodness which we will then be able to make more precise in each case by

certain determinations. The relationship between the human and
divine goodness is not defined in relation to a third term which is
more or less known to us. There is no third term. Strictly speaking, we conceive only the creature. When we name God, the
"signified" remains uncircumscribed. Nonetheless, the affirmative propositions which we form are also true by virtue of the
relationship which unites the creature to God.[39]

Analogy is therefore not simply a matter of a resemblance between
creatures and God; it is rather a way of affirming a relation between
them. That relation is unique, and implies resemblance and also
transcendent difference. The qualities we affirm of God do not
"represent" him, but they do *signify* him: they are symbols which
refer to God. They signify, however, precisely by the negation of
the mode of signifying: for our mode of knowing is finite and
sensible, while God is infinite and transcendent. Analogy is a judgment, in which we affirm the real relationship of the creature to
God, by which it is "similar" to him, while at the same time denying
the limitations of the creature when its quality is affirmed of God.
We affirm that God is the source and the pre-eminent reality of a
positive quality which is known *to us* in creatures, in a limited way.
We know God, then, in symbols. This is necessarily a mediated and
indirect knowledge, so that analogy always implies the negation of
the finitude of our way of knowing.

The Transcendental Foundation of Analogy

What we have said up to this point stresses the negativity of all
our analogous knowledge of God. (In this "negative theology" we
are on common ground, thus far, with the Hindu tradition, in its
emphasis on the absolute transcendence of God as "Nirguna Brahman," the Absolute of whom no "attributes" may be predicated.)
But if the content of any concept must be negated in applying it to
God, how can we say that it speaks of him at all?

The negative knowledge of God by analogy is in fact founded in
a positive knowledge which is prior to it. This prior knowledge is
not any content of our consciousness, since all such contents are
drawn from sensible experience, but is rather the knowledge implicit in the *a priori* element in consciousness: in the "*notion*" or
Vorgriff of being, which is the capacity of mind for the infinite, and
which manifests itself above all in the action of judgment.

While no concept or idea of ours applies directly to the Absolute, there is something in our knowledge which does have an unlimited range: namely, that dynamism which is a striving toward being, which is open to the unrestricted, and which reaches the unconditioned in a virtual way in judgment. Thus it is not concepts which are analogous, but the process of judging. There is no concept whose range extends to include God; it is the saying of the "is" of judgment which refers to him, intends him.

This is to say: our transcendental reflections have revealed that in the dynamism of intellect and freedom itself, in the *a priori* element which is the condition of possibility for all knowledge and love, there is a positive (although non-objective) *presence* of God as the Absolute. Without this presence in the unlimited range and intentionality of judgment, the negative way of analogy would be impossible; we would have no way of distinguishing what is not God from God himself, had we not some prior "standard" of knowledge.[40] As Bouillard says:

> If God were not present to our spirit, we would be unable to know that he transcends our spirit. We would not know that God is the totally other if he were not the secret principle of all knowledge in us.[41]

We return again to Augustine's description of God as *interior intimo meo et superior summo meo*—a presence which is both interior and transcendent. It is because of this radical (but unthematic) presence of God in the dynamism of spirit that we have a capacity for the unlimited and a capacity for being in general. This radical presence is why we have a "notion" or "pre-apprehension" of what pure perfection is in itself, even though we can never grasp it conceptually. The *a priori* dynamism which is expressed in the affirmation of being is a presence of the infinite which becomes limited as soon as we speak of it. Therefore our analogous knowledge of God is real, even though we can never enclose him as the content of our consciousness.

As Coreth states, whatever we *conceive* about God is hopelessly inadequate; but what we *mean* or *intend* really refers to God as he actually is;[42] for his real being is the goal implicitly present in our fundamental drive toward being.

The reason for man's ability to make true affirmations about the Absolute, then, resides in the mystery of consciousness as the faculty of the Absolute: the openness to the "all" which is already a presence of God. This presence is classically explained in terms of the category of "participation." All being, insofar as it exists, "participates" in God's being (not, of course, in a material sense, as though creation could be thought of as a "part" of God; but in the sense that there is no being "apart from" or "outside" God, so that there would be "more" being than the being of God). If God is *esse per essentiam*, all other existence is *esse per participationem*. But conscious being is in a more particular way a participation in the divine being. In the "agent intellect," the capacity for reaching the unconditioned, we see a participation in a way of being which imitates God's being on a level beyond that of things: being-for-self, "luminous" or self-transparent being.[43] (This is why even in man loving and knowing are a mode of being, and not a mere matter of "perceiving" or confronting objects interiorly. Consciousness is a participation in the "divine light," in the self-present being of the Idea of Being, and not simply a matter of confrontation between objects. For this reason consciousness can only be known through itself, through a heightening of its own activity; it is irreducible to merely objective being.)

It is the notion of participation which underlies the theory of judgment we have arrived at in transcendental method. The absoluteness of judgment, in the reaching of a virtually unconditioned, is possible because the formally Unconditioned, the Absolute, is present and active in the dynamism of our knowing, continually creating our "intellectual light" (the Thomist image for the agent intellect) as a finite participation of his own essential "light." That essential light is the very intelligible Being of God, which "enlightens" being and gives it intelligibility. That is, the pre-condition for the identity of spirit and being (knowledge) in us is the existence of an absolute identity of Spirit and being (the Idea of Being, God): the identity in us participates in that absolute identity, which is complete spirituality or selfhood. The "demonstration" of the existence of God is nothing other than the recognition of this fact: that the Absolute is the unthematized but inescapable pre-condition of our capacity for being, knowing, and loving, and that our existence is thus a finite "sharing" in his being. It is in the light of that sharing that we are able to speak really, although symbolically and analogously, about God.

THE "ATTRIBUTES" OF GOD

Then Moses said to God, "If I come to the people of Israel and say to them, 'The God of your fathers has sent me to you,' and they

ask me, 'What is his name?' what shall I say to them?" God said to
Moses, "I AM WHO I AM."

Ex. 3:13–14

Not by speech, not by mind,
Not by sight can He be apprehended.
How can He be comprehended
Otherwise than by one's saying, "He is"? . . .
When he has been comprehended by the thought, "He is"
His real nature manifests itself.

Katha Upanishad

The process of "naming" God, of saying *what* God is, is an explicitation of the same unthematic presence by which we know *that* God is; we do not know God by his essence, but we can set forth the implications of what is co-affirmed and co-loved in every spiritual act of man. The "attributes" of God are simply the conceptual implications of the fact of God's existence. Just as his existence may be inferred from different starting points in man's spiritual experience, so he may be named in diverse ways, as he is related to the various aspects of our anticipation of him.

The Transcendentals

God may be named analogously through many images and concepts, so long as we maintain the process of negation and eminence. All aspects of finite being which manifest transcendence may be used with reference to God, whether within the realm of common sense (mytho-poetic metaphor), theory, or interiority. But the most basic attributes of God will be derived from what is contained or implied in our "memory" of God as the ground of our spiritual being. The fundamental names of God, that is, will be derived philosophically from our spiritual dynamism toward him, rather than from images which refer primarily to persons or relations or objects within the finite world and limited to it. These fundamental names are traditionally called the "transcendentals."

The transcendentals are so called because they are terms which reach beyond the limits of individual beings, and refer to the necessary notes which appear in all beings, insofar as they "have" being.

They therefore also intend or refer to that Being who is the fullness of "having being," the ultimate Reality that all beings participate in insofar as they are. The transcendentals refer to the objective of the unrestricted dynamism of conscious and free being. That objective is ultimately one: God; but it may be named under different aspects, because of *our* multiplicity. Thus the one objective may be spoken of insofar as it is viewed "in itself," or in relation to our intellect, or our freedom, or our integral personal dynamism; and each relation will yield a different "note" or aspect of the same reality.

The traditional enumeration of the transcendentals includes: Being; Unity; Truth; Goodness; and for some, especially philosophers in the Platonic tradition (among transcendental philosophers notably J.-B. Lotz), Beauty. (Other suggestions include Reality, Identity, Quiddity, Similarity, etc. These, however, seem to be reducible to the traditional designations.)

It should be clear that the "transcendentals" are in fact what we would call, in Lonergan's vocabulary, transcendental *notions:* they are materially identical with the notion or *Vorgriff* of being, the pre-apprehension of the unlimited goal of the spiritual dynamism. They therefore intend not only the being, unity, goodness, and beauty of all beings and of the formal horizon of being-as-such, the one-as-such, goodness-as-such, etc., but also they co-intend the *subsistent* Being, One, Good, and Beautiful as the condition of the horizon itself and of all existents within it. The *Vorgriff* is of course a single dynamism; but when we speak of it, we may call it by different names according to the aspect under which we consider it. Likewise, the pure notion of being, etc., as an *a priori* and unthematic anticipation, has no "content," although it underlies all contents of consciousness.[44] But when we advert to it and name it in its various relations, we obtain a heuristic notion which is thematic and has a "content" insofar as it refers—analogously—to the being, goodness, unity and beauty of proportionate beings.

Every being, insofar as it is ("has" being), is one: i.e., is an intelligible whole, is what it is and no other, is an identity, a self. In this fact is based the principle of non-contradiction. Every being, insofar as it is, is true—i.e., is what is affirmed in rational judgment as somehow unconditioned. Every being, insofar as it is, is good—i.e., is what is loved in an act of rational, responsible decision. Every being, insofar as it is, is beautiful—i.e., is what is desired and sought as the fulfillment of spiritual being. Thus the transcendentals intend the reality of all beings. Yet the qualification of "insofar as they are

. . ." must be added; for the primary intention of the notion of being must be that Being which fully answers to the orientation: God.

Implications of the Idea of Being

We may now more explicitly apply the transcendental notions to God as the fullness of what is intended by them. In drawing out the implications of these notions, we will come to a fuller knowledge of what we are saying when we affirm that God exists. In speaking of the attributes of God, we are again making explicit what is implicit in the necessary co-affirmation of God as the goal of our free subjectivity. A first level of explicitation allows us to justify the reasonability of the affirmation of God; this second level allows us to say more clearly and fully what that affirmation comports.

[We may say that, since we have no intuition of the essence of God, all our rational knowledge of him is simply the explicitation of what we know in saying *that* he exists. In this sense, the attributes of God, like the demonstration of his existence, are merely statements about the goal of our spiritual dynamism, before that goal has been reached. We should note, however, that our anthropology has been following what Lonergan calls a "moving viewpoint." We are not able to speak of every element of the existential situation at once. There may be a yet higher viewpoint on man's relation to God and his/her knowledge of him than we have reached up to this point (the viewpoint of revelation—faith). But since our present perspective is foundational and provides the criteria for attaining any higher viewpoint, the insights of the latter will build upon, and not contradict, what is revealed in the metaphysical perspective.]

In our use of transcendental method we arrived at God as the necessary condition for the intelligibility of being, given in our experience of ourselves as conscious, knowing, loving beings. Let us resume the process as explicitated by Lonergan. The examination of the indubitable datum of our own consciousness reveals the intelligibility of being: we are led to the insight that the world is completely intelligible. Intelligibility and being (the object of the pure desire to know) are identical. Therefore, there are no mere matters of fact without explanation (for a mere matter of fact would be apart from intelligibility, and thus apart from being; but apart from being, there is nothing). From this follows the existence of God. For every proportionate being is a conditioned that happens to have its conditions fulfilled—i.e., is contingently existent. But being is intelligible; therefore no mere happening, no contingence, can be the final word about being; it needs an explanation. All proportionate being, however, is contingent. The explanation, therefore, must be in some other being that is ultimate and non-contingent. That being must be transcendent and self-explanatory (not a mere matter of fact), and must be the ground of explanation for everything else.[45] In this way we arrive at God as the Idea of Being: the content of an act of complete intelligibility: the spiritual act which knows Itself and in Itself all about everything, and is therefore the ground of its own intelligibility and the ultimate explanation of the intelligibility of all being whatever.

From this, there follow certain necessary attributes of God, which Lonergan enumerates in a celebrated section of *Insight*.[46] We shall follow the general line of Lonergan's exposition with some omission of detail and some addition of complementary insights.

There are first of all certain qualities which are implied by the notion of the Idea of Being itself. This primary Idea is an unrestricted act of understanding. It is by identity the primary Intelligible and the primary Truth; that is, it understands Itself, and because it is unrestricted, it understands Itself as absolutely unconditioned, and therefore correct and true (since truth resides in the grasp of the unconditioned). Thus in speaking of the Idea of Being, we have said that traditional language names "Truth" as a transcendental.[47] The Idea of Being is self-explanatory. If it were not, it would be incomplete in intelligibility; and that of course is incompatible with an unrestricted act of understanding. The Idea of Being is its own reason for being; there can be no "why?" beyond God. He is the ultimate reason for himself.[48] In his understanding of himself, the Idea of Being understands also everything that exists by participation—that is, everything that is.

What is known by correct and true understanding and affirmation is being; and therefore the primary intelligible is also primary Being. (Note, however, that God should not be said to be *a* being;[49] nor is he "being-as-such," in the sense of the formal horizon of being; God is rather Absolute Being, *esse subsistens, das zweifach absolute Sein.* God does not fall within the world of beings as we know them, nor "alongside" beings, as the supreme among them. (It is therefore also true to say that God is both "above" being, in the sense of the horizon of being or any content of being that we know, and "within" all being, since there is no limitation to his being.) The primary Being must be perfect being, without any defect. If there were any imperfection in God, it would be grasped by the unrestricted act of understanding; but this would be the grasp of a restriction in the unrestricted act, a lack of intelligibility in the pure intelligible, which is contradictory. God must also be infinite Being—i.e., Being which transcends the finite world and all contingency. (To say that God "transcends" the world, however, must not be understood as an exclusion, or a *delimitation* of God, as though he were "All" *except* the finite; infinite Being must "include" the world as "participating" in its Being; otherwise God's being itself would be finite.) Because the divine Act of intelligibility or being is unrestricted, it includes no limits. God is thus Being in all its fullness.

God must also be unconditional being; for if he depended on anything else, he would not be self-explanatory. For the same reason, God's being is necessary: He cannot be in any way contingent, because he would then need an explanation outside himself. God is therefore the absolutely Unconditioned, on which every virtually unconditioned depends. The faculty of judgment in man is a "participation" in God's unconditioned being, insofar as we are able to recognize the virtually unconditioned only in the light of the formally unconditioned present and active in our very consciousness as its ground.

It follows from the unconditioned character of God that his being must also be completely simple. The absolute or unconditioned being cannot contain parts or divisions: for such parts would have to be finite, and a being composed of finite parts would itself be finite, and hence not unconditioned. The Absolute Being must be infinite fullness in simple unity—the One. The Absolute is therefore immutable or unchangeable.[50] Change always presupposes both unity and difference: a steady and stable element, and a mutable element which is "added" or "subtracted." But this implies duality, which is impossible in the subsistent One. Furthermore, change could not occur in the infinite Being and unrestricted Act of understanding; for any change would mean a decrease or increase, which would only be possible if the being in question was not already unrestricted. For the all-intelligible, there is no more intelligibility, and therefore no more being, to be had; there are no limits to be surpassed; and thus there is no possibility of change.

Because he is beyond development, the One is not "composed," as finite being is, of potentiality and actuality. As the Scholastics say, God is pure Act: his essence is his existence; he "has" his being all at once, without succession. This implies that God must also be immaterial, since matter is the principle of potency and change. By the same token, Absolute Being is non-spatial and non-temporal, because space-time supposes contingency. Space and time are the *a priori* categories of sensibility—i.e., of a mode of knowing which depends upon materiality and upon the reception of empirical data. This mode of knowing is necessary for the finite knower, whose being is not simply identical with the known; but an unrestricted act of understanding cannot be dependent upon sensation or matter. The knowledge of the Idea of Being must be non-receptive; it is purely knowledge by *identity*, for otherwise it could not be unrestricted and non-contingent. The One is therefore beyond the world of relativity defined by the *a priori* of space-time. God is *eternal*—which is not to say that he exists in indefinitely extended time (which could not exist without space), but that his existence is entirely "present," a "now" without past or future. The One is also absolute Spirit: that is, the Being of God is being on the supreme level of "having" being, which is more analogously similar to the existence of persons than that of things. God is being as self-possession, being-for-self, "luminosity." (This follows directly from the identity of the One with the Idea of Being.) Furthermore, we may now say that Absolute Spirit is *pure* spirit, as it excludes spatio-temporality and therefore also materiality.

As we have seen, the good is transcendentally identical with intelligible being; therefore the primary Intelligible and primary Being will also be the primary Good. But the absolute Good is not merely goodness on an objective level; it is good as spirit, as conscious good. As we have also seen earlier in this chapter, this implies freedom in the transcendental sense: the ability of self-disposition, being-for self. The Absolute, then, is the Good not only as lovable, but as freely self-posited or loved. God is the perfect act of loving or freely affirming the primary Good.

God's love of his own perfection is the necessary act of love, identical with his very being as free, self-conscious and absolute existence. But God is also the source and goal of contingent being. By definition, such being is not necessary. On the other hand, neither can the existence of finite being be arbitrary, since everything, insofar as it "participates" in being, is intelligible and good. Since finite beings exist contingently and at the same time intelligibly, we must say that they exist by virtue of an act of intelligent and responsible *positing* in being—i.e., they are created by God. But the free act of positing or affirming the being of another is precisely what is meant by "love." From the standpoint of his relation to finite being, therefore, we must also conclude that God is Love.[51]

Because God is the Idea of Being and the Act of Love, he is the perfection of spiritual being as personal. For this reason he may also be called absolute Beauty—the absolutely desirable and lovable. Again, however, God is not Beauty in the mode of an object, but in a spiritual, conscious mode. God is the beautiful as conscious of itself, knowing itself and loving itself. God is therefore also perfect personal fulfillment, self-conscious Beauty or Joy. God is not a sterile perfection, but is the fullness of what we experience in ourselves as the height of being: joyous, self-fulfilled being, happiness. The Sanskrit name of the Ultimate Reality, Brahman, is Saccitananda: *sat:* being; *cit:* consciousness; *ananda:* bliss or joy. We have arrived transcendentally at the same attributes. What we mean by God, and co-affirm in every spiritual act, is Absolute Being, Absolute Meaning, Absolute Love, Absolute Spirit, Absolute Joy. Because these qualities in us are what make us persons, we may also say that God is supremely Personal.

We have thus far considered God principally as he is anticipated in our transcendental notions by which we "participate" in his being and are similar to him. We may also name God according to the essential difference between his necessary being and the contingency of our participated being. In this perspective, we affirm God as the transcendent source and goal of the world, or as creator. If we ask the basic metaphysical question "Why is there something rather than nothing?" we find that the ultimate answer is "God." If we then proceed to ask "Why is there something *other* than God?" the answer is "Creation." All finite being is necessarily related to and dependent upon God in every aspect of its existence. That relation has three principal aspects, all of which are forms of "causality."

God is first the "exemplary cause" of the world. That is, all the perfections of finite being pre-exist in God in an eminent way, so that God is (to speak in imaginative language) the "model" for all being. Every finite being is in some sense an image of the infinite divine being; God is the source of the analogy of being. In Platonic terminology, we speak of the "participation" of all beings in God to signify his exemplary causality.

Second, God is the "efficient" cause of the world. All finite beings are brought about by God's free action, which makes them to be from a state of non-being. Everything is created by God. Since God is the Idea of Being and the Act of Love, "to be created" is equivalent to being known and loved by God.

[It should be noted that God's knowledge and love are *creative*, not receptive. That is, God does not know and love things because they exist; rather, they exist because he freely posits them—that is, knows them and loves them as real. For us, the material finite universe is first in the order of knowing and loving: all our knowledge and love depend upon objectivity and receptivity; as the Thomist dictum states, *nihil est in intellectu quod non erat prius in sensu.* But God is absolute Subject; Mind is first, not matter. From the theist point of view, objects ultimately exist in reality because they are posited by absolute Mind or Spirit. (This is why Marxist philosophy calls every theistic system an "idealism." The believer in creation by a totally spiritual God does in fact hold that thought or spirit is prior to matter. On the other hand, the Marxists recognize Thomist metaphysics as a kind of "objective" idealism, because the priority of thought to matter is only on the divine plane; for us, the existence of things in thought derives from the existence of objects in the world, not vice versa.)

This explains how God—the Idea of Being—can know all things, but without changing. He knows all in his pure creative eternal act, which is identical with himself. God knows things by consciously causing their existence. The existence of any thing is identical with its being caused by God. But all that God "does," he is; and all that he is, is conscious. Therefore God knows what he creates precisely in creating; or, put the other way around, God creates all things in knowing them.⁵²]

Third, God is to be conceived as the "final" cause of the world—i.e., the last end or goal (Latin *finis*) of all finite beings. God is the source of the world's meaning, the ground of its value, by being the objective of all its striving, the ultimate "beloved" of all things. God is the supreme answer to the question "Why?" which we ask of existence. Each form of causality answers the question under a different aspect. Exemplary causality tells "why" in the sense of "how is it that?": God is the "model" of the universe in its being and goodness. Efficient causality tells "why" in the sense of "where from?": God is the source of the universe. Final causality tells "why" in the sense of "what for?": God is the goal of the universe. Finality is a form of causality because it gives a reason, an intelligibility, to being. For Aristotle, indeed, it was the major form of causality: God moves the world ὡς ἐρώμενον: as the One who is loved or desired by the movement in all things. The whole world is "in love" with God, on various levels. In transcendental philosophy likewise, because we begin with the dynamism of consciousness, we discover God first as the final cause of our existence, the goal of the unrestricted desire to know and love.

As Rahner points out,[53] the notion of God as "creator" is immediately implied by our transcendental experience. In every spiritual act, we co-affirm Absolute Being as the real ground and goal of existence. In subsequent reflection, we recognize the essential difference between this grounding Reality and all finite being, including my own: God is absolute and infinite reality, while all finite being is dependent. God therefore cannot need the world, while the world is in every aspect totally dependent upon God's freedom. (This total and permanent dependence is the meaning of the traditional phrase, creation "out of nothing"—*ex nihilo*. There is no other metaphysical principle of creation besides God.)[54]

The notion of God as "creator" radically distinguishes his action from any other form of causality. God creates the world; he does not act as a "secondary cause" within the world. God creates the whole, as a whole; he is not simply a factor within the working of the world. The conception of God as creator, then, raises again the question: Is God only present to man as the horizon, the cause, and is he known and loved by us only in a way which is mediated by creation? If this is so, then man's highest relation to the Absolute will be what Rahner calls a "devotion to the world" as the medium in which God is encountered.[55] Or is it possible that there is for man a dialogue and encounter with God "in himself," beyond the mediation of the relation of creation?

THE ABSOLUTE MYSTERY: THE GOD OF POSSIBLE REVELATION

Because God is always the one who cannot be encompassed by any concept, nor by any larger "horizon" within which he could be defined, we know and can speak of him only as the infinite, ineffable, and undefinable goal of our transcendence.[56] We know him, then, as absolute "Mystery."

In speaking of "mystery," as Gabriel Marcel points out,[57] we are designating an intelligibility on the level of personal and interpersonal knowledge. "Mystery" refers to what is *intelligible*, but *not comprehensible*. The mysterious is not absurd or irrational; neither is it merely "as yet" unknown. It has an intelligibility, but not of a kind that can be "possessed" objectively; it is rather a kind of meaning into which we are invited, and in which we must grow. "Mystery" ultimately refers, therefore, to the elusive character of subjectivity: for what I cannot totally objectify is precisely the reality of myself (and others) as subject. It is because man is "subject" that he/she is "mystery" to him/herself.

From the foregoing it is clear that the mysterious character of man's being, the "luminosity" which cannot be possessed in the manner of an object, stems from our essential orientation to the participation in the supremely intelligible yet incomprehensible being of the Absolute. (Here we may perhaps find an opening for dialogue with the classical Hindu identification of "Atman," the "soul," and "Brahman," the Absolute.) Since my own being—and that of every person—is not "self-contained," but is essentially constituted by a relation to a "beyond," I remain, in the depths of my being, ungraspable to my own objectifying reason. I am "mystery" by virtue of the fact that what I am is defined by an orientation to the Absolute Mystery, the goal of human spirit. Because human being is not closed, but "open" to the Absolute, it remains mysterious just as the being of God is Mystery. In knowing myself as "subject," then, I know myself as the being who co-intends and co-loves the unconditioned Ground of all spiritual acts, the absolute Subject, the source and goal of freedom and the Mystery of being.

[Because God is known as the source and goal of human freedom, Rahner speaks of him as the "holy" Mystery:

> If free and loving transcendence goes toward a goal which itself creates this transcendence, then we can say that the unconditioned, nameless and absolutely all-conditioning Reality itself is present to us in loving freedom; and this is exactly what we mean when we speak of the "holy mystery." ... For what else could "holy" refer to, to whom could it be more fundamentally applied, than to this infinite goal of love?[58]

For the "holy" is what man worships; and to stand before God as Mystery, in the silent adoration of inescapable love, is to worship him with our very being, prior to every religious articulation.]

To proceed from the notion of God as "holy Mystery" to that of the God who may reveal himself is merely a matter of drawing out the implications of what we have already stated. Man stands before God as a finite personal subject confronting the infinite and personal ground of existence and the goal of transcendence. It would be thoroughly intelligible for man's finality to be simply an "asymptotic" approach toward the ground of our being. On the other hand, we have seen that man is essentially a "natural desire for God," which is to say, a desire to possess and be possessed by God *in himself*. (This remains true even if the natural desire for God had for man no absolute fulfillment: that is, in the case of man's being as an "asymptotic striving" toward God. In this case, the "natural desire" would still be the necessary ground of man's transcendence and his self-realization in and through the finite world.) Man's being cannot "demand" God as its end; but it is, by its very essence, a "question" to God and a capacity for him as end.

How man's question to God is "answered" depends upon the sovereign freedom of the Absolute. God—the holy Mystery—is Person, and therefore he cannot be known positively and in himself except by self-revelation; for as we have seen, the essential being of God is transcendent to every creaturely mediation; he is known to human reason transcendentally, as goal and source, and not "directly." A direct and immediate knowledge of God in himself is conceivable only as the result of God's own initiative, as a freely bestowed gift to man.

Man stands before God, then, as freedom facing Freedom. God is free to remain "silent" for man—i.e., to be for man always the "horizon," the remote Mystery which, unknowable in itself, grounds all human knowledge and love and gives meaning to existence. Such "silence" on God's part would itself be revelatory for man. It would mark our being in and for the world as our definitive mode of being and the sphere of the finality of our striving. On the other hand, it is possible for God to "speak" to man, revealing a further dimension of existence and a further depth of his Mystery and our own. God's free positing of the universe is the primal act of love; and for transcendental philosophy, God is affirmed as identical with Love, both "in himself" and in his relation to the world.[59] All that constitutes man as person and as freedom is grounded in and participates in the being of God as infinite Person and Freedom, and is consequently "open" to that infinite Personhood. It is possible, then, that God may invite man to a participation in his being which surpasses the mediation of the world; such a goal cannot be excluded by the limits of human nature, even though it is in no way an exigency of that nature. If God "speaks" to man, revealing himself in a way beyond what is implied in the relation of creation, he initiates a new sort of dialogue with man's spirit—a dialogue which partakes of the intimacy of "friendship." God may address to man a new "word," making himself not merely the "horizon" of human existence, but its "partner" in dialogue. Such a word of invitation to man would not merely fulfill our essence, but would raise it to a new plane of existence, unattainable to the creature as such, and ungraspable by a merely conceptual analysis of human nature.

We have reached at this point the central conclusion of Rahner's anthropology as presented in his *Hörer des Wortes:* man is always, and by our very essence, one who awaits in history and "listens for" the speech or the silence of God. Because man is free spirit, we are capable of "hearing" such a revelation; because God is free Spirit, he is capable of initiating it. Man is thus the finite spiritual being who listens for a revelation from God, an invitation to a further "dialogue" which would engage and fulfill man's basic desire for knowledge and love. Man seeks for God as the ultimate personal Other who can perfect our drive to be in relationship. All of man's being as person is an implicit participation in the luminous and mysterious subjectivity of God; man seeks and listens for a word from God which would indicate a deeper participation and more intimate sharing in a union of unmediated love.

VII. SALVATION AS REVELATION

GOD'S WORD AS SALVATION

We know that the Law is spiritual, but I am physical, sold into slavery to sin. I do not understand what I am doing, for I do not do what I want to do; I do the things that I hate. But if I do what I do not want to do, I acknowledge that the Law is right. In reality, it is not I that do these things; it is sin, which has possession of me. For I know that nothing good resides in me, that is, in my "flesh"; I can will, but I cannot do, what is right. I do not do the good things that I want to do; I do the wrong things that I do not want to do. But if I do the things that I do not want to do, it is not I that am acting, it is sin, which has possession of me. I find the law to be that I who want to do right am dogged by what is wrong. My inner nature agrees with the divine law, but all through my body I see another principle in conflict with the law of my reason, which makes me a prisoner to that law of sin that runs through my body. What a wretched man I am! Who can save me from this doomed body? . . .

Rom. 7:14–24

The idea that man needs salvation depends, in fact, upon two simpler ideas whereof the main idea is constituted. The first is the idea that there is some end or aim of human life which is more important than all other aims, so that, by comparison with this aim, all else is secondary and subsidiary, and perhaps relatively unimportant, or even vain and empty. The other idea is this: that man as he now is, or as he naturally is, is in great danger of so missing this highest aim as to render his whole life a senseless failure by virtue of this coming short of his true goals.

Josiah Royce, *The Sources of Religious Insight*

175

THE NEED FOR SALVATION

We have seen by transcendental analysis that our being as luminous and free constitutes man as a possible partner in dialogue with God. To be "open" to God is the ultimate meaning of being human; it is of man's "essence." We have also seen, however, that man does not simply "have" being as a given; we must also achieve freedom by our performance: we are responsible for our being. Man's openness to God, then, is not simply a "fact";[1] we will fulfill our essence as "listener" for God to the extent that we live responsibly, freely, as knowers and lovers. Man must by intelligence and love "face" God and be "open" to God's speech or his silence.[2] Human life will be genuine or authentic before and toward God, insofar as man lives by transcendence: insofar as we constitute our life by true judgments and good decisions by following the "transcendental precepts"[3] of being attentive, intelligent, rational, and responsibly loving.

Here, however, there arises a problem. Although we may speak of man's "essence" as freedom and transcendence, we find existentially that there are distressing and frequent obstacles to authentic living and the realization of that essence. With disturbing regularity we find ourselves not living by intelligent and responsible norms, but by others which somehow superimpose themselves on our basic desires. Only too often we do not find ourselves achieving ever further openness toward God, but rather "closing" ourselves in narrow horizons and small concerns. "What we struggle with are the small things, and our very victories make *us* small," as the poet Rilke writes.

Moreover, we find ourselves in some senses *unfree.* Although we may be transcendentally constituted as "finite freedom," our categorical freedom is limited by many factors besides mere finitude. We discover that our actual freedom to fulfill our "essence," our drive toward the good, is frustrated and, most distressingly of all, is frustrated by ourselves: by our own lack of willingness to pursue the good and our own lack of insight into it. We experience in ourselves the paradoxical situation described by St. Paul: made for the good and wanting it with the deepest desire of our being, we nevertheless wander from it. Our freedom itself seems to be trapped in unfreedom; for we cannot live the authenticity we know to be our goal. Made to be transcendent, seeking ever higher integrations of our lives, we seem to block progress by perverse attachments to lower viewpoints and by willful blindness to the ultimate good. In short, man faces a problem of *evil:* in our "situation," in the world, and, above all, in ourselves.

The Blocking of Transcendence: the "Biases"

Bernard Lonergan names "biases" those intellectual blind spots which frustrate man's drive to transcend by preventing the emergence of "higher viewpoints" in human living.[4] Human life, on both the individual and the communal levels, is based upon insight— intellectual and moral—into concrete situations. In order to act or react responsibly and lovingly, man must understand the situation. But such understanding itself is not automatic; its occurrence depends not only upon the subject's intelligence, but also upon a prior willingness to understand. Insight can in fact be unwanted or even excluded; for although man is a questioning being, one can in the concrete refuse to ask the questions which would lead to new perspectives.

The exclusion of insight, however—like the positive act of understanding or love—has implications which go beyond the individual act. For human knowledge and freedom are progressive, and the attainment of higher and broader viewpoints depends upon the achievement of more fundamental ones. The exclusion of understanding does not merely preclude a single answer to a single question; it also excludes all the further questions which would be raised by this answer, and all the further insights and questions which would flow from them; ultimately, it undermines the possibility of arriving at a more comprehensive grasp of truth. The lack of intellectually and morally higher viewpoints, however, can lead man to forms of behavior which run counter to the drive for transcendence. If we do not progress, we regress; if we do not seek freedom in the ultimate good, we entrap ourselves in the snares of lower influences.

Lonergan discusses four levels of operation of the "biases" in common sense human living. On a first level, there is what he calls the "dramatic" bias of subjectivity. By this he refers to psychological or personality disorders which are caused by the refusal of insight. Lonergan attempts to show that the understanding of modern psychology and psychoanalysis concerning human personality may be positively correlated to and deepened by a philosophical view of personality based upon the reality of transcendence. As the psychologist Abraham Maslow notes, "Freud's greatest discovery is that *the* great cause of psychological illness is the fear of knowledge of oneself."[5] (This is not to imply, of course, that there are no other causes: chemical, physical, environmental, etc.) The fear of self-knowledge is parallel to a fear of the "outside" world. It is, in fact, a fear of living, of having to act, of being responsible for one's existence. It is related (as modern psychologists like Ernst Becker have shown) to the existential *Angst* described by Kierkegaard. In psychological terms, this fear may be called "defensive," for it is a means of protecting one's self-esteem by creating a tendency to avoid challenge situations—situations which call for personal growth, and by doing so may produce feelings of awe, of weakness, or of inadequacy. Insights into one's own limitations may be unwanted because they are threatening: they demand a revision both of one's view of him/herself and of his/her behavior. The threatened subject therefore exercises what Freud calls "censorship": he/she represses certain perspectives which would lead to the emergence in awareness of unwanted insights. By this process the subject develops "blind spots" in the personality: areas where he/she cannot (because he/she will not) come to the insights required for personal development.[6]

The process of repression, however, is fraught with danger for the subject. The contents of the thematic awareness of consciousness are not products of a self-standing and independent spirit; man's conscious acts are founded on the lower manifolds of physical and psychic being. The neural processes which arise from man's sensation, and are the means of contact with the world, demand and need psychic manifestation and integration into awareness. When repression takes place, the need for psychic representation is frustrated; for the subject has determined to neglect certain areas of experience. These areas nevertheless press for conscious attention. If the frustration is sufficient, the neural demand functions will seek other means of asserting themselves—means associated, perhaps, with incongruous contents of consciousness, since the proper representation has been denied (thus dreams, for example, may carry affective meanings far beyond their literal import). The dramatic bias or refusal of insight thus ends in a lack of integration in the subject's sensitive and psychic life. This may result in compulsions, anxieties, and psychological malfunction; at the limit, it may become the condition of neurosis or pyschosis.[7]

On a higher level (from the standpoint of the conscious involvement of the subject) Lonergan distinguishes the "individual" bias, or the bias of egoism. Egoism, for Lonergan, is the interference of spontaneous self-interest with an intelligent seeking for the good.

The egoist attempts to make the self, as it were, the center of the universe: he/she, attempts to be the goal of his/her own spiritual dynamism. As we have seen in discussing the "paradox" of the good,[8] there is indeed a sense in which self-interest is inevitable and necessary. Man's approach to the good is always through being as a subject: the good must be apprehended as good "for me." Nevertheless, man's being as a subject receives fulfillment and perfection precisely in its orientation "outward" toward God and others: it is in "losing" life that man "finds" it,[9] because man's being is defined by an unrestricted drive to transcend present being, in love. The very essence of subjectivity is its "ecstatic" character: consciousness is made for the "other."

The egoist, however, seeks to avoid the paradox of the good. He defines the good for him/herself in terms of the immediate and palpable self. He/she refuses to seek beyond the world of immediate desire for a more "true" self; and thus he/she "cuts short" the drive toward the good, refusing to pursue it past a certain limited viewpoint: that of immediate self-interest. Thus, as Lonergan points out, egoism is also a refusal of insight. The egoist refuses to ask further questions about the good. The foundation of morality as formulated in the "golden rule" of all the major religions, as also philosophically in Kant's "categorical imperative," is that no finite individual taken in him/herself can be the ultimate norm for free decision. One must always ask: Can this kind of decision be generalized? What if everyone were to behave in this way? How does this affect the others—who must be recognized as being subjects just as I am, with equal rights? The true good, that is, can never be a good *merely* "for me." To put it in another way: my selfhood must be defined in terms of the good, and not vice versa. That is, I must discover my true selfhood and fulfillment in the light of the ever-transcendent object of the dynamism toward being and the true; I cannot define the good in terms of my immediate and isolated "self." Man's being, as we have seen, is radically communitarian—not merely in the sense of being a "social animal," but in the profound sense that what makes man human is exactly our dialogical openness to the transcendent. It is this which the egoist neglects.

On the other hand, the egoist does not simply follow "animal" instincts; these, after all, are highly social and inter-subjective. The egoist really uses intelligence, and can function with intellectual detachment. But he/she puts aside insight once he/she reaches a certain point. Unlike the victim of the psychological bias or scotosis, the egoist does not live in a world of compulsions and dreams. As

Lonergan says, "the cool schemer, the shrewd calculator, the hard-headed self-seeker are very far from indulging in mere wishful thinking."[10] Indeed, the children of the world may be a good deal more shrewd in attaining their ends than are the children of the light.[11] The egoist deals with reality; for he/she intends to manipulate and use it. But egoism stops short with an incomplete truth and a truncated development of human spirit.

Parallel to the bias of egoism is what Lonergan calls the "group bias." This third level is an extension of the individual bias to include some kind of social grouping. It is based not on the "I", but on the "we"; but the "we" is only a limited section of the human community. As in individuals, so also in human societies there exist blind spots which prevent the emergence of insights which would be threatening to the apparent good of the group. Societies—from the level of the family to large alliances of nations—tend to avoid perspectives which might reveal that their well-being is in conflict with the just expectations of others, or that their term of existence has been over-extended. The group—be it family, tribe, or nation—can make its small intersubjective world into the whole horizon of existence. Anthropologists point out examples of primitive tribes whose names for themselves mean simply "the people" or "the human beings"—so that non-members of the tribe are not considered human; among more culturally advanced people, G.B. Shaw remarks that "the more ignorant men are, the more convinced are they that their little parish and their little chapel is an apex to which civilization and philosophy has painfully struggled up." The glorification of the group may serve many beneficial purposes. It can be a remedy to individual egoism and can provide a context for genuine human concern—but only within the limits of the group. Since, however, the concentration on one group is in general at the expense of others, the group bias produces ill effects on the large scale. It works against wide collaboration among people; it leads to conflict between rival classes, interest groups, or nations; and it promotes, in consequence, a social order in which power, rather than the common good, is the principal goal and determinant of policy.[12]

The operation of the group bias can also be detrimental to individuals within the group. Arnold Toynbee writes:

> One generic evil of an institution of any kind is that people who have identified themselves with it are prone to make an idol of it. The true purpose of an institution is simply to serve as a means for promoting the welfare of human beings. In truth it is not sacro-

sanct but is "expendable"; yet, in the hearts of its devotees, it is apt to become an end in itself, to which the welfare of human beings is subordinated and even sacrificed if this is necessary for the welfare of the institution.[13]

Just as individuals may fear the challenge of growth because of the demand for change, so groups or societies may resist the insight that their true usefulness is limited or has ended. They may obstruct the changes needed to meet new social conditions because social progress would mean the diminution or the end of this particular institution.

Finally, there is the level of bias which Lonergan names "general." It is the intellectual short-sightedness which results from an exclusive attention to the "common sense" realm of mind. The legitimate concern for the here and now, the concrete and practical, leads to a disregard for larger issues, long-term results, and more ultimate perspectives. People come to despise "theoretical" and "abstract" forms of thought which have no immediate and concrete relevance. The realm of theory, however, is the only means man has for dealing with universal and long-range problems. What is "irrelevant" to the common sense of the moment may nevertheless be crucial to the process of human progress as a whole. Thus, for example, the study of the past may seem a sterile pursuit to the common sense mind; yet those who do not learn from history, as Santayana remarked, are doomed to repeat it. In our own culture, the "common sense" concern with the present has led to neglect of long-term perspectives in such areas as energy, food production, and ecology, with the result that the very survival of our civilization is threatened.

The operation of the biases, and especially of the "general" bias, has far-reaching effects. As human evolution continues and knowledge advances, there is an increased need for a human contribution to history; man must discover and control the world process of "emergent probability."[14] Man becomes increasingly the master of the world—or, at least, of the human world—and the emergence of situations which will lead to ever higher integrations of life comes to depend more and more on human intelligence and good will. But if intelligence is neglected and transcendence blocked, such new situations cannot arise. Instead of progressing, man becomes involved in a "dialectic of decline,"[15] the inverse of the needed higher integrations. Human society becomes riddled with conflicts. As man constructs and constitutes a world, blind spots become objectified in the structures of society and behavior. There thus arises a kind of communal context—which Lonergan names the "social surd"—in which a lack of intelligibility is inherent.

The existence of this context partially explains the vulnerability of human freedom and the paradoxical situation of the person who wills the good but cannot perform it. Human spirit is never pure freedom. Man is embodied spirit, spirit in the world; and this means not only the physical world, but also a human environment: the world of community and history brought about by man. Every person's decisions take place in and have an effect upon this world. Human freedom does not remain interior to spirit, but becomes "objectified" in the situations man creates by decisions: physical situations, and, even more significantly, the spiritual situation of the meanings man mediates and constitutes. The objective and inter-personal situation thus created becomes the context or horizon in which *others'* freedom must operate. The concrete possibilities open to any person's freedom have always been in large measure pre-determined by the previous insights (or blind spots) and decisions of others. The operation of the biases, however, means that at least some of those decisions have been based on inadequate and narrow viewpoints. The horizon of an individual's freedom, there-fore, may already be narrowed by a blockage of transcendence transmitted through the community.

Moreover, since the attainment of transcendent living is pro-gressive and cumulative, every blockage of transcendence elimi-nates whole series of possible goods. Hence the biases block higher progress and the attainment of the good is made more difficult. Every person comes into a human situation, then, in which the wrong choices of others have been objectified in a world which is now the material for the person's free decisions. The concrete possibility of good decisions for this individual is therefore threat-ened; freedom is seduced by the apparent ease of wrong and the difficulty of right; intellect is misguided by lack of insight and confusion of values. Because no evil is totally evil, and because in a world infected with the "social surd" the best option may simply not be available, it becomes difficult to make clear choices, and motiva-tions become mixed. Even morally good decisions are made in a context which is already to some extent infected with ambiguity, and the subjectively good intention of the actor can never totally change the objective effect of the action. Thus even morally good acts may remain ambiguous; good choices may lead to tragic dead-ends; and good people may find themselves at cross-purposes in their choices. If one thinks of this condition as being existential and permanent for man, as Karl Rahner points out, one has discerned the condition which the Christian tradition names "original sin": the existential co-determination of my freedom by the guilt of others.[16]

Sin

The evil in man, however, is not merely something that "happens" to us and that can be explained from outside causes. For all the limitations of human freedom, we are nonetheless transcendentally free, and capable of some restricted categorical realization of that freedom. Although human responsibility may with some frequency be diminished or even removed by circumstances, man experiences a basic responsibility for making decisions. Furthermore, man's freedom is exercised "before God"—at least in the sense of a pre-conceptual awareness of the Absolute Good as the binding norm and goal of our freedom. (This pre-conceptual awareness may take the form of the recognition of moral norms even by the non-theist.) The evil in man therefore has, at its limit, the character of personal "sin": the free, responsible rejection of the good before God. We experience evil not merely as a happening or a circumstance in which we are involved; we experience also the guilt of evil, and know ourselves to be—to some extent—its cause, and not only its victims. If we look for the source of evil, we must look not only outside, but also within ourselves.

But precisely here there arises a problem for our understanding of man: How is it possible for man knowingly to seek evil, to sin, if we are for and necessarily tend toward the good as the transcendental horizon of all our being?

[At this point we are touching upon one of the great problems of human existence: the problem of evil and its relation to God, the transcendent source and goal of existence. It would be presumptuous in this brief treatment to attempt to arrive at even a provisional "solution" to this problem. Much less can we address the anguish of people actually involved in suffering and pain, or attempt with a mere intellectual formulation to meet the human reality of alienation and the existential feeling of evil. Nevertheless, we cannot ignore the difficulty which the fact of evil poses to the metaphysical position we have outlined, and we must attempt at least some minimal understanding. How is evil metaphysically possible, if, as we have maintained in our transcendental analysis, being is identical with the good? Or, to put the question in the theist perspective:

How can evil exist in a world entirely created ("from nothing") by a completely good God?

In order to account in some way for the seeming contradiction of evil, we must return momentarily to our transcendental analysis of being.[17] We stated that everything that exists, *insofar as it exists,* is good. The qualifying phrase means that we were constrained to distinguish between, on the one hand, Being "as such," that mystery which is revealed in the *Vorgriff* of being, and, on the other hand, *finite* being. The pre-grasp of the Absolute allows us, as we saw, to know the contingent, the being of proportionate experience. The contrast between proportionate being and the Absolute pre-thematically known is crucial to the affirmation of the existence of God; for each "demonstration" of God's existence restates in a different way the fundamental principle that there must exist a complete intelligibility and goodness, but that the intelligibility and goodness of the world is incomplete.[18] What is not the Absolute—namely, all the being of our experience—is not being in itself, nor completely one, nor totally intelligible, nor thoroughly good. It rather *participates* in the qualities called the transcendentals. Hence there arises the analogy of "having" being, goodness, etc.

This means that finite being is of its very essence dependent or contingent being—which is to say, *relative* being. It is not being as a self-contained unity, but being as a dynamism toward the Absolute. Hence, the qualities of being are shared by finite beings in a relative and dynamic way; and the transcendentals, when applied to the finite, may be stated in terms of *relational* categories. The intelligibility of the finite is not the complete and actual intelligibility of the Idea of Being, but the partial intelligibility of a world which attains its ultimate meaning only by reference outside itself—that is, in God. The being of the finite is being-in-becoming, or process—not Pure Act, but the dialogue of act and potency. Its good is not self-sufficient Goodness, but proper relationship to an end; and hence its love and freedom partake of the quality of ἐρος. Its unity is not simplicity, but order; its beauty is not pure Bliss, but proportion.

It is precisely the relational character of finite being which admits the possibility of evil. Because the finite good is a good of order or relationship, and because the beings making up that order are partial, there is the possibility of a *lack* of proper relation: that is, the possibility of "evil." For, on the Thomist and transcendental metaphysical position, evil cannot be being, but must be a lack of being. Being, insofar as it is, is good; it is the absence of being, or of the proper relationship between beings, which constitutes evil.

The actual world, moreover, is an *evolving* order. The process of emergent probability is good as a whole, for it leads to the further increment of being and higher levels of perfection; yet it contains dead ends and failures, as well as lower stages which are the imperfect but necessary conditions for the eventual appearance of a greater order. In such a world, Teilhard de Chardin claims, "physical evil" such as physical pain, conflict, destruction and death is necessary and unavoidable.[19]

Physical evil, however, remains indifferent morally until one enters the realm of meaning or consciousness. It is here that the real problem of evil arises. All of the shortcomings of the world-order of emergent probability are, in the long run, a part of a potential for the good, and hence are good when seen in context. In the light of God as final cause of the whole dynamism, the evil which consists merely in the lacks of a finite world is relativized, so that for the person who is in love with God, all things, even in their imperfection, are perceived as working toward the good[20] and thus as good in themselves.

Physical evil is defined by shortcomings which must be transcended. True evil, however, is not merely what should not *remain,* but what should not *be.* It is not simply a lesser degree of the good, but a denial of the good; not a lower stage of the dynamism, but an opposition to the dynamism; not a movement (even if dialectical) toward transcendence, but the rejection of transcendence. Evil in this sense can only be the result of the working of finite freedom; that is, it is identical with the reality of sin.[21] Here we return, however, to our original question: How is sin possible, if spiritual consciousness is made for God and necessarily seeks him as its end?]

From the difficulty of this question arises the "Socratic" notion of sin: the evil that man performs is simply a mistake. Man necessarily seeks the good; anything whatsoever that we will, we will as a good. If a particular choice is "evil," it is merely because man has chosen the wrong good; the intellect has been obscured, and one's desire and action are correspondingly misdirected. Evil (and likewise virtue) thus becomes a totally intellectual matter—an error of understanding. The elimination of evil is simply a matter of attaining the proper insights.

This notion of sin, attributed by Kierkegaard to Socrates, but also widely found in both Hinduism and Buddhism, ultimately eliminates the possibility of real guilt. "Sin" becomes an accident of lack of education or wisdom. With the elimination of guilt, however, coincides the elimination of human freedom of choice. "Willing" becomes simply an automatic process following upon understanding.

If, however, categorical freedom is taken seriously, then decision must mean more than an affirmation pre-determined, as it were, by "intellect" alone; it must be a real accomplishment of self-determination. While it is true that man has a necessary and essential orientation toward the good (and ultimately toward God), the mystery of freedom consists in the fact that we can and must *achieve* by decision what we "are" by essence. Finite "will" (which we should not regard as a separate faculty of man, but as the culminating level of consciousness) is precisely that which can posit its own being, can collaborate in the conscious creation of its being, can be its own (secondary) source of being.[22]

Categorical freedom is thus essentially the capacity to accept and to affirm the true good as known through rational judgment, but it includes also and necessarily the possibility of the refusal of acceptance. The possibility of the "no" is the unavoidable guarantee of the freedom of the "yes." That freedom must manifest itself categorically as *choice* follows from the finitude and hence the complexity of human consciousness. The categorical in man cannot be identical with the transcendental. On the level of freedom, human decision does not coincide completely with *volonté voulante* or "willing will" which is a natural desire for the good. This lack of identity is the mark of the essential incompleteness (or, from another point of view, the dynamic nature) of man as a finite being. It is this incompleteness which makes possible and needful freedom of choice. Because man is directed to the *absolute* Truth and Good as the final horizon, our willing cannot be completely determined by any lesser or categorical good. (Again to cite Augustine's phrase, the human heart is made for God, and cannot rest except in him.) No object of finite choice can ever be *the* good which is the object of man's transcendental and necessary desire; and therefore there exists a radical possibility of accepting or rejecting any particular good, that is, of choosing. Likewise, because man's being is incomplete, we exist in time, and have a future. Because our knowing is incomplete, that future is unknown and (as far as man is concerned) undetermined; it can therefore be the object of choice or self-determination. (In this sense we may recognize, with Rahner, the "positive function of human ignorance"; for if we had—*per impossibilem*—an absolute and certain knowledge of our future acts, we could not act freely.)[23]

That human freedom reaches the good through conscious and responsible decision implies ineluctably not only the possibility of intellectual error, but also the possibility of conscious failure to decide properly: that is, the possibility of sin. If we live with the moral imperative to accept and make our own the goal of the transcendent orientation of our being, this means that we *can*—although we must not—reject that necessary orientation. We can never, indeed, reject it completely: even in performing evil, man must seek it insofar as it is (or is perceived as) a good, and therefore as something sharing in the ultimate Good or God. To contradict completely the drive for God, we would have to will ourselves entirely out of existence; for anything which is willed or desired must be or lead toward being, even if only a narrow and truncated being; and being coincides with the good; and every good anticipates the final good, or God.

Man cannot escape the thirst for God, mediated by the need to choose being as a good. But man can settle for lesser goods rather than greater; we can distort the goodness of beings by willing them outside their true relation to God and to the order of rationality; we can attempt to construct our own order of relation in which we ourselves are the ultimate end: our own god. In this sense, sin is not a "mistake," but a lie: the refusal to acknowledge the real good. In order to be sin, the negation of the good must be conscious—not merely an error of judgment, but a deliberate ignoring or contestation of a good which is known, at least in a pre-thematic way. It is clear, then, that ill will is necessarily self-contradictory; for its decision must be made as a "good" for the subject acting, even while that subject is aware of its conflict with the true good. The choice of evil, therefore, always represents a discord within human consciousness—between the implicit *volonté voulante* and the explicit *volonté voulue*. It is also clear that sin, far from being explainable as the result of an intellectual apprehension, is thoroughly irrational. As Lonergan insists, sin is by its nature absurd; it runs counter to man's deepest drive toward the good and therefore counter to the intelligibility which is identical with goodness. Sin is therefore, as Lonergan says, the root of the irrational in man's rational self-consciousness,[24] and, by extension, it is the root of the irrational, the meaningless, in man's alienated situation. Intellect can understand the nature of sin only by means of an inverse insight—that is, by realizing that there is no intelligibility to be grasped.[25] If it had a reason, it would not be sin; for, as Lonergan again points out, sin consists not in yielding to reasons, but in failing to do so—even though the reasonable course is known.[26]

In this connection we must also follow Lonergan in noting that sin is by its nature the negative in human decision, not a positive content. It is in its essence a *failure* to will, an absence of response to moral obligation. The root of all sin is the sin of omission; for even in the morally evil act which is positively chosen, the evil lies not in the being or act, but in what is lacking to it: namely, the proper relation to the self, to others, the world, and God. The sinful act, insofar as it is sinful, is not an event or being (although it takes place in and through an event), but is a failure of being and the lack of an act. It is namely the failure of will to respond reasonably and lovingly to obligatory motives. Sin, *as sin,* has no goodness, no intelligibility, and hence no cause; it is simply the surd, the irrational. As evil, it is non-being, the absence of relation (even though, again, it takes place *in* a being).

In this sense we may say that all sin is basically the denial of transcendence. It is the human will's refusal to go "beyond" in accord with its drive toward the transcendent good, and the consequent choice instead of an incomplete goodness and intelligibility. St. Augustine characterizes the fundamental attitude of sin as "pride," for it is the refusal to be a creature, that is, to have one's end outside oneself. Our spirit knows in its depths that *the* good is God, the Absolute, and that every other good can be so only in relation to him. Sin is the effort to remove a particular good from that relation. It is a matter of making into an end in and for itself (*honestum,* in Augustine's terminology) what in truth always points beyond itself toward the only final good in which spirit can find completion.[27] (It is in this context that we must understand Augustine's definition of sin as a "turning away from God and toward the creature" [*aversio a Deo, conversio ad creaturam*]: not in the sense that God is a rival with his creatures for our love, but in the sense that every true love shares in and implicitly contains the love of God.)

The sinner refuses to transcend the finite good's incompleteness. He/she desires to "stop" within a narrow perspective, rather than see him/herself and all things in the viewpoint of ultimacy. He/she absolutizes what is in truth relative (that is, directed to God). Insofar as sin rejects transcendence, we may agree with Kierkegaard's characterization of sin as "despair";[28] it is the refusal to believe in the greatness of man's destiny. By sin, man "settles" for something less than we are made for; we commit the ultimate folly of rejecting our own good.

Every analysis of sin, however, is insufficient; for sin in reality cannot be "explained." It is by its nature irrational. As Kierkegaard remarks, "How sin comes into the world, every man knows of himself. If he would learn it from another, he *eo ipso* misunderstands it." Each person must experience in him/herself the reality of freedom and his/her own capacity and responsibility for evil. I experience the alienation of personal sin at least as a real possibility, if not as an actuality; and if I am not guilty of sin in its radical form of disrelation to God, I know it at least in an analogous form in the many ambiguous choices and mixed motivations of my life.[29] Every person knows at heart that the achievement of transcendence is radically threatened, not only from without, but from one's own freedom. Each knows, as Royce says, that it is possible for us so to miss the one necessary thing that life itself would become a meaningless failure. And each intuits that if for me evil is somehow transcended, then it is by virtue not of achievement but of gift.

Evil as a Problem Before God

The recognition of evil as an existential problem in the human situation and in myself already contains implicitly a new perspective in reflecting on man and his relation to God. In our previous considerations, we had recognized that man is by nature a "listener" for God's word. God, as free and personal, is capable of revealing himself, and man, as unlimited openness, is capable of "hearing" him. The reality of evil, however, makes us see man as more than a merely possible dialogue partner with God. Man *needs* God's "answer" to the problem of evil. Existentially we cannot by our own powers achieve the transcendence to which we know ourselves called; we need to receive openness as a gift from God. We have spoken previously of the question *about* God being transformed to a question *to* God. In the light of man's existential dilemma, the "question" to God becomes an urgent prayer: for God's "answer" now takes on the aspect not merely of man's ultimate completion, but of salvation.

Moreover, man can and does expect from God the revealing "word" which will address the problem of evil and of authentic existence. For, as Lonergan notes,[30] evil is only a *problem* in the light of our anticipation of God's solution. Apart from God's existence, evil would be a mere fact. In a world without any ultimate intelligibility, the irrationality of evil would be only one facet of the general meaninglessness and brute facticity of existence. But if God exists, then there is an ultimate intelligibility and goodness, and evil cannot be the last word. As long as our perspective is limited to man, evil and sin remain merely the surd; there is no further intelligibility to be sought. But if God exists, then evil is genuinely a problem—that is, something about which a question can be asked, and to which there is an answer. For if God exists, then the entire actual order of the universe, in all its aspects, is the product of limitless intelligence, power, and love. Therefore Lonergan is able to reason boldly from the problem of evil, in the light of God's existence, to the existence of a "solution" for man: "Because God is omniscient, he knows man's plight. Because he is omnipotent, he can remedy it. Because he is good, he wills to do so."[31] The question then becomes: What is God doing about the problem of evil? Man is now seen not only as the essential listener for God's word, but as the one who seeks existential salvation in God's answer to the problem of evil and of authentic existence.

FINDING GOD'S WORD

It was little by little and in different ways that God spoke in old times to our forefathers through the prophets, but in these latter days he has spoken to us in a Son, whom he had destined to possess everything, and through whom he had made the world.

Heb. 1:1–2

In the history of the Universe, in so far as human insight has been able to probe the mystery of it so far, we can see events that have been decisive and therefore significant: the successive geneses of our galaxy, our sun, and our planet; the epiphany of Life on this planet; the epiphanies of the Vertebrates, of the Mammals, of Man. These are all instances in which a particular creature has, in fact, served as the instrument or vehicle for a decisive event at a particular point in Space-Time. If it is not incredible that the Earth may have been singled out circa 2,000,000,000 B.C. for becoming a home of Physical Life, it is neither more nor less incredible that Abraham may have been singled out circa 1700 B.C. at Ur, or Israel circa 1200 B.C. at the foot of Mount Sinai, for becoming a vehicle of God's grace to God's creatures. If it is not incredible that the first Adam may have been created, circa 1,000,000 or 600,000 B.C., at some point, not yet located by pre-historians, on the land-surface of this planet, it would be neither more nor less incredible that a Second Adam may have become incarnate in Galilee at the beginning of the Christian Era.

Arnold Toynbee, *An Historian's Approach to Religion*

THE HEURISTIC ANTICIPATION OF GOD'S SOLUTION

If God is in fact presenting to man a "solution" to the problem of evil, it should be possible for us to discern, by a kind of transcendental deduction, what the essential characteristics of God's saving "word" must be. Prior to examining the conflicting claims of religions about God's revelation to man, we can construct what Lonergan calls the "heuristic structure" of the solution.[32] We cannot say a priori what God's "answer" to the problem will be; but we know what the problem itself is, and, since the solution must be fitting to the problem and its context (the order of the world and the nature and capacities of man), we can from the problem itself determine the minimal elements which the "answer" must have. This heuristic structure will not identify God's word, but it will show us how to recognize it. We shall summarize briefly the main points of Lonergan's statement of this heuristic anticipation.

First of all, God's "answer" must be in harmony with the actual order of the universe. More accurately, it is the actual order of the universe, discerned from the highest viewpoint. It is clear from the simplicity and absoluteness of God that his action cannot be in any literal sense a "response" to a pre-existing situation, or an "afterthought" to creation. Whatever God's plan of salvation may be, it is not to be conceived as something "added on" to an already complete world. (Within our moving viewpoint, indeed, we may look first at the problem, and then ask about its solution; but such a procedure is, as we have already noted, of necessity "abstract," in that it cannot consider every aspect of the existential situation at once.) It is the total and actual which is metaphysically "prior," for God knows and loves in a single creative act. Hence the "solution" is really co-existent with the problem itself—although it is "hidden," in the sense that its apprehension by human consciousness depends upon the attainment of certain higher viewpoints on human existence.

[It is this fact which justifies and necessitates the technique of the moving viewpoint. We are, as we have seen from the start, already involved in the dialogue with God prior to our examination of it. It is in the light of God's "answer," as Tillich says, that we ask our questions about him. Nevertheless, because of our finitude and the complexity of our minds, we must go through the process of actually asking the questions in order to discern the answer. The questioning and abstracting process itself is an element in our collaboration with the solution. It is in order to assume rational responsibility for our existential stance that we must analyze and abstract from the total and actual situation.]

Like the problem itself, the solution must be an "existential": a universal and permanent condition of human existence, prior to man's explicit knowledge, and not derivable from the human "essence," but occurring within the "ontological" realm of man's actuality as a conscious and self-determining being. That is, the condition of being faced (at least implicitly) with the offer of God's saving "word" is an ontological determinant of man's existence prior to free decision and explicit recognition.

The solution must also be in man, and must be in continuity with those structures which we have discerned as belonging to our "nature": i.e., our fundamental openness to being and the good. The answer to the human dilemma, that is, must occur by introducing a higher dimension in human life. It cannot consist in replacing man with another species, for example (for this would not solve the problem, but avoid it). Nor can it consist in taking man out of the world in which the problem occurs. That is, the solution cannot be simply in an "afterlife" which will rectify the injustices and alienation of this life. Our analysis of man as spirit does, indeed, imply a hope for a dimension of existence beyond the end of biological life. We have seen that spirit is an unrestricted desire to know and love (in Scholastic terms, a natural desire to "see" God). This drive is not merely an unlimited curiosity; it is the desire to *be* and to be conscious of being, to be as spirit. It is the rebellion of consciousness against the threat of extinction. We have also seen that man's essential drive to being and the good transcends the world of proportionate experience, and this leads us to hope beyond death for an eternal validity.[33] Man hopes to "rest" finally in God, the goal of our striving. Nevertheless, the means to this goal cannot simply be identical with the goal itself. The solution to the problem of human life cannot be in the postponing of meaning in life until after death. If there is a solution to the problem of evil, it must operate in the realm of the problem, i.e., in the world. For, as we have seen, man only attains spirituality in and through being-in-the-world. The present world, with its existential situation, is the necessary space of man's becoming transcendent by knowledge and love. Therefore if man has, in fact, an eternal destiny, we can only attain to it by our being in history.

Whatever we are to *be* for eternity, we must *become* in time. The value for eternity of human life in the world stems from the essential constitution of man as spirit-in-the-world, that is, as spirit which comes to subjectivity through the mediation of the non-subjective (matter). Therefore, although a solution and answer to the problem and question of human life must *point beyond* history, to the ultimate fulfillment of transcendence in God (in some as yet undetermined way), it must also be realized *in and through* history. Man can attain a trans-historical value only by means of inner-worldly action and responsibility. We must therefore reject from the outset any notion of salvation which simply negates human experience in the world or counts it as valueless or illusory. We can say at this point that the world must be *at least* the locus in which man attains salvation; it is not yet clear to what extent the world itself may actually form a part of that salvation.[34]

Although salvation must be for man and begin within the human world, it must also transcend man's means; for it is God's answer to what is insoluble within the merely human horizon. A solution must provide a yet higher integration of life, including the irrationality of evil and sin. Evil itself must somehow become a potency for good, insofar as it is transcended and integrated into a higher system (which, again, is the actual order of the world, under-stood from the highest viewpoint).

The higher integration, since it occurs within the actual dynam-ic world order and within the dynamic of human spirit, will be a dynamic ordering. We may expect it, as a higher integration, to be more similar to the higher integrations of life—intelligence, psyche, etc.—than to lower levels of integration like the physical and chemi-cal. Since higher integrations leave intact the lower manifolds on which they are built and which they transcend,[35] God's answer to man will leave man's "nature" intact: that is, it will come to man as an intelligent, rational, free and responsible being. The solution for man must therefore come to us through our own apprehension and consent. Since man is an historical being, involved in both the process of general emergent probability and the particular human history which is man's contribution to it, God's solution must have history as its locus. It must come to man, therefore, within human-ity's historical conditioning, and hence in accord with the varying possibilities of occurrence. For the possibility of actual human rec-ognition of and consent to a word from God is not invariable. Although human nature may remain constant as a *potentia obedien-tialis* for God, it is obvious that man's actual realization of our nature as spirit is historically conditioned. There is not only the evolutionary development in which the brain is progressively freed for the function of thought, but also the cultural and social development in which man progressively built worlds of language and meaning to express self-understanding. The basic human capacity to ask questions and to grasp answers is limited by the potentialities of the "language" (in its largest sense) at hand. Man's actual performance as a perceptive, intelligent, rational and loving being capable of "hearing" a revelation from God will therefore be conditioned both by physical and cultural evolution.

It is therefore to be expected that salvation will imply a "fullness of time"[36]—a full realization which does not simply descend from the blue, but awaits the required development for human recognition and collaboration. We may then anticipate not only God's solution, but also a whole series of "emergent trends" (as Lonergan calls them) through which that solution's effective realization in man becomes possible and probable. Hence the appearance of salvation will be multiform, having different historical stages of evolution and preparation and different degrees of perfection and realization, all leading to its final achievement.

Since it comes as a fulfillment of man's spiritual being, God's word must include a higher integration of human freedom, i.e., a new dimension of love. Our metaphysics has shown that the entire universe is "in love" with God, with the exception of the irrationality of sin. God, that is, is the "final cause" or necessary goal of the universe, as well as the implicit and unavoidable end of all human desire. Sin is that which contradicts the dynamism toward God. The solution must overcome this contradiction by somehow bringing the surd of evil into the dynamism of love. Evil, like every "counterposition," calls out for its own reversal; for it contains the implicit contradiction of an absence of good within an orientation which is toward the good and implicitly affirms it. Sin is rooted in the refusal of transcendence and the blocking of higher integrations; its reversal will involve a movement toward the accomplishment of selfhood by means of transcending self in and for God. This movement is love; and love must restore the dynamism toward the good by providing a motivation for man to respond to evil with good, thus turning even the irrationality of evil into a potency for transcendence. Such love will be in some sense "self-sacrificial," for it is not only "ecstatic" in seeking a final good outside the self, but it does so in the face of a concrete lack of a proportionate good.

The act of love also necessarily involves man's mind; for freedom is the highest level of rational self-consciousness. Love is always connected with meaning and truth, just as evil is at its root a lie and a surd. The solution to the problem of evil must therefore involve a higher collaboration with God and with others in pursuit of the true meaning of existence. Because man is an historical and social being, the pursuit of truth must necessarily have a communal dimension; and historical progress as a community of knowers involves a continuity, a tradition. People cannot and do not each begin from an absolute "point zero" in the search for meaning and freedom; rather, each enters into a world in which many meanings are already constituted. The assent to such meanings and their appropriation as one's own implies the human reality of belief, which is pre-supposed by all collaboration.[37] Thus the solution implies some (yet undetermined) sort of "faith," since it involves a basic trust in a collaboration or dialogue which goes beyond one's own self-generated knowledge. It would seem that this collaboraton, in order to perdure through history, would also have to have some kind of institutional existence. (At this point, however, we cannot more exactly determine what kind of institution would be needed; the "institutional" dimension of the solution might consist in such natural institutions as the family, the political structure, etc.)

Man must not only apprehend and accept God's word, but must actively collaborate with it. For the solution to the problem of evil is not to replace humanity nor to take man out of the world, but to bring man to a new and higher integration. This integration will presuppose (as the Scholastics also put it) all of man's "nature." If God's word comes to man as a free, intelligent, rational being who constructs a life with others, then it cannot simply be "imposed" on man or "added on" to human living; the project of human life will be an integral part of the solution. Human life, however, involves the dialogue of persons, the interchange of influences, and the progressive humanization of the world. Thus man is called to realize and further the solution by becoming a part of it: by making it known, formulating it in the available language and insights, adapting it to different cultures, explaining it to oneself and others in terms of the basic "given" of inter-subjectivity and the ever-changing "given" of the situation.

Because man operates consciously on many levels, the solution must have many dimensions. It must integrate not only the higher reaches of human intellect and freedom, but also living on the practical, common-sense level and intellection on the mythical and symbolic level. Man is a bodily and sensitive being, and the human spirit flows from animal existence. The solution will not be the introduction of a dichotomy in man, in which a part is left behind; it will rather address the whole person. God's word must therefore also address man in the dimensions of imagination, affectivity, and sensitivity. It will exist, then, on an aesthetic level. Indeed, we may expect that man will apprehend it principally on this level; for there is in human life a priority of the poetic and symbolic over the conceptual. Man faces the mystery of existence and of God and speaks of it above all in the analogies not of metaphysics, but of art.

Because human freedom and intellect remain whole, man's collaboration with God and with others will be imperfect; error and sin can be expected to remain even within God's solution, insofar as man is not only the recipient, but the means of its realization. Nevertheless, the solution will be God's word working in man, and will therefore be finally invincible.

Lonergan concludes his heuristic anticipation of God's action in man by recalling the limits of the heuristic structure itself. What can be anticipated *a priori* about God's word is only what can be known from the problem. But God's solution may go beyond a mere answer to the problem. Since God is free and personal, and man is constituted by an essential desire to know God, it is possible that salvation will be more than salvation—that is, that it will open up a new and unanticipated dimension of existence for man. In any case, the actuality of the solution will go beyond what can be deduced heuristically; if the solution should be in some sense "super-natural," going beyond the natural proportion of the creature, it will contain elements which transcend completely the nature of an "answer," and which constitute a free creative initiative from God. (This free initiative will, of course, "subsume" the whole of God's word, and will be the metaphysically prior cause of the whole). The introduction by God of a "super-natural" mode of existence for man would greatly increase the tensions which always appear when lower levels are transcended and subsumed into higher ones.

As Rahner ends his *Hearers of the Word* with the imperative for man to "listen" in history for a possible revelation from God, so Lonergan ends *Insight* with the imperative of intellect to seek for faith. Man is not only a potential dialogue-partner with God, but is the being who is existentially called to find his salvation in a higher collaboration of love with God and others.

THE FINDING OF THE SOLUTION

Following Lonergan one step further, we find that once we have formulated a heuristic structure of the solution, there remains the task of identifying and accepting that solution in its actual operation.

This task will differ for each person. For the actual identification of God's word cannot be heuristically deduced from the problem; it must be received precisely as God's revelation of himself. Every person is responsible before God, and must direct him/herself as a "listener" for the word of salvation which is spoken in history. But the solution exists not only in its fullness, but also in a series of "emergent trends," and therefore each individual's possibility of identifying and accepting the solution will be conditioned by his/her own historical setting, as well as by his/her personal disposition. The actual act of acceptance and identification of God's word is accomplished only in the very act of entering into the dialogue with God. Thus the act of accepting God's solution is itself a part of the solution; although it is man's collaboration, it is at the same time God's gift.

Insofar as each person is already involved in a personal dialogue with God (whether positive or negative), he/she is already in contact with God's revelation. Insofar as a person is actually engaged in a self-transcending and authentic life, i.e., in loving and intelligent existence, he/she is already collaborating with God's solution; for the activity of the solution on a pre-thematic level is prior to any thematic identification. Insofar as each person not only presupposes an ultimate meaning and value to life, but finds evidence for his/her lived faith in experience, despite the surd of sin, he/she is already involved in the reality of "transformation" or "conversion," has at least implicitly identified and accepted God's love in history, and has expressed it in some sort of language of transcendence. The task of identifying the solution thematically is therefore a matter of advancing to a new level of collaboration. It is a question of justifying and naming a faith and love which are implicitly lived and (to some degree) explicitly formulated. The process of identification allows the subject to "give answer" for his/her life, to humanize the option for God by taking fuller responsibility for it, to integrate it with the mind, psyche, and emotions, and to make it more communicable to others, thus entering into a dialectic of purification. For the thematic identification of God's word confronts the subject with the foundations of his/her own faith experience, and allows him/her to compare his/her actual faith-"language" with the historically identified revelation of God. He/she may then engage in the process of advancing those positions and formulations which accord with the solution, and of reversing those which contradict it.

If it is true that the solution is an existential which is actually operative in the lives of all (at least as an "offer" on God's part), and which is experienced as the basis for "conversion," or the life of transcendence, then we should be able to say something about the identification of the solution which on the one hand goes beyond the merely heuristic anticipation, but on the other hand does not yet involve entry into the dialectic of comparing and evaluating the various identifications given in the history of religions. In seeking to identify thematically the solution which is God's historical word, we must seek a correspondence not only with the nature of man and of the problem, but also with man's internal experience of conversion, i.e., with the solution actually at work in one's own life. The concrete existential *experience* of the transformation of life in dialogue with God and in love of others will provide certain criteria for identifying the characteristics of God's word as an historical-social reality; what is implicit in our collaboration with God will, if made explicit, allow us to say more exactly what we are "looking for" in history as the full expression of salvation, and will thus allow us to enter even more fully into the collaboration.

Concretely, our progressive reflections up to this point have left us with two important unanswered questions regarding God's relation to man. First: in the light of man's unlimited openness to the mystery of being, we have seen that the only possible final goal of human existence is God—that man is, by nature, a "question" to God. But an examination of human nature could not disclose whether that question has a final attainable "answer," that is, whether God remains always for man the asymptotic goal of all finite striving (but without any arrival), or whether God's "word" to man includes an "answer" which is a participation in God's own being, at a new level beyond the mediation of the finite world.[38] The second question is intimately tied to the first: our statement of Lonergan's "heuristic structure" of God's solution to the problem of evil leads to the affirmation that history and the world must be the "locus" of God's word; but it could not be determined by the heuristic method to what extent human history in the world would actually constitute the solution.[39] We are therefore left with the questions: Is there an immediacy of God to man, beyond the mediation of the world? and In what way and to what extent does the world mediate God's word and presence to man?

A priori, God's self-revelation and solution to evil could take a multitude of forms. As Rahner points out, and we have already noted, even God's "silence" would be a revelation for man. God's "response" to evil need not *per se* include an "elevation" of man to immediacy with God: God's "word" of salvation could remain on a level proportionate to man's finite nature. God's communication with man and his collaboration in love could take place entirely through the mediation of the world; God's "word" would then be no other than the word of continuous creation expressing God's solution ("providence"), while God as the ultimate mystery would remain "silent": the constant source and asymptotic goal of transcendence. The "healing" of man would then remain within the horizon of a finite creature. On the other hand, because God is the free and absolute mystery, and because man is an unlimited openness (*potentia obedientialis*), it is possible that God's "word" be in some sense "super-" natural: that is, beyond the natural proportion of the finite creature. This would mean that the healing of man would also be a transformation of the human horizon, bringing man into the sphere proper to God alone: an immediacy with the Absolute.

We cannot deduce *a priori* what kind of word God does in fact address to humanity for our salvation. But whatever it is, it is (in some measure) operative already: we are already experiencing it as the existential offer of salvation or as the reality of our conversion. We can therefore apply a kind of transcendental reduction as the first step in the task of identifying God's solution: we can examine our actual experience, and then ask what the conditions of possibility of that experience must be. By this process we can attempt to resolve the interrelated questions of the "supernaturality" of God's word and of the place of the present world in it.

The question, then, is one of fact: Is our experience of the Absolute such that the highest point of our transformation cannot aspire beyond a complete "devotion of the world"?[40] Is God's "word" to us so entirely mediated by creatures that it is really experienced as the "silence" of a God who reveals our salvation, but not himself? Or does our experience evidence the tension of a calling "beyond" the human horizon? Is God's "word" in reality not a merely external communication, but a sharing of his own proper life? And, if the latter is the case, does the immediacy of the Absolute preclude every mediation by the world, so that the finite becomes a locus and means of salvation only by its own negation? Or does the world maintain a positive role in salvation even in the case of a "supernatural" relation to the Absolute?

Every person must answer such questions for him/herself. First of all, do I, or do I not, experience what I may dare to call an immediacy and intimacy with the Absolute? No one can answer this question for another. But others' explicitations of their experience may point to and allow us to name our own. For an immediate experience of God by definition is a transcendental, non-objective experience, and is therefore "hidden" from and disproportionate to our objectifying thematic consciousness.[41] If we are thematically to discern such an experience, it can only be by a transcendental reduction: we must find whether our actual performance as intelligent and loving beings implies the presence of a "supernatural intentionality"[42.] that is, whether our spiritual being, our rational self-consciousness—precisely in its most rational and responsible acts—contains elements which are inexplicable except on the condition of a self-communication of God. But the spiritual testimony of mankind does in fact attempt to point to such experiences. Karl Rahner returns to this theme in both his spiritual and theological writings:

> If someone perseveres in final faithfulness to his conscience, even when there is no reward; when someone manages to love selflessly, so that it is no longer merely a question of getting along with someone, or a union of egoisms; when someone allows himself to be drawn into the night of death calmly and without a last protest; when the whole of a person's life—despite all the contrary experiences and disappointments—quietly opts for the light and the good; when someone—perhaps in apparently total hopelessness and doubt—nevertheless hopes that he hopes ... there human freedom has become identified with that hope which is the fundamental structure of man's existence: the hope which constantly underpins human freedom through all the individual events of life. In such hope there is already unthematically experienced and known that which is really meant by "God," even if this word is lacking in the normal vocabulary of such a person. ... God himself is the most profound dynamism of this unlimited movement of hope toward himself. And insofar as God in grace makes himself the dynamism and the goal of our hope, revelation is already taking place.[43]

In our most authentic moments we find ourselves living by something beyond ourselves, something experienced as gift and as mystery, and at the same time as the expression of our own freedom. We find ourselves living by convictions, hopes and commitments which are implicitly rational and responsible, and yet have not sufficient reasons within the finite world. Our actual performance in the collaboration of conversion with God and others implies the presence of an unspoken "supernatural" motivation.

> Have we ever kept silent, despite the urge to defend ourselves, when we were being unfairly treated? Have we ever forgiven another although we gained nothing by it and our forgiveness was accepted as quite natural? Have we ever made a sacrifice without receiving any thanks or acknowledgment, without even feeling any inward satisfaction? Have we ever decided to do a thing simply for the sake of conscience, knowing that we must bear sole responsibility for our decision without being able to explain it to anyone? Have we ever tried to act purely for love of God when no warmth sustained us, when our act seemed a leap in the dark, simply nonsensical? Were we ever good to someone without expecting a trace of gratitude and without the comfortable feeling of having been "unselfish"?
>
> If we can find such experiences in our life, then we have had that very experience of the Spirit which we are after here—the experience of the Eternal, the experience that the Spirit is something more than and different from a part of this world, the experience that happiness in this world is not the whole point of existence, the experience of trust as we sink into darkness, the experience of a faith for which this world provides no reason....
>
> Now if we have *this* experience of the Spirit—by accepting it—then we who live in faith have in fact experienced the supernatural, perhaps without quite realizing it.[44]

If there is an implicit presence in man of an immediacy to God, it is perhaps most clearly seen in the living of agapic love toward our neighbor.[45] Rahner again proposes that an absolute love bestowed unconditionally on a human being implicitly affirms, as its condition of possibility, the presence of God himself, the Absolute, within the sphere of human activity. For every human being is finite, and can therefore only be a *virtually* unconditioned value or object of love.[46] Moreover, the life of the beloved is changeable; the values affirmed in the act of love can be altered by the free options of the person loved. There is a certain inevitable possibility of "fickleness" inherent in any finite free person; no finite being can, *per se*, be worthy of an unreserved trust. *In se*, then, man cannot justify an *absolute* love, in which one commits self unconditionally and entrusts oneself completely to the other. *In se* man—our neighbor—can only be loved *conditionally: if* the conditions (of value) are fulfilled, then the act of love is grounded. Only God is the unconditioned value which can ground a completely unconditioned or absolute mode of love. But if we in fact experience within ourselves a call to an absolute love *of our neighbor* (and whether we do so, each person must answer for him/herself), then the implication must be that the love of this finite being is somehow identical with the love of the Absolute and Unconditioned: that the love of neighbor *is* the love of God. Only thus could an *absolute* love be justified. If we do experience a summons to an absolute love of neighbor, therefore, we must recognize that such love implies a "supernatural" intentionality: that it has as its proper object God himself, somehow united with the finite object of love. Rahner is saying, then, that in every total act of our spiritual nature as free beings we are directed implicitly not only toward God as transcendent and asymptotic horizon, but toward an immediate presence of God.[47]

[We must note again that the experience of which we are speaking is a *transcendental* one, and one that is therefore incapable of being known unambiguously on the reflexive level, or with thematic certitude. As the presence of an immediacy to God which is not (yet) total immediacy (i.e., the "vision" of God), such an experience could not reflexively be adequately and certainly distinguished from man's unlimited natural dynamism toward God. Nevertheless, although such an experience of the self-communication of the Absolute "cannot indeed in individual cases (prescinding from possible exceptions) be known with an *unambiguous* reflexive certitude, nevertheless such an experience is not simply and absolutely unavailable to reflection."[48]

In the case of Rahner's examples of action for the sake of a motivation which goes beyond the finite, for example, it is true that we can never know our deepest and truest motivations for any single act with direct reflexive certitude. But in the whole series of such acts, we encounter a convergence of probabilities which becomes decisive for reflection. And we reach the "supernatural" character of the experience not by simple psychological introspection, but by transcendental reduction.

"We are in reality dealing with a transcendental experience which manifests itself in human existence and realizes itself in that concrete existence."[49] While the sort of reflexive knowledge that we can have of the supernatural is not absolutely certain, it suffices (from the perspective of our "moving viewpoint") to lead us to *look for* a historical confirmation of the self-gift of God in history, or (from the perspective of people "giving answer" for their faith) to *recognize* the experience once it is presented and interpreted by historical religion.]

If what we have said thus far about the implications of our existential experience of involvement in salvation is correct, then we have already indicated the direction of a response to our second unanswered question as well as the first. For the context in which we experience the mysterious "more" which points to immediacy with God always seems to be some form of commitment to the world. If God's word is one in which he gives himself to man, then God is man's absolute Future. But does unity with God belong entirely to the future—or does history in the world tend toward that goal because it is already *within* the goal—i.e., by God's immediacy coming to man in and through history, so that the world is not only the "locus," but also the means of God's self-communication? Only in this case, Rahner claims, can man have a genuine hope for and commitment to the world.[50]

But how is it possible to speak of an "immediacy" to God in which the world serves as a "means"? First of all, we must recall that we are speaking of an immediacy *of the transcendent Absolute*—that is, of that which is in no wise "on the same level" as finite being. "Mediation" and "immediacy" will take on a special meaning in relation to God. Secondly, let us recall that even within the sphere of proportionate existence we have an experience of what Hegel calls "mediated immediacy" (*vermittelte Unmittelbarkeit*): namely, in the experience of our own subjectivity. We come to consciousness of ourselves as subjects by means of awareness of objects. The objective content of consciousness "mediates" the immediate presence of the subject to him/herself.[51] Likewise, the presence of God as the transcendent ground and horizon of all knowing and loving (which is already a kind of "immediacy" to God in his omnipresence, although not the "supernatural" immediacy of which we are now speaking) takes place through the mediation of finite objects.[52] Similarly, a supernatural immediacy of the Absolute to a finite creature cannot be thought of otherwise than as a "mediated immediacy"—for at least the finite subject's own subjectivity must serve as a limiting medium in and through which the Absolute is experienced. Rahner writes:

> It is easy to perceive that immediacy of God in himself (however this is to be understood more exactly) either is completely impossible, or is not prevented by the fact that there is also some kind of mediation. If there is immediacy to God at all—that is, if we really can have to do with God, in himself—then this immediacy cannot depend on the fact that the non-divine simply disappears....

> Mediation and immediacy are not simply contradictories; there is,
> with regard to God, a real mediation of the immediacy.[53]

Of course, in the case of an immediacy to God which is "be-yond" his presence as horizon and ground of being, we cannot think of the mediation by a creature as being such that the creature's very existence makes present the intimate selfhood of God: "The individual being as such in its categorical individuality and finiteness, can only 'mediate' God in so far as in the experience of this thing, the transcendental experience of God takes place also."[54]

The analysis of our existential experience, then, points toward and expresses a hope for a genuine "word" of self-communication of God which nevertheless does not simply negate the experience of the finite world, but takes place in and in some sense "through" the latter. This word is at the same time salvation, or God's solution to the human dilemma. We have seen that we should expect such a solution to come to man in accord with the emerging probabilities of human history and culture, so that there would be "emerging trends" toward the fullness of salvation. If salvation is a real self-communication of God in history, however, there must also be a point where the solution is completely and definitively present and victorious over evil. There must be a point at which the "word" is truly God's own, and not merely man's always relative and provisional attempt to express categorically his transcendental experience of the Absolute. In order to be a true presence of God in history, the fullness of salvation must have the character of historical "event" in which man experiences the human essence as question really and absolutely answered by God's definitive gift of himself.[55] (Such an event—whose more precise character cannot here be determined—would be the fullness of the solution and the "final cause" of the whole process of human collaboration with God and others on its many levels.) We may then say that our existential experience induces us to anticipate in history an "absolute saving event" (which has either already occurred or is yet to come) in which God's self-gift and the human acceptance and collaboration with it are finally and definitively present.

The task of identifying God's solution, as we have said, implies actually entering into the collaboration with God. This act we may now identify with Lonergan's phrase, "being in love with God in an absolute way."[56] This mode of loving is human consciousness on its highest level—that of decision or freedom; but it is this level given a new basis: a supernatural intentionality. The motivation of love is now an unconditioned value present as God's self-gift: "God's love flooding our hearts."[57] By it we experience the freedom of those who choose the good because they are "in love" with it. We experience our orientation toward the Absolute Mystery of love as being in some sense fulfilled, and thus serving as the dynamic principle of our actions. The full and free acceptance of this change in horizon is man's "fundamental option" for God.

The religious dimension of conversion—"being in love with God in an absolute way"—is in itself an unthematic and transcendental experience. It cannot, therefore, stand alone, but must seek to objectify and thematize itself in language, community, and history—i.e., in interaction with the world. For this reason, religious conversion cannot remain isolated; it calls for integration with the whole person. It therefore demands a progression into moral and intellectual conversion as well.[58] These three "levels" of conversion, as Lonergan calls them, are distinct; but they call for each other, and each cannot ultimately be true to its own dynamism except by progressing toward the others. When the conversion experience thematizes itself in community and history, it enters the world mediated by meaning; it seeks interpretation of itself. This interpretation coincides with what we have called the identification of the solution. Man looks to history in search of a "word" of God which embodies and explains what is anticipated in the experience of the solution as an absolute mode of being in love: we seek, in other words, an "absolute saving event."

Our anthropology has led us thus far to three major statements about man. First, man is a being capable of God—that is, man is by nature open to the infinite, and stands as a "question" to the Absolute. Second, man needs God: confronted with the existential dilemma of evil and sin, man looks to God for salvation. Third, man experiences the working of salvation in life, and in this experience implicitly anticipates from God an absolute saving event by which God communicates himself in history.

Man's identification of that saving event normally takes the thematic form of religion. For the Christian believer, it takes the form of Christian religion: the affirmation of Jesus as God's eschatological presence, the absolute saving event in its primal moment and the "sacrament" of universal salvation. The entry into the dialectic of religious beliefs and the justification of faith in Jesus demands a study of its own, to which this volume stands as introduction and foundation. But what we have attempted here is already in large measure a step toward answering not only for religious faith in general, but particularly for Christian faith. In an age in which the Christian claim to a unique and definitive revelation is largely dismissed by secularists as mythology, it is crucial to show that it is not incredible that God should reveal himself, and that that revelation should be as particular and decisive an event as any of the various thresholds in evolution which have brought about human existence. In an age in which the same Christian claim is flaunted by fundamentalists as the banner of irrational, anti-humanist and exclusivist religion, it is crucial to show that the claim of Christ not only does not deny, but most deeply corresponds to our humanity, and that it not only does not exclude the universality of grace, but is the condition for it.

NOTES

1. I am indebted in this section to the lectures given by J.-B. Metz in his course, *Die Verantwortung des Glaubens an Jesus den Christus*, given at Münster in the summer semester of 1968.

2. The word "ideology" is used here in the pejorative sense which has become widespread particularly in the context of Marxist philosophy: a system of thought which is purely abstract, and unconscious of its own motives and reasons for being. Cf. Engels: "Ludwig Feuerbach and the End of Classical German Philosophy"; "Letter to Franz Mehring"; Marx and Engels: *The German Ideology*.

3. See Paul Tillich, *Systematic Theology*, I (Chicago: University of Chicago Press, 1951). For a "revisionist" model of the task or correlation, cf. David Tracy, *Blessed Rage for Order* (New York: The Seabury Press, 1975), pp. 45, 79–80, and *passim*.

4. On man's being constituted by his faculty of questioning, see below, Chapter II. Cf. also Karl Rahner, *Spirit in the World* (Montreal: Palm Publishers, 1968), p. 58.

5. Tillich, *op. cit.*, p. 4; for Tillich, the "situation" is "the totality of man's creative self-interpretation in a special period."

6. Cf. *ibid.*, pp. 18–28, for Tillich's ideas on the relationship prevailing between philosophy and theology.

7. On the contrast between "classical" culture and the modern world, see Bernard Lonergan, "Belief: Today's Issue," pp. 91–99, and "The Future of Christianity," pp. 160–161, both in *A Second Collection* (London: Darton, Longman & Todd, 1974); "The Revolution in Catholic Theology," in the *Proceedings of the Catholic Theological Society of America*, Vol. XXVII (1972), pp. 19-20; "Philosophy and Theology," in the *Proceedings of the American Catholic Philosophical Association*, Vol. XLIV (1970), p. 19. For the integration of theology and philosophy in the modern context, see "Philosophy and Theology," p. 27; *Method in Theology* (New York: Herder and Herder, 1972), pp. 338–340; *Philosophy of God, and Theology* (London: Darton, Longman & Todd, 1973), esp. pp. ix–x, 11–15, 19, 50–59.

8. C.S. Lewis gives a good personal account of this bias, which he calls "chronological snobbery," in his autobiography, *Surprised by Joy* (New York: Harcourt, Brace & World, 1955), pp. 206–208, 212–213.

9. Reflections of this type of thought may be traced through popular culture, especially in the optimistic youth movements of the 1960's, which proclaimed, in the words of the rock-musical *Hair*, "the dawning of the Age of Aquarius."

10. See Karl Rahner, "The Man of Today and Religion," in *Theological Investigations*, Vol. VI (Baltimore: Helicon Press, 1969), p. 3.

11. An example may be drawn from the consideration of belief in the contemporary world. It has become common in some circles to proclaim that the modern world is undergoing a crisis of religious belief, and that there has been a radical decline in belief in recent years, as compared with earlier periods in history. Clearly, it is true that the quality of religious belief has undergone modifications in response to the particular characteristics of the modern situation—as, indeed, is true of religion in every new age and situation. There is, however, no clear way of making a judgment on the *quantity* of belief in the modern world; indeed, even if it were not very difficult to formulate a working definition of "religious belief" which would permit a sociological estimate of its quantity today, there would be no adequate basis of comparison with the past, since no such sociological data are available from previous eras of history. (For a variety of sociological views of the question, see Rocco Caporale and Antonio Grumelli, eds. *The Culture of Unbelief* [Berkeley: University of California Press, 1971]).

On the other hand, what seems to be consistent is that in *every* age—including those that described themselves or are described by others as "Christian"—the person of faith is seen as "alone" in the midst of an opposing world. When Elijah on Mount Horeb declares to the Lord, "I, even I only, am left, and they are seeking to take away my life" (1 Kgs. 19:8ff), he expresses the perennial situation of the faith facing the power of the "world"—no less in the "Christian" Denmark of Kierkegaard, who saw in his day's "Christian" education the major obstacle to real Christian belief, or in the "Christian" Europe of Abélard, who declared that faith was everywhere dead in his time, than in ancient Israel, confronted with the secular might of unbelievers. Although there are certainly cultural and historical factors which affect belief, and which make the believer feel more or less "at home" in the surrounding world, and although the modern situation contains many elements which have a direct bearing on the context of belief, among them the factors we are here examining; nevertheless, it is gratuitous to assume that faith today finds itself in a totally unprecedented and unique situation. The problem of belief facing unbelief, the problem of authenticity within belief, is a permanent factor, present in every age. Clearly, as we shall see, it cannot be denied that a highly integrated culture, in which social forms of Christian faith were promoted, no longer exists in most of Western society. This means that unbelief as an individual act of choice—as, likewise, belief as an individual choice—becomes a more *recognizable* phenomenon; but it does not necessarily mean that either form of choice itself is radically more predominant than in the past.

12. See Bernard Lonergan, "The Transition from a Classicist WorldView to Historical-Mindedness," in *A Second Collection*, pp. 1–9.

13. Metz, *op. cit.*, p. 9.

14. "The man of science has learned to believe in justification, not by faith, but by verification"—T.H. Huxley, *Lay Sermons, Addresses and Re-*

views, p. 18; quoted by Frederick Copleston, *A History of Philosophy*, Vol. 8 (Garden City, New York: Doubleday and Co., 1967), p. 127.

15. For this concept, see Bernard Lonergan, *Insight* (New York: Philosophical Library, 1957), pp. 25–32.

16. Karl Rahner, "Reflections on Methodology in Theology," in *Theological Investigations*, Vol. XI, p. 70.

17. Antonio Grumelli, "Secularization: Between Belief and Unbelief," in Caporale and Grumelli, *op. cit.*, p. 83.

18. On the word "God" as the unifier of all human exerience and the means for facing the question of its meaning, see Karl Rahner's "Meditation on the Word 'God'" in *Foundations of Christian Faith* (New York: The Seabury Press, 1978), esp. p. 47.

19. Metz, *op. cit.*, p. 11.

20. Rahner, "Reflections on Methodology," p. 73.

21. Karl Rahner, "A Small Question Regarding the Contemporary Pluralism in the Intellectual Situation of Catholics and the Church," in *TI*, Vol. VI, p. 22. See also *Foundations of Faith*, pp. 8–10.

22. See among others Caporale and Grumelli, *op. cit.;* Harvey Cox, *The Secular City* (New York: The Macmillan Co., 1965); Louis Dupré, *The Other Dimension* (Garden City, N.Y.: Doubleday & Co., 1972); Peter Berger, *A Rumor of Angels* (Garden City, N.Y.: Doubleday & Co., 1969) and *The Sacred Canopy* (Garden City, N.Y.: Doubleday & Co. 1967); Langdon Gilkey, *Naming the Whirlwind* (Indianapolis and New York: The Bobbs-Merrill Co., 1969).

23. Sociological opinion seems now to be tending away from the strong affirmation of secularity, the decline of religion, etc., and toward a reaffirmation of the perdurance of religious values and sacral experiences, even within "secularist" societies. Nevertheless, the basic notion that the public sphere of life has undergone a significant change in its relation to the religious is unquestioned. For some of the many sociological and theological views on the subject, see Caporale and Grumelli, *op. cit.*

24. *Ibid.*, pp. 180–181.

25. Rahner, "The Man of Today and Religion," pp. 5–7.

26. Quoted in Martin E. Marty, *Varieties of Unbelief* (Garden City, N.Y.: Doubleday and Co., 1966), p. 55.

27. Walter Kern, "Atheismus. Eine philosophiegeschichtliche Information," in *Zeitschrift für Katholische Theologie*, 97 Band, Heft 1/2, 1975, pp. 13f. Kern notes that the recognition that the Judaeo-Christian *Entgötterung der Natur* (desacralizing of nature) permits the grounding of an independent secular sphere and the consequent "emancipation" of modern man is already present in Hegel, Schiller, Schelling, Goethe, etc.

28. Joseph Ratzinger, *Introduction to Christianity* (New York: Herder and Herder, 1973), p. 24.

29. Rahner, "The Man of Today and Religion," p. 11.

30. *Ibid.*, pp. 18–19.

31. Cf. Tracy, *op. cit.*, chapter 5: religious language is "limit" language.

32. Thus Lonergan shows in *Insight* (pp. 527ff) how the Scholastic theological distinction between faith and reason, nature and grace, permitted and logically led to the development of the empirical sciences as independent fields of inquiry.

33. Metz, *op. cit.*, p. 6.

34. The term is taken from R.A. Knox's *Enthusiasm* (Oxford: Clarendon Press, 1950), p. 2. Knox tells of a young man "who protested that he would never so much as cross the street unless he had a [supernatural] guidance about it" (p. 156).

35. Rahner, "Theological Reflections on the Problem of Secularization," in *TI*, Vol. X, pp. 321, 325.

36. The word is used here in a sense somewhat wider than that of the Hegelian-Marxist concept. Cf. Tracy, *op. cit.*, p. 243.

37. *Theses on Feuerbach, XI.*

38. "Praxis" itself, in the sense of the critical relationship of theory to action, is not identical with "practice," but the evaluation of "praxis" must take into account the actual conditions produced by the attempt to implement a system's beliefs and values. In this sense, the question of praxis is not identical with, but includes an examination of practice.

39. Werner Heisenberg, *Physics and Beyond* (New York: Harper & Row, 1971). The same principle lies behind the critique of Marxism by the "new right" in France, and indeed, behind the independent attitude of the French and Italian Communist Parties themselves with regard to the Soviet Union and its "orthodoxy."

40. Karl Jaspers, *The Future of Mankind* (Chicago: University of Chicago Press, 1961), p. 260.

41. Compare Lonergan's notion of "cosmopolis," developed in *Insight*, pp. 238–242.

42. There still exist, of course, philosophical systems which lie outside this general context: neo-Scholasticism, for example, or various systems of Oriental philosophy. Perhaps, above all, the dogmatic philosophy of Marxism (at least as practiced in the Soviet Union) would have to be excluded.

43. This notion will be developed later; see Chapter V.

44. Lonergan, *Method in Theology*, pp. 81–85.

45. Lonergan, *Insight*, p. 294.

46. *Ibid.*, p. 175.

47. *Ibid.*, p. 294.

48. The example of "Eddington's tables" is familiar to all readers of *Insight*. It was also used by José Ortega y Gasset in the ninth lecture of his 1932–33 course in Metaphysics at the University of Madrid, recently published as *Unas Lecciones de Metafísica* (Madrid: Alianza Editorial, 1966).

49. Lonergan, *Method in Theology*, p. 83.

50. Lonergan notes that the most common differentiation of consciousness is not common sense–theory, but common sense–transcendence,

as may be observed, for example, in the masses of Asian peoples. "An Interview with Fr. Bernard Lonergan, S.J.," in *A Second Collection*, pp. 428f.

51. Lonergan, *Method in Theology*, pp. 95f.

52. *Ibid.*, pp. 94–95.

53. Cf. Laplace's famous reply to Napoleon.

54. This is not to deny the perennial need of faith to speak also—and, indeed, principally—to the common sense mentality. More than ever, faith has need of aesthetic expression which can speak to the whole of human existence. But faith must also respond to the development of mind, in the form of theology.

55. See Avery Dulles, *A History of Apologetics* (New York: Corpus, 1971).

56. This is not to imply that the realms of commonsense and theory are left behind; these stages are progressive, in the sense that each later builds upon the earlier; but they are also contemporary and simultaneous, both within pluralist cultures and within individuals.

57. Cf. Lonergan, *Method in Theology*, pp. 19–20.

58. See the post-conciliar document "On Dialogue with Unbelievers" (*Humanae Personae Dignitatem*, AAS 60 [1968]), in Austin Flannery, O.P. (ed), *Vatican Council II* (Northport, N.Y.: Costello Publishing Co., 1975), pp. 1010f.

Chapter II

1. On the philosophical turn from the study of substances to the study of the subject, see Bernard Lonergan, *The Subject* (Milwaukee: Marquette University Press, 1968).

2. See José Ortega y Gasset, *¿Qué es Filosofía?* (Madrid: Ediciones de la Revista de Occidente, 1958). On consciousness as the determinant of subjectivity, see also Ortega's *Unas Lecciones de Metafísica* (Madrid: Alianza Editorial, 1966); Jörg Splett, art. "Consciousness," *SM*, I, pp. 414–416; Bernard Lonergan, *Insight* (New York: Philosophical Library, 1957), *passim; "Existenz* and *Aggiornamento,"* in *Collection* (New York: Herder and Herder, 1967), p. 241; "Christ as Subject: a Reply," *ibid., passim;* Karl Rahner, *Foundations of Christian Faith* (New York: Seabury Press, 1978), pp. 18ff.

3. There are different views concerning when the historical turn from "substance" to "subject" took place in Western thought. The study of man as "substance" concentrates on the examination of the "soul," which is the "first act" of the organic body (see Aristotle's *De Anima*). The classical exposition proceeds from the objects of the soul's activity to its acts, and hence to its habits, potencies, and, finally, its nature or essence. The results of such a study are "objective" and universal; it prescinds from the actual states of consciousness of concrete persons, which are "accidents" and hence irrelevant to the "essence" of the soul. The study of the subject, on

the other hand, is concerned precisely with the self as conscious; hence it ignores the notion of the "soul," its essence, potencies, habits, etc., because these are not directly given in consciousness. Lonergan: *The Subject,* pp. 5–8.

According to Lonergan, awareness of the subject was already implicitly present in Aristotle and St. Thomas, but came to be neglected in the era of rationalism and conceptualism ("Christ as Subject," p. 192), only to be rediscovered in the age of idealism.

Ortega y Gasset, on the other hand, credits Descartes with the "discovery" of subjectivity in philosophy, and sees Aquinas and Aristotle as representing the objectivizing tendency *par excellence,* in contrast to the more subjective line of thought, anticipating Descartes, which derives from Christianity and runs through thinkers like Augustine. *¿Qué es Filosofía?,* Lección viii.

4. Ortega y Gasset, *Unas Lecciones de Metafísica,* p. 45.

5. *Loc. cit.*

6. Heidegger makes the distinction in the first chapter of *Sein und Zeit.* Cf. also Sartre's distinction between *l'être-pour-soi* and *être-en-soi* in *L'Être et le Néant* (Paris: Gallimard, 1943). Eng. trans.: *Being and Nothingness* (trans. Hazel E. Barnes) (New York: Philosophical Library, 1956).

7. Ortega, *Unas Lecciones . . . ,* pp. 45–46; cf. Lonergan, "Christ as Subject," pp. 176–177.

8. Splett, *art. cit.,* pp. 414–416.

9. José Gómez Caffarena, *Metafísica Fundamental* (Madrid: Ediciones de la Revista de Occidente, 1969), p. 114.

10. See Maurice Blondel's classic work, *L'Action* (Paris: Ancienne Librairie Germer Baillière et Cie., 1893). Cf. Ortega's distinction *pensamiento reflejante—pensamiento reflejado* (*¿Qué es Filosofía?,* p. 168), and Lotz's *begleitende Reflexion—ausdrückliche Reflexion* (Johannes B. Lotz, S.J., *Die Identität von Geist und Sein,* Rome: Università Gregoriana Editrice, 1972, p. 136).

11. Bernard Lonergan, *De Verbo Incarnato* (Roma: Pontificia Universitas Gregoriana, 1964), p. 280.

12. Cf. Rahner, *Foundations of Christian Faith,* pp. 18–19.

13. *Ibid.,* pp. 15–16. Rahner notes that it is the error of rationalism to insist that reality is present for man only in objectifying consciousness, while it is the fault of "modernism" to hold that the concept is absolutely secondary, so that reflection could be dispensed with entirely.

14. Ortega, *Unas Lecciones . . . ,* p. 79.

15. Splett, *art. cit.,* p. 415.

16. Gómez Caffarena, *op. cit.,* p. 114.

17. Ortega, *Unas Lecciones . . . ,* pp. 48–50. On the notion of horizon, see Bernard Lonergan, *Method in Theology* (New York: Herder and Herder, 1972), pp. 235f.

18. Cf. Ernst Bloch, *Tübinger Einleitung in die Philosophie,* I (Frankfurt a.M.: Suhrkamp Verlag, 1963): *"Ich bin. Aber ich habe mich nicht.*

Darum werden wir erst." (p. 11). ("I am. But I do not have myself. Therefore we first come to be.")

19. *Loc. cit.*

20. Gómez Caffarena, *op. cit.,* p. 127.

21. Ortega, *Unas Lecciones . . . ,* p. 74.

22. Gómez Caffarena, *op. cit.,* ch. viii.

23. *Ibid.,* pp. 148, 197. Ernst Bloch expresses the radical unrest of
human spirit, the need to be always "underway," as "hunger"—a spiritual
phenomenon which is both analogous to and an extension of man's physical
need. Bloch, *op. cit.,* pp. 12–15.

24. Ortega, *Unas Lecciones . . . ,* p. 53.

25. Lonergan, *Insight,* p. 10.

26. See below, Chapter V.

27. I summarize here the first chapters of Lonergan's *Insight.*

28. Lonergan, *Insight,* pp. 70ff.

29. *Ibid.,* pp. 87ff.

30. *Loc. cit.*

31. *Ibid.,* pp. 88–89.

32. *Ibid.,* p. 101.

33. *Ibid.,* pp. 103–115.

34. *Ibid.,* pp. 13–19, 257.

35. Barry Commoner, "Energy," in *The New Yorker,* Feb. 2, 1976, p.
42.

36. Lonergan, *Insight,* pp. 205–206.

37. Note, however, that the recognition of the legitimacy and need
for higher viewpoints, including a science of man and his consciousness, is
not yet an answer to the doctrines of "dialectical" materialism, as taught for
example in the Soviet Union today. Modern theories of the laws of materialist dialectic acknowledge qualitative changes in nature that produce real
novelty, resulting in a real difference between higher and lower orders in
the world, and also the presence of "ontological surplus values" which can
only be explained by progressively higher systematizations. This is what, in
its own view, distinguishes dialectical from "vulgar" materialism. See Gustav A. Wetter, *Soviet Ideology Today* (London: Heinemann Educational
Books Ltd., 1966), especially Chapters 3 and 4.

38. Lonergan, *Insight,* pp. 451–452. Cf. the Hegelian notion of *Auf-
hebung.*

39. *Ibid.,* pp. 125–126.

40. *Ibid.,* pp. 118–124.

41. *Ibid.,* pp. 126–128.

42. *Ibid.,* p. 126.

43. Commoner, *art. cit.,* p. 43.

44. Pierre Teilhard de Chardin, *Comment Je Crois* (Paris: Editions du
Seuil, 1969), p. 125. Eng. trans.: *How I Believe* (trans. René Hague) (New
York: Harper and Row, 1969).

45. We may say that "man" is the culmination of the world, provided,

of course, that we understand by "man" any intellectual and free material being, and not simply *homo sapiens.*

What we have presented here represents Teilhard's view of the evolutionary process; but it is not completely new. Compare, for example, St. Thomas Aquinas' statement in the *Summa Contra Gentiles* (III. 22): *"Ultimus.... generationis totius gradus est anima humana, et in hanc tendit materia sicut ultimam formam ... homo enim est finis totius generationis."* ("The final stage of all generation is the human soul, and it is toward this that all matter tends as its final form..... For man is the end of all generation.") Aquinas, of course, is not thinking in terms of an evolutionary world view, but of metaphysical causality; still, the application of the notion of final causality to the human soul's relation to matter represents in essence an anticipation and a philosophical counterpart to the biological theory of evolution. We may also see precursors of Teilhard's thought in Augustine's notion of the *rationes seminales,* as well as in Bonaventure's theory of the successions of forms in man (anticipating the modern biological observation that "ontogeny recapitulates philogeny").

46. Karl Rahner, "Christology within an Evolutionary View of the World," in *Theological Investigations (TI),* V, translated by Karl-H. Kruger (Baltimore: Helicon Press, 1966), p. 167.

47. The production of the human "soul," therefore, need not be looked upon, from a theological point of view, as some kind of miraculous intervention by God on the level of secondary causes, once the proper "matter" has been prepared; rather, it is a real part of the evolutionary process. Spirit is "created" as a part of the general creative "concursus" of God with the world.

48. Blaise Pascal, *Pensées* (Paris: Editions Garnier Frères, 1964), no. 347 (p. 162). Eng. trans.: *Pensées* (trans. A.J. Kraikheimer) (New York: Penguin, 1966).

49. Cf. Gen. 1:27–30.

50. Christianity is, in the suggestive title of a sermon by Karl Rahner, "faith that loves the world."

51. Boris Pasternak, *Doctor Zhivago* (New York: New American Library, 1958), p. 417. The lifting of man above the universe, as an exception to its laws, without providing a vision of any really transcendent reality beyond the death which makes us a part of nature, is one of the great failures of the Marxist ideology which condemned Pasternak, Solzhenitsyn, and others in the Russian spiritual tradition.

52. Lonergan, *Insight,* p. 210.

53. *Ibid.,* p. 196.

54. Pierre Teilhard de Chardin, *The Phenomenon of Man* (New York: Harper & Brothers, 1959), p. 71.

55. The notion of "ontological surplus value" is taken from Marxist philosophy, where it is the accepted phrase for qualitatively higher forms of being. Note that the basic metaphor, in line with the fundamental Marxist insight, is economic.

56. The notion of man's being "thrown" into the world, although it received currency with the existentialists, and particularly Heidegger's concept of *Geworfenheit*, is a common theme going back to early Gnosticism. See Hans Jonas, *The Gnostic Religion* (Boston: Beacon Press, 1958), especially the fascinating epilogue on "Gnosticism, Existentialism, and Nihilism," and in particular p. 334.

57. Bertrand Russell, *"Why I Am Not a Christian" and Other Essays on Religion and Related Subjects* (New York: Simon and Schuster, 1957), p. 107.

58. Rahner, *Foundations of Christian Faith*, pp. 44–51.

59. We cannot here go into the question of how far the various expression for God in different languages, religions, and philosophical systems are in fact "synonymous." It is obvious that there are different *conceptions* as well as *images* of the nature of the ultimate reality. To the variety and the convergence of these conceptions we shall return at a later point. What is significant here, however, is that these expressions arise from the same basic human experience and questions, and point to some ultimate answer, however it may be conceived and named.

60. Rahner, *Foundations of Christian Faith*, p. 45.

61. I am indebted in much of the following to a series of lectures given by Karl Huber, S.J., on *"l'analysi linguistica del discorso cristiano su Dio"* at the Pontifical Gregorian University in the Spring semester of 1973.

62. On this point, a distinction might be drawn between the words for the supreme Reality which were originally the "personal" names of single gods among many in a pantheon, but which eventually came to be synonymous with the notion of the Absolute or Deity itself, and, on the other hand, the more "theological" or conceptual titles which refer directly to the absolute ground, however conceived. To the former group would belong the names of Siva, Vishnu, Yahweh, Zeus, Olodumare, etc. To the latter would belong the more general words such as the Indo-European *deva* (θεός, Deus, Dieu, etc.) and God (Gott, etc.—apparently deriving from the Sanskrit root meaning "to invoke"), the Brahman of Hindu philosophy, the Chinese T'ien, and the LXX translation of God's "personal" Hebrew name as O ΩN. It should be noted that the former group, when they pass from a polytheistic and anthropomorphic stage to the designation of the one transcendent Being, takes on the linguistic characteristics of the more "abstract" titles, even if remnants of mythological "personality" remain.

63. See below, pp. 43, 156ff.

64. On "heuristic" concepts, see below, pp. 130, 135.

65. See below, pp. 156ff.

66. See below, Chapter V.

67. Karl Heim, *Glaube und Denken* (Hamburg: Furche, 1957), pp. 219f. Heim continues: "Speaking in the second person is the form in which the movement toward the eternal Thou is really accomplished, and in which I enter with my being into this relationship. As long as I only speak of God in the third person, the turning toward him remains only a possibili-

ty. . . . Only *in actu,* in the movement toward him, is the way to him opened for me. Only when I undertake to speak with God and to listen to him, do I see with illuminating clarity what the word God means."

68. When Moses asks God's name (Ex 3:14), the reply which is given is "ehyeh asher ehyeh." Although the meaning of the passage is obscure, on one level the reply may be taken as an affirmation by the sacred theologian of God's absolute thou-ness: he is not to be contained in a name, but can only be known as himself, i.e., in the encounter with him.

69. See Thomas Aquinas, *Quaest, Disp. de Pot., VII, V, ad XIV: "ex quo intellectus noster divinam substantiam non adaequat, hoc ipsum quod est Dei substantia remanet, nostrum intellectum excedens, et ita a nobis ignoratur: et propter hoc illud est ultimum cognitionis humanae de Deo quod sciat se Deum nescire, inquantum cognoscit illud quod Deus est, omne ipsum quod de eo intelligimus, excedere."* See also below, pp. 225f.; translation, p. 226.

70. Rahner, *Foundations of Christian Faith,* p. 65.

Chapter III

1. See below, Chapter VII, on the "biasis"; also p. 116.

2. See Sarvepalli Radhakrishnan and Charles A. Moore (eds.), *A Sourcebook in Indian Philosophy* (Princeton, N.J.: Princeton University Press, 1957). On the schools of Hinduism, see also Heinrich Zimmer, *Philosophies of India* (Princeton, N.J.: Princeton University Press, 1951); R.C. Zaehner, *Hinduism* (Oxford: Oxford University Press, 1962); Max Weber, *The Religion of India* (New York: The Free Press, 1958). On Buddhism, see, besides the above, Edward Conze, I.B. Horner, David Snellgrove and Arthur Waley (eds.), *Buddhist Texts Through the Ages* (New York: Harper and Row, 1964), and Edward Conze, *Buddhism: Its Essence and Development* (New York: Harper and Row, 1959.

3. The name "Hinayana," meaning "lesser vehicle," is a title which derives from the Mahayana (= "greater vehicle") tradition. Southern Buddhists prefer the name Theravada.

4. See Radhakrishnan and Moore, *op. cit.,* pp. 289f.

5. Note, however, that the doctrine of complete "annihilation" and non-existence after death was early regarded as a heresy (see the *Samyuttanikaya*). One interpretation of this, however, would be that one cannot speak of the "annihilation" of what which cannot properly be spoken of as "existing" in the first place. See Radhakrishnan and Moore, *op. cit.,* pp. 286ff.

6. Zimmer, *op. cit.,* pp. 314–315.

7. Sarvepalli Radhakrishnan, *Eastern Religions and Western Thought* (London: Oxford University Press, 1940), p. 134.

8. Sarvepalli Radhakrishnan, *Indian Philosophy* (London: George Allen and Unwin Ltd., 1929), p. 37 n.

9. Zimmer, *op. cit.*, p. 393.

10. Geoffrey Parrinder, *Avatar and Incarnation* (New York: Oxford University Press, 1982), p. 131.

11. *Ibid., loc. cit.* See also Conze, *op. cit.*, pp. 38ff.

12. Geoffrey Parrinder, *Mysticism in the World's Religions* (New York: Oxford University Press, 1976), p. 56.

13. *Ibid.*, pp. 54ff. On worship in Buddhism, see, by the same author, *Worship in the World's Religions* (Totowa, N.J.: Littlefield, Adams and Co., 1976), Chapters 6 and 7.

14. Parrinder, *Mysticism*, p. 60.

15. Conze, *op. cit.*, p. 39.

16. Thus in Indonesia, for example, where atheism, in the wake of the 1965 failed Communist coup, is considered a crime, the Buddhists insist that they believe in God, although they use other terms. See Heinrich Dumoulin (ed.), *Buddhism in the Modern World* (New York: Collier Books, 1976), p. 152.

17. Soyen Shaku, *Sermons of a Buddhist Abbot* (trans. Daisetz Teitaro Suzuki) (New York: Samuel Weiser, Inc., 1971), p. 25.

18. Daisetz Teitaro Suzuki, *Outlines of Mahayana Buddhism* (New York: Schoken Books, 1963), p. 219; cf. p. 30.

19. *Idem, On Indian Mahayana Buddhism* (ed. Edward Conze) (New York: Harper and Row, 1968), p. 109.

20. See for example the dialogue reported by Klaus Klostermaier in his *Hindu and Christian in Vrindaban* (trans. Antonia Fonseca) (London: SCM, 1969), Chapter 3.

21. Radhakrishnan, *Eastern Religions*, p. 21.

22. For further reflections on these lines, see Bede Griffiths, *Vedanta and Christian Faith* (Los Angeles: Dawn Horse Press, 1973), pp. 4–5, 45, and *passim*.

23. For a survey of existentialism, particularly in relation to Christian belief, see Francis M. Tyrrell, *Man: Believer and Unbeliever* (New York: Alba House, 1974), pp. 51–66.

24. Chapter II, p. 23 and note 6.

25. Martin Heidegger, *Die onto-theo-logische Verfassung der Metaphysik*, p. 71; Eng. translation, *Essays in Metaphysics*, p. 65; quoted in Cornelio Fabro, *God in Exile*, translated and edited by Arthur Gibson (New York: Newman Press, 1968), p. 926.

26. For a critique of Sartre's phenomenology from two different Christian points of view, see Fabro, *op. cit.*, who accuses Sartre of reducing being to phenomenon or appearance (p. 939), and William A. Luijpen, *Phenomenology and Atheism* (Pittsburgh: Duquesne University Press, 1964), Chapter 6, where the phenomenological method is accepted, but Sartre's conclusions are disputed.

27. Jean-Paul Sartre, *Being and Nothingness*, trans. by Hazel E.

Barnes (New York: Philosophical Library, 1956), Introduction. See Luijpen, *op. cit.*, for a critique of Sartre's phenomenological reduction to the thing "in-itself" and his abstraction from the"thing-in-itself-for-us."

28. See Henri Duméry, *Foi et Interrogation* (Paris: Ed. Téqui, 1953), pp. 76ff; Luijpen, *op. cit.*, pp. 264ff.; William A. Luijpen and Henry J. Koren, *Religion and Atheism* (Pittsburgh: Duquesne University Press, 1971), pp. 141, 152ff.

29. Duméry, *op. cit.*, p. 99.

30. Jean-Paul Sartre, *Existentialism and Humanism* (London: Methuen, 1948), pp. 26ff.

31. Sartre, *Being and Nothingness*, p. 580.

32. Luijpen, *op. cit.*, p. 277; cf. Luijpen and Koren, *op. cit.*, p. 144.

33. Sartre, *Being and Nothingness*, pp. 257ff.

34. Luijpen and Koren, *op. cit.*, p. 154.

35. Sartre, *Being and Nothingness*, p. 428.

36. Luijpen and Koren, *op. cit.*, p. 153.

37. Sartre, *Being and Nothingness*, p. 493.

38. *Ibid.*, pp. 90ff.

39. *Loc. cit.*

40. *Ibid.*, p. 91.

41. *Loc. cit.*

42. *Ibid.*, p. 566.

43. *Ibid.*, p. 615.

44. As we shall see, "Marxism" and "dialectical materialism" are not necessarily synonymous. The latter term includes the philosophical doctrines of Engels, while Marxism may refer to a much wider collection of movements. For our purposes, however, the terms may be used interchangeably, since we shall restrict our purview to those forms of Marxism which accept the materialist system as their theoretical basis.

45. A.D. Makarov, S.I. Popov, L.V. Slavnova (eds.), Marksistsko-Leninskaya Filosofii (Moskva: "Thought" Editions, 1972), pp. 277–298. See also the discussion of Sartre in the official text published by the Philosophical Institute of the Soviet Academy of Sciences, and edited by F.V. Konstantinov, Osnovy Marksistsko-Leninskoi Filosofii (Moskva: Editions of Political Literature, 1976), p. 427.

46. Karl Marx, *Theses on Feuerbach*, XI. This and other important documents of Marxist philosophy may be found in Karl Marx and Friedrich Engels, *Basic Writings on Politics and Philosophy* (ed. Lewis S. Feuer) (New York: Doubleday, 1959).

47. See Gustav A. Wetter, *Die Umkehrung Hegels* (Köln: Verlag Wissenschaft und Politik, 1964), esp. Chapter 2.

48. Marx and Engels, *The German Ideology*, in *Basic Writings*, pp. 288ff.

49. *Loc. cit.*

50. *Loc. cit.*

51. *Loc. cit.*

52. The first translation of the manuscripts available in the United States (by T.B. Bottomore) forms the bulk of the volume by Erich Fromm, *Marx's Concept of Man* (New York: Frederick Ungar, 1961).

53. Marx, *Economic and Philososphical Manuscripts*, in *ibid.*, p. 96.

54. *Loc. cit.*

55. *Ibid.*, p. 98.

56. *Ibid.*, p. 99.

57. *Ibid.*, p. 100.

58. *Ibid.*, pp. 101ff.

59. *Ibid.*, p. 163.

60. Marx, *Toward the Critique of Hegel's Philosophy of Right* (1893) in *Basic Writings*, p. 303f.

61. Marx, *Economic and Philosophical Manuscripts*, p. 128.

62. Marx, *Toward the Critique of Hegel's Philosophy of Right*, p. 305.

63. Marx, *Theses on Feuerbach*, III, p. 284.

64. See, for example, Frederick C. Bender, *The Betrayal of Marx* (New York: Harper and Row, 1975), Introduction, pp. 1–52.

65. See, for example, the quotations in the famous "little red book": *Quotations from Chairman Mao-Tse Tung*, ed. Stuart R. Schram (New York, Bantam Books, 1967).

66. Francisco Lage Pessoa, "Brasil: La Iglesia y el Movimiento Revolucionario," quoted in Donald Eugene Smith (ed.), *Religion, Politics, and Social Change in the Third World* (New York: Macmillan, 1971), p. 248. Fr. Lage Pessoa is a Brasilian Catholic priest who professes the possibility of Catholic Marxism. Historically, however, it is clear that Marx's atheism predated his social ideas, and was, to some extent, the foundation of them. See Hans Küng, *Does God Exist?* trans. Edward Quinn (New York: Doubleday, 1980), pp. 218–223.

67. Camilo Torres, "Message to the Communists," in *ibid.*, pp. 246ff.

68. Ernst Bloch, *Das Prinzip Hoffnung* (Frankfurt a.M.: Suhrkamp Verlag, 1959), vol. 3, p. 1628.

69. Engels himself speaks of "materialist dialectics"; the term "dialectical materialism" dates from the era of G.V. Plekhanov, who apparently first used it in 1891.

70. On Engels' misunderstanding of Hegel, see Gustav A. Wetter, *Storia della Teoria Marxista* (Roma: PUG, 1972), pp. 132ff.

71. *Ibid.*, pp. 133f.

72. It should be noted that Engels' own position on materialism is far from consistent; he seems to fluctuate between various meanings of the term, attempting to reconcile the priority of matter with a real "ontological difference."

73. The clearest statement of Engels' position—including its inconsistentices—is found in his *Ludwig Feuerbach and the Close of Classical German Philosophy*. (Karl Marx and Friedrich Engels, *Selected Works*, Vol. I [Moscow: Cooperative Publishing Society of Foreign Workers in the USSR, 1935]. Selections also in *Basic Writings* and in Bender, *op. cit.*). See

also Engels' *Anti-Dühring (Herr Eugen Dühring's Revolution in Science)* (Peking: Foreign Languages Press, 1976).

74. See Engels, *The Dialectics of Nature* (Moscow: Progress Publishers, 1966).

75. This eventually led Engels to the logical conclusion of epistemological relativism and to historical determinism—both of which were subsequently abandoned in the official philosophy of the USSR.

76. A position insisted upon by modern Soviet philosophy. See Konstantinov, *op. cit.*, Chapter IV.

77. Stalin imposed his own formulation on the whole system of dialectical materialism, restating Engels' laws by dropping the third and adding two of his own (the law of totality or unity of the world, and the law of progress). After Stalin's death, Engels' formulation was resumed.

78. Ignace Lepp, *Atheism in Our Times.* (New York: Macmillan Co., 1964), p. 82.

Chapter IV

1. On the "ecstatic" dimensions in man, see José Gómez Caffarena, *Metafísica Fundamental* (Madrid: Ediciones de la Revista de Occidente, 1969), Chapter VI.

2. See Bernard Lonergan, *Method in Theology* (New York: Herder & Herder, 1972), p. 157.

3. This point will be discussed at greater length in our treatment of "transcendental method."

4. Gomez Caffarena, *op. cit.*, p. 153.

5. Heidegger, for one, claimed that the Christian who is really a believer cannot genuinely philosophize, that is, cannot really ask the radical question about existence, because he/she claims to have the answer. In Heidegger's view of philosophy, the Christian can only "theologize." To this it might be replied that it is precisely because he/she believes in God's "answer" that the Christian *must* ask the radical questions; for an answer makes no sense except to the person who asks seriously, i.e., personally. Furthermore, "faith" is never simply the possession of an "answer"; it is a commitment which transcends the rational content of the believer's mind, and which therefore needs to come to self-understanding and appropriation.

6. For the notion of "dialectic" in theological method, see Lonergan, *op. cit.*, Chapter 10.

7. The revisability of which we speak here is a theoretical and epistemological possibility: that is, it has to do with the methodical openness of all questions. Whether, and in what sense, the presupposition of meaningfulness—at least the meaningfulness of questioning itself—is not revisable, but absolutely unavoidable and irreversible, so that its rejection ends in absurdity and self-contradiction, must await the outcome of our investigation. At the outset, in any case, we must on principle be open to

whatever revision may prove warranted. Likewise, whether and in what sense "faith"—once it is an *existentielle* reality, and not merely a series of received opinions —can be radically "revised" by a particular person without "sin" is a theological question from which we must prescind here.

8. Our treatment of these possibilities certainly was not of sufficient depth to make any of them real alternate options for the reader; rather, we presuppose a basic knowledge and experience of some forms of the non-theistic stance toward life, and have attempted in our examples to summarize and synthesize several major tendencies, in their broad lines, for the sake of confrontation with our own basic positions. Our purpose has been more of "reminding" than of informing about the non-theistic alternative.

9. It would of course be a mistake to presume that we can now be finished wth the non-theistic alternative. Even if our presuppositions can be justified, a theistic solution to the dilemma of existence be validated, and the option of belief given a rational foundation, it will be necessary for a fundamental theology to return, in much greater detail, to the stance of the non-believer: first, in order to clarify our own position, both by contrast and by the recognition and acceptance of truths within these systems which we may overlook; and, second, in order to dialogue with them, both on the level of theory and in the realm of practical cooperation.

10. For this distinction, see above, Chapter I.

11. *Summa Contra Gentiles,* lib. 1, cap. XIII; *Summa Theologica,* p. I, q. 2 art. 3.

12. *Summa Contra Gentiles,* cap. XI.

13. On this point, see Jacques Maritain, *Approaches to God* (New York: Collier Books, 1954), p. 24.

14. *Summa Contra Gentiles,* lib. 1, cap. XXII.

15. *Ibid.,* lib. 1, cap. XII.

16. *Loc. cit.*

17. Maritain, *loc. cit.* Maritain cites *De Potentia,* q. 7, a. 2, ad 1; *Summa Theologica,* I,, q. 3, art. 4, ad 2.

18. This will lead to the theological question of the existential need of "grace" or conversion for the personal discovery of God.

19. Maritain, *op. cit.,* p. 18.

20. *Ibid., loc. cit.* and p. 19.

21. See *ibid.,* p. 20.

22. Anselm of Canterbury, *Proslogion,* 228 (my translation). Migne, t. 158, cols. 223–247. For English version of the relevant passages, see M.J. Charlesworth (ed.), *St. Anselm's Proslogion* (Notre Dame: University of Notre Dame Press, 1979).

23. *Loc. cit.*

24. See, for example, the series of articles collected by Alvin Plantinga in *The Ontological Argument* (Garden City, N.Y.: Doubleday & Co., 1965), or Charles Hartshorne, *Anselm's Discovery: A Re-examination of the Ontological Proof for God's Existence* (LaSalle, Ill.: Open Court, 1965).

25. This is why, as we shall see, all of Kant's arguments against the

"proofs" for God's existence are directed at the ontological argument, and why this same argument becomes central, on the other hand, to the idealist system of Hegel.

26. *Summa Theologica*, I, q. 2, art. 1, ad 2.

27. *Ibid.*, c.

28. We leave open the question of whether Anselm himself actually referred, in his "proof," to an *experience* of God which is obtained *ex aliunde*, i.e., from faith. This is the position taken by Karl Barth in his *Anselm, Fides Quaerens Intellectum* (London: SCM Press, 1960).

29. L.N. Tolstoi, *Voina i Mir;* 1 (Minsk: Narodnaya Asveta, 1976), p. 353 (my translation). A good English translation is that by Constance Garnett, *War and Peace* (New York: Thomas Y. Crowell Co., 1976).

30. *Summa Theologica*, 1, q. 2, art. 3, c.

31. *Enn. in Ps.*, CXLIV n. 13; ML 37, 1878-9.

32. *Sermo* CXLI, cap. 1 et 3; ML 38, 776. (English trans. in *The Fathers of the Church*, Vol. 38) (New York, Fathers of the Church, Inc., 1959).

33. *Confess.* lib. XI, c. IV, n. 6; ML 32, 811. (Latin text and English trans.: *Confessions*, ed. W.R. Connor and John Gibb) (Salem, N.H.: Arno, 1979).

34. *Loc. cit.*

35. *Physics* 1, VII and VIII.

36. Aquinas here modifies Aristotle's thought slightly, at least as regards terminology. For Aristotle, no being whatever can "move" itself, as this would imply the contradiction of being in potency and in act in the same respect; God, or the first Mover, is therefore "unmoved" and "unmoving," or immobile—i.e., he is neither moved by another, nor does he move himself, being essentially actual (and therefore unchanging, unmoving). Aquinas notes, however, that one can also take the word "motion" in a wider sense, as Plato does. In this way, one could say that God "moves" himself insofar as he understands and wills himself. This, however, is exactly what Aristotle actually means: "Nihil autem differt devenire ad aliquod primum quod moveat se, secundum Platonem; et devenire ad primum quod omino sit immobile, secundum Aristotelem." ("There is no difference between arriving at a primal being which moves itself, in Plato's terminology, and arriving at a primal being which is totally immobile, in Aristotle's terminology.") *Summa Contra Gentiles*, lib. 1, cap. XIII. In our exposition we have avoided this terminological difficulty by referring the argument to the impossibility of any *finite* being moving itself.

37. *Loc. cit.*

38. *Summa Theologica*, 1, q. 46, art. 2; opusc. *De Aeternitate Mundi Contra Murmurantes*, 2 dist. 1, q. 1, a. 5; *De Potentia*, q. 3, a. 13-17; *Quodlib.* 3, a. 31; 12 a. 7; *Summa Contra Gentiles* II, 31-38. Aquinas holds that *in fact* the world had a beginning; but this is only known through revelation, and is not philosophically demonstrable. Thus Aquinas' philosophical position (as distinguished from his theological reading of the Book

of Genesis) is compatible with any of the modern scientific theories of the origins of the world.

39. *Summa Contra Gentiles*, 1, cap. XV.

40. Avicenna, *Metaphysices Compendium (Nadjât)*, lib. I, pars II, tract. II, cap. 1–3 (Trad. Carame. Rome: Pont. Inst. Orient. Studiorum, 1926, pp. 91–100).

41. Plato, *Symposium*, 210e–211d.

42. Cf. Avicenna, *Metaphys.*, lib. II, tract. VIII, cap. III init.

43. *De Fide Orthodoxa*, lib. I, cap. III. MG 94, 796 c, d.

44. Cf. *Summa Contra Gentiles*, I, cap. XLII.

45. Augustine, *Sermo* CXCVII; ML 38, 1022. English trans.: see note 32.

46. Augustine: *De Diversis Quaestionibus LXXXIII, q. XLV Adversus Mathematicos*, n. 1. ML 40: 28–29. Eng. trans.: *83 Different Questions* (trans. David L. Mosher) (Washington, D.C.: Catholic University of America Press, 1982).

47. *De Veritate*, q. 22. a. 2, ad 1.

48. *Ibid.* ad 5.

49. *Itinerarium Mentis in Deum, cap. III. (S. Bonaventurae Opera Omnia* [A.C. Peltier, ed.]: Paris: Ludovicus Vivès, 1864; vol. XII). English translation: see note 52, below.

Bonaventure holds, in fact, like St. Anselm and in opposition to Thomas Aquinas, that the existence of God is "per se notum," or self-evident, even though it is not *explicit* and can be doubted, because of the defectiveness of our intellects. For a discussion of Bonaventure's views, see Frederick Copleston, S.J., *A History of Philosophy*, vol. 2, part I (Garden City, N.Y.: Doubleday & Co., 1964), pp. 280–287. On the difference of St. Thomas' views from Bonaventure's, Copleston remarks: "St. Thomas admitted an implicit knowledge of God, but by this he meant that the mind has the power of attaining to the knowledge of God's existence through reflection on the things of sense and by arguing from effect to cause, whereas St. Bonaventure meant something more by implicit knowledge, that is, virtual knowledge of God, a dim awareness which can be rendered explicit without recourse to the sensible world" (p. 284).

50. *Itinerarium Mentis in Deum, cap. II (Opera*, vol. XII, p. 8).

51. *In Lib. Primum Sententiarum*, q. II (*Opera*, vol. I, pp. 148–150).

52. Bonaventure, *The Soul's Journey into God*, trans. Ewert Cousins (New York: Paulist Press, 1978), pp. 73–74.

53. *Itinerarium Mentis in Deum, cap. III (Opera*, vol. XII, p. 11).

54. *Ibid., cap. V (Opera*, vol. XII, p. 16). Cf. Augustine, *De Div. Quaest., LXXXIII, q. DII, n. 2, 4.* Eng. trans.: see note 46, above.

55. See Bernard Lonergan, *Insight* (New York: Philosophical Library, 1957), pp. 412ff.

56. Immanuel Kant, *Kritik der Reinen Vernunft* (Hamburg: Felix Meiner, 1956); A 643, B 671. All citations from this work follow the pagination of the original German first (A) and second (B) editions. Translations

are my own. An English edition which shows the original pagination is the translation by F. Max Müller, *Critique of Pure Reason* (New York: Doubleday & Co., 1966).

57. *Ibid.*, A 682–85, B 710–13.

58. *Ibid.*, A 567, B 595; A 702, B 730.

59. *Ibid.*, A 686, B 714.

60. *Ibid.*, A 614, B 642.

61. *Ibid.*, A 619, B 647.

62. *Loc. cit.*

63. *Ibid.*, A 630, B 664.

64. *Ibid.*, A 637, B 666.

65. *Ibid.*, A 639, B 667.

66. *Ibid.*, A 701, B 729.

67. *Ibid.*, A 574–76, B 602–04.

68. *Ibid.*, A 580, B 608.

69. *Ibid.*, A 580, B 608.

70. *Ibid.*, A 583, B 611, note.

71. *Ibid.*, A 579–80, B 607–08.

72. *Ibid.*, A 583–84, B 611–12.

73. *Ibid., loc. cit.* As we shall see, Kant finds such circumstances in moral duty.

74. *Ibid.*, A 590–91, B 618–19.

75. *Ibid.*, A 592, B 620.

76. *Ibid.*, A 592–93, B 620–21.

77. *Ibid.*, A 598, B 627.

78. *Ibid.*, A 600, B 628.

79. *Ibid.*, A 601, B 629.

80. *Ibid.*, A 604–5, B 632–33.

81. *Ibid, loc. cit.*, note.

82. *Ibid.*, A 609, B 637.

83. *Ibid.*, A 612, B 640.

84. *Ibid.*, A 607–08, B 635–36. Frederick Copleston points out that Kant's reasoning on this point is far from convincing, even though the majority of historians of philosophy seem to accept uncritically Kant's reduction of the cosmological proof to the ontological. Kant assumes that "the argument based on experience brings us, not to an affirmation of the existence of a necessary being, but only to the vague *idea* of a necessary being. For in this case we should have to look about, as Kant puts it, for a determining concept which would include existence in its content, so that existence could be deduced from the determined idea of a necessary being" (Copleston, *A History of Philosophy*, Vol. 6, Part II [New York: Doubleday & Co., 1964], p. 91). This, of course, would be the "ontological" argument; but it may be questioned whether the cosmological proof does in fact merely lead to a vague idea, rather than to existence of the necessary being. In any case, even leaving aside the determination of the idea, the process of reasoning to God's existence will be "ontological" for Kant on other

grounds, namely because of his epistemological presuppositions about the limits of the categories of causality. Since Kant presumes, moreover, that the only valid judgments of existence stem from empirical intuition, and that all reasoning will necessarily end in *ideas* only (whether determinate or not), it is clear that any judgment of God's existence will involve an illegitimate leap from the ideal order to the real.

85. *Ibid.*, A 614–17, B 642–45.

86. *Ibid.*, A 623, B 651.

87. *Ibid.*, A 620, B 648.

88. *Ibid.*, A 622, B 650.

89. *Ibid.*, A 625f., B 654f.

90. *Ibid.*, A 622, B 652.

91. *Ibid.*, A 624, B 652.

92. *Ibid.*, A 627–29, B 655–57.

93. *Ibid.*, A 642, B 671.

94. *Ibid.*, A 640, B 668.

95. *Ibid.*, A 792, B 820.

96. *Ibid.*, A 641f., B 669f.

97. *Ibid.*, A 798, B 826. The notions of freedom of the will and of the immortality of the soul derive from the transcendental ideas of the world and the self. They are more fully treated by Kant in his *Kritik der Praktischen Vernunft* (Hamburg: Felix Meiner, 1963). See, e.g., pp. 238f. (original pagination). Eng. trans.: *Critique of Practical Reason* (trans. Lewis W. Beck) (Indianapolis: Bobbs-Merrill, 1956).

98. Kant, *Kritik der Reinen Vernunft*, A 799–800, B 827–28.

99. *Ibid.*, A 811, B 839.

100. *Ibid.*, A 813, B 841.

101. *Ibid.*, A 815, B 843.

102. *Ibid.*, A 827, B 855.

103. *Ibid.*, A 828, B 856.

104. *Loc. cit.*

105. *Ibid.*, A 588–89, B 616–17.

Chapter V

1. José Gómez Caffarena, *Metafísica Fundamental* (Madrid: Ediciones de la Revista de Occidente, 1969), p. 168.

2. This phrase translates Gómez's somewhat more evocative *"Vivencia metafísica."Ibid.* pp. 168–169. An important figure in the development of a philosophy which attempts to expose the basis of metaphysical experience is Maurice Blondel, whose philosophy of "action" must be by-passed here because of limitations of space and time, but which is vital to a modern theological anthropology.

3. Immanuel Kant, *Kritik der Reinen Vernunft* (Hamburg: Felix Meiner, 1956); A 14, B 28. English translation: *Critique of Pure Reason*, trans. F. Max Müller (New York: Doubleday & Co., 1966).

4. The relationship between Blondel and Maréchal would be fascinating to pursue; unfortunately, their correspondence, which had been preserved in the library of the University of Louvain, was destroyed in the war. Edouard Dhanis, S.J., who had made a study of this correspondence, recalls that in one letter Maréchal wrote to Blondel that if he were to go a little farther, he would be a transcendental philosopher; to which Blondel replied that he had no wish to be one, as the purpose of his philosophy was quite different.

5. 2nd edition: Bruxelles: L'Edition Universelle, 1949. Sections from this work are translated in Joseph Donceel, ed., *A Maréchal Reader* (New York: Herder and Herder, 1970).

6. Emerich Coreth, *Metaphysics* (ed. Joseph Donceel) (New York: Herder and Herder, 1968), p. 40; cf. p. 49.

7. On thematic and unthematic consciousness, see above, Chapter II, pp. 38–39.

8. Coreth, *loc. cit.*

9. The notion of self-appropriation (or, more fully, the "appropriation of one's rational self-consciousness") is most developed and insisted on by Bernard Lonergan. See his *Insight* (New York: Philosophical Library, 1957), pp. xvii–xxiii, xxviii.

10. Cf. *ibid.*, p. xix.

11. See Coreth, *op. cit.*, p. 36.

12. *Ibid.*, p. 37.

13. *Ibid.*, p. 39

14. *Ibid.*, pp. 48–52.

15. *Ibid.*, p. 53.

16. *Ibid.*, p. 54.

17. *Ibid.*, pp. 56f.

18. *Ibid.*, p. 62. Compare Lonergan's "notion" of being: *Insight*, p. 641, and below, p. 136.

19. *Ibid.*, p. 63.

20. *Loc. cit.* Compare Lonergan's self-affirmation of the knower; see below, pp. 133ff.

21. *Loc cit.*

22. *Ibid.*, p. 65.

23. *Loc. cit.*

24. *Ibid.*, p. 66.

25. *Ibid.*, p. 67.

26. *Ibid.*, p. 65.

27. *Ibid.*, p. 171. Coreth points out that it is not the hypothetical necessity of the principle of identity—"*If* something is, then it necessarily is"—which establishes the necessity of being, but the apodictic necessity of real being in which the logical necessity is rooted.

28. *Loc. cit.*

29. Cf. Lonergan's notion of the "virtually unconditioned." See below, p. 132.

30. *Ibid.*, p. 137.
31. *Ibid.*, p. 174.
32. *Loc. cit.*
33. *Ibid.*, p. 175.
34. *Ibid.*, p. 176.
35. *Ibid.*, p. 97.
36. *Loc. cit.*
37. *Ibid.*, p. 98.
38. *Ibid.*, pp. 176, 177.
39. On primary and secondary causes, see *ibid.*, p. 99.
40. *Ibid.*, p. 177.
41. *Ibid.*, pp. 99–100.
42. *Ibid.*, pp. 100–101.
43. See above, p. 85.
44. Coreth, *op. cit.*, p. 179.
45. This argument is perhaps better and more clearly stated by Lonergan in terms of the "Idea of Being." See below, pp. 140ff.
46. See above, pp. 95ff.
47. Coreth, *op. cit.*, p. 180.
48. *Ibid.*, p. 181.
49. *Ibid.*, p. 182.
50. *Ibid.*, p. 183.
51. Cf. St. Thomas, above, p. 96.
52. Karl Rahner, *Hörer des Wortes* (München: Kösel-Verlag, 1963 [originally appeared in 1941; the new edition was edited by J.-B. Metz]). There is an English translation of this work, but I have found it awkward and sometimes misleading. Rahner's argument for God appears nowhere so fully as in this early work, but his basic line of thought is repeated many times in other works. See, for example, most recently, his *Foundations of Christian Faith* (New York: Seabury Press, 1978), pp. 51–71, esp. 69 and 70. It will be noted that Rahner here approaches the question more in the context of religious experience.
53. Rahner, *Geist in Welt* (3rd edition; unchanged from the second) (München: Kösel-Verlag, 1964 [first published 1939; second edition revised by J.-B. Metz in collaboration with the author]). English translation, based on the second edition: *Spirit in the World*, trans. William Dych, S.J. (Montreal: Palm Publishers, 1968).
54. *Ibid.*, pp. 14–15; English, p. liii.
55. Cf. *Summa Theologica*, 1, q. 84, a. 7, ad 3.
56. Rahner, *Geist in Welt*, pp. 396–397; English, pp. 396–398.
57. Rahner, *Hörer des Wortes*, pp. 51–53.
58. *Ibid.*, p. 53.
59. *Ibid.*, p. 55.
60. *Ibid.* pp. 55–57.
61. *Ibid.*, p. 59.
62. Rahner, a student of Heidegger, echoes the latter's insistence on

the "ontological difference": *being* for Heidegger is a properly human act; it is improper to speak of things as "being." Heidegger therefore says, *"das Ding dingt; die Welt weltet"*—for the word *"ist"* belongs to man, conscious being. See J.B. Lotz, S.J., *Metaphysica Operationis Humanae* (Romae: Pontificia Universitas Gregoriana, 1972), p. 152.

63. Rahner, *Hörer des Wortes,* pp. 57–62, 64–65.

64. *Ibid.,* p. 68.

65. *Ibid.,* pp. 68–69.

66. *Ibid.,* pp. 71–73.

67. *Ibid.,* pp. 74–75,

68. *Ibid.,* p. 76.

69. *Ibid.,* p. 77.

70. *Ibid.,* p. 78.

71. *Ibid.,* p. 76.

72. *Ibid.,* p. 79.

73. *Ibid.,* p. 83.

74. *Loc. cit.* We may also speak of a "pre-apprehension" of God; but such would not be identical formally with the pre-apprehension of being; God is not to be identified with *esse simpliciter.* It seems to me that Rahner therefore eludes the criticism leveled against his argument by Louis Dupré in his book *The Other Dimension* (Garden City, N.Y.: Doubleday & Co., 1972), pp. 133–134; for Rahner, the thematic affirmation of God is a step beyond and transcendentally implied by the recognition of the absoluteness of being as the mind's horizon.

75. Rahner, *Geist in Welt,* pp. 193–194; English, p. 184.

76. Rahner, *Hörer des Wortes,* p. 84.

77. *Ibid.,* p. 85. See above, p. 96.

78. See above, p. 23.

79. Johannes B. Lotz, S.J., *Die Identiät von Geist und Sein* (Roma: Università Gregoriana Editrice, 1972), p. 224; *Metaphysica Operationis Humanae,* p. 102.

80. Lotz, *Die Identität,* p. 233.

81. *Ibid.,* pp. 233–234.

82. Lotz, *Metaphysica,* pp. 50, 109.

83. Lotz, *Die Identität,* p. 235.

84. *Ibid.,* p. 236.

85. Lonergan's intellectual background differs in some respects significantly from that of the other major transcendental philosphers. He shares with them a grounding in Thomism and some exposure to Maréchal, although the latter's influence on Lonergan was less direct and less far-reaching. But while Lotz and Rahner were students of Heidegger, and the continental tradition tends to take its starting point in the existentialist notion of the "ontological difference," Lonergan was comparatively unaffected by existentialism until late in his career. On the other hand, Lonergan is firmly grounded in the British empirical tradition and in modern science, and is by training a mathematician. Hence the emphasis on empiri-

cal fact is much stronger in Lonergan; he does not begin with the assertion of the identity of spirit with being, but with cognitional facts, and only gradually and carefully arrives at the affirmation of spirit.

86. Edward MacKinnon, S.J., "The Transcendental Turn: Necessary But Not Sufficient," in *Continuum*, 6 (1968), p. 226.

87. Otto Muck, S.J., *The Transcendental Method*, trans. William D. Seidensticker (New York: Herder and Herder, 1968), pp. 189–190.

88. Lonergan and Coreth have reflected explicitly on their differences with regard to transcendental method. See Lonergan's "Metaphysics as Horizon," in *Gregorianum*, 44 (1963); also in *Collection: Papers by Bernard Lonergan* (New York: Herder and Herder, 1967), and also printed as an afterword in the English edition of Coreth's *Metaphysics*. Coreth's view is presented in "Immediacy and the Mediation of Being: An Attempt To Answer Bernard Lonergan," in *Language Truth and Meaning. Papers from the International Lonergan Congress 1970*, edited by Philip McShane, S.J. (Notre Dame: University of Notre Dame Press, 1972).

89. Lonergan, *Insight*, p. xxvii.

90. Rahner states that the aim of transcendental method is to give an operative definition of the basic concepts of metaphysics, "with the fundamental-ontological claim that being is to be conceived in terms of its 'transparency' (*Gelichtetheit*) in man. What the very being of being is can be worked out only in terms of man's fundamental understanding of being. This understanding of being is, at the same time, man's own self-understanding." Muck, *op. cit.*, p. 190.

91. On the "positions" see *Insight*, pp. 387–388; for an example of the necessity of the philosophical positions to ground the dogmas of faith, see Lonergan, *De Verbo Incarnato* (Romae: Pontificia Universitas Gregoriana, 1964), p. 6.

92. Muck calls this the "classical critique" of skepticism, or the process of "retorsion." Muck, *op. cit.*, p. 129; *cf. Insight*, p. xxvi.

93. See above, p. 17.

94. Lonergan, *Method in Theology* (New York: Herder and Herder, 1972), p. 83. Cf. *Insight*, p. xxiv. Lonergan's later division into three questions seems more clearly to describe his procedure than the two mentioned in his introduction.

95. Lonergan, *Insight*, pp. 3–6.

96. Lonergan breaks cleanly with the Scotist tradition, which holds that concepts "cause" understanding, rather than vice versa.

97. Lonergan, "A Note on Geometric Possibility," in *Collection*, p. 107.

98. Lonergan, *Insight*, p. 9.

99. *Loc. cit.*

100. *Ibid.*, p. 44.

101. *Ibid.*, p. 45.

102. *Ibid.*, pp. 15–17.

103. Lonergan, *Verbum. Word and Idea in Aquinas*, edited by David

B. Burrell, C.S.C. (Notre Dame, Ind.: University of Notre Dame Press, 1967), pp. 65–66.

104. Lonergan, *Insight*, pp. 271–272.

105. *Ibid.*, p. 280.

106. *Ibid.*, pp. 280, 284.

107. Note the similarity to Rahner. See above, pp. 123f.

108. Lonergan, *Insight*, p. 273.

109. *Ibid.*, p. 319.

110. *Ibid.*, pp. 327–328.

111. *Ibid.*, p. 328.

112. *Ibid.*, p. 332.

113. Pierre Rousselot, S.J., *The Intellectualism of Saint Thomas*, trans. James E. O'Mahony (New York: Sheed and Ward, 1935), p. 28.

114. See Joseph J. Flanagan, S.J., "Lonergan's Epistemology," in *The Thomist*, Vol. XXXVI, No. 1 (Jan. 1972), p. 88.

115. Lonergan, *Insight*, p. 348.

116. *Loc cit.*

117. *Ibid.*, p. 349.

118. *Ibid.*, p. 350.

119. *Loc. cit.* For a critical view of Lonergan's treatment of being and the "notion of being," see William A. Van Roo, S.J., "Lonergan's Method in Theology," in *Gregorianum*, 55, No. 1 (1974), pp. 135–144.

120. The entire question of the intellectual knowledge of being in the human intellect, which belongs to the realm of spirit only as potency, is treated by Lonergan from a somewhat more limited perspective and in summary form in "*Insight*. Preface to a Discussion" (in *Collection*, pp. 152–168). Here Lonergan specifically addresses himself to the fact that man does not possess an "intellect" in the full sense of the term (p. 156) and therefore is simply a dynamism toward the knowledge of things by essence (p. 157). Cf. Rousselot, *op. cit.*, p. 63.

121. Lonergan, "Christ as Subject: A Reply," in *Collection*, p. 189.

122. That the formal object of human intellect is being "cannot be demonstrated by showing that man does understand everything. But it is clear from the fact that man wants to understand everything about everything . . ." *Loc. cit.* But cf. Van Roo, *op. cit.*, pp. 143–144.

123. This is even clearer in Lonergan's *De Constitutione Christi Ontologica et Psychologica* (Romae: Pontificia Universitas Gregoriana, 1956), where he speaks of *ens* as the object of intellectual nature. The "quiddity" of *ens*, however, is the divine nature itself (p. 9). Here also, being is defined in terms of knowledge, and God is conceived as the "Idea of being."

124. Rousselot, *op cit.*, p. 71.

125. Or between what is called in more classical language the *notio entis naturalis* and the *notio entis reflexiva, analytica*. Cf. Lonergan, *De Intellectu et Methodo* (mimeographed student notes of a course given at the Pontifical Gregorian University, 1959).

126. Flanagan, *op. cit.*, p. 88.

127. Lonergan, *Insight,* p. 354.

128. *Ibid.* p. 355.

129. *Ibid.,* pp. 359–360.

130. *Ibid.,* pp. 361–362.

131. *Ibid.,* p. 377.

132. Lonergan, *Verbum,* p. 7.

133. Lonergan, "Cognitional Structure," in *Collection,* p. 230.

134. The full analysis of "objectivity" and the judgments on the actual existence of distinct subjects and objects, and their metaphysical composition, occupies chapters XIII–XVI of *Insight.*

135. Lonergan, *Insight,* p. 635.

136. *Ibid.,* p. 637.

137. *Ibid.,* pp. 638f.

138. *Ibid.,* p. 640.

139. David Tracy, *The Achievement of Bernard Lonergan* (New York: Herder and Herder, 1970), p. 172.

140. Lonergan, *Insight,* p. 642.

141. *Loc cit.* Like Malebranche, Lonergan identifies the Absolutely Transcendent (God) with the "idea of being." Malebranche, however, believed that we have the idea of being. For Lonergan, we do not know God immediately in this life; what we have is only a notion of being, a kind of anticipation of the immediate knowledge of God. See Desmond Connell, "Fr. Lonergan and the Idea of Being," in *Irish Theological Quarterly,* Vol. XXXVII, No. 2 (April 1970), pp. 119–120.

142. Lonergan, *Insight,* pp. 657f.

143. *Ibid.,* pp. 668f.

144. *Ibid.,* pp. 651.

145. *Ibid.,* pp. 652–653.

146. *Ibid.,* pp. 653–654.

147. *Ibid.,* p. 272.

148. Lonergan, "Response," in *Proceedings of the American Catholic Philosophical Association* (Washington: Catholic University of America Press, 1967), p. 259.

149. Lonergan, *Insight,* pp. 673f.

150. *Ibid.,* p. 674.

151. *Ibid.,* pp. 675–676.

152. *Ibid.,* p. 683. Lonergan notes that the misuse of the name "God" can lead to the explicit rejection of God by those who really adore him by seeking the unconditioned.

153. *Ibid.,* p. 678.

154. Joseph Ratzinger, *Einführung in das Christentum* (München: Kösel-Verlag, 1968), p. 115. English trans.: *Introduction to Christianity* (New York: Herder and Herder, 1973), pp. 105f.

155. *Ibid.,* p. 116.

156. *Ibid.,* p. 120.

157. *Loc cit.*

Chapter VI

1. On man as "question," see above, p. 25.

2. Karl Rahner, *Grundkurs des Glaubens* (Freiburg im Breisgau: Herder, 1976), pp. 103ff; English translation, *Foundations of Christian Faith* (New York: Seabury Press, 1978), pp. 93ff. See also Rahner's article, "Freedom: III. Theological," in *SM*, pp. 361f; *Hörer des Wortes* (München: Kösel-Verlag, 1963), pp. 117ff.

3. Rahner, *Hörer des Wortes,* pp. 107–110. Rahner states that we posit our own being with a "kind" of absoluteness. Using Lonergan's terminology, we may specify the absoluteness as that of a "virtually" unconditioned: a conditioned whose conditions are in fact met. That is: my being is not a necessary value, but it is in fact a value, and is absolutely affirmed or willed as such (just as I necessarily affirm my own existence, but affirm it as a virtually unconditioned, and not as necessary being). The sufficient reason for the act of positing one's self is in the act itself, which is an act of value apprehension or of being *for* self. The positing of one's self goes beyond the intellectual self-affirmation of the knower, in that the value affirmed is that of commitment to one's own being, which takes place in the very act of positing. In the act of freedom, the self wills its own existence precisely as one who wills; therefore the sufficient reason for the act cannot be found in man's "objective" being.

4. In using the word "will," I wish nevertheless to avoid association of the term with a "faculty" psychology in which Intellect and Will are regarded as two separate and parallel faculties or functions of the "soul." Such a treatment frequently leads to a lack of integration of freedom and knowledge.

5. Rahner, *Grundkurs, loc. cit.; Foundations, loc. cit.* It must be recalled, of course, that man's fundamental and transcendental freedom —like every transcendental reality for man—realizes itself only in and through categorical acts, and is therefore not independent of the sociological and psychological dimensions of freedom. See Rahner, "Freiheit und Manipulation in Gesellschaft und Kirche," in *Toleranz in der Kirche* (Freiburg im B.: Herder, 1977), pp. 70ff. Eng. trans. in *Meditations on Freedom and the Spirit* (trans. Rosaleen Ockenden, David Smith, Cecily Bennett) (New York: Seabury, 1978).

6. Rahner, *Hörer des Wortes,* pp. 123f.

7. See above, pp. 25, 33ff., 57f.

8. It becomes apparent, therefore, why even from a philosophical point of view love or good will is necessary for the attainment of the knowledge of the existence of God—even if that knowledge is conceived of as "natural." The knowledge of God proceeds from the evidence of our own subjectivity; but that subjectivity is existentially incomplete if it is lacking the dimension of love precisely toward the Mystery of being.

9. See above, pp. 25, 36f., 43, 135. Lonergan expands upon the

dimension of human existence as freedom and love in his *Method in Theology* (New York: Herder and Herder, 1972), esp. Chapters 2, 3, and 4.

10. For an analysis of freedom on the thematic level, see Bernard Lonergan, *Insight* (New York: Philosophical Library, 1957), pp. 596ff.; also, *Method in Theology*, Chapter 2: "The Human Good."

11. Lonergan, *Insight*, p. 598.

12. *Ibid.*, p. 599.

13. *Ibid.*, pp. 596–597; also *Method in Theology*, pp. 34–41.

14. We have reached here the transcendental basis for the notion of a moral "fundamental option" for the good or for God, realized in and through the choice of particular values.

15. See Bernard Lonergan, "Openness and Religious Experience," in *Collection* (New York: Herder and Herder, 1967), p. 199.

16. See Lonergan, *Method in Theology*, pp. 39–40, 43–46, 47–52.

17. Aquinas, *Summa Theologica*, I IIae q. V art. 8, speaks of "happiness" as the necessary and natural end of the will's activity. Pascal expresses the idea forcefully: "[Man] wishes to be happy, and wishes only to be happy, and cannot not wish to be happy ..." (*Pensées*, 169); "All men seek to be happy; this is without any exception: however different may be the means they use, all tend toward this goal. ... The will never makes the slightest motion, except toward this object. It is the motive of all the actions of all men, even those who go and hang themselves" (*ibid.*, 425).

18. On this, see Maurice Blondel's treatment of the inevitable transcendence of will toward the "one necessary thing" in *L'Action (1893)* (Paris: Presses Universitaires de France, 1950), pp. 339ff.

19. See the treatment of de Lubac's *Surnaturel* in Juan Alfaro, *Cristología y Antropología* (Madrid: Ediciones Cristiandad, 1973), pp. 259–272.

20. See especially the classic statement in Miguel de Unamuno, *Del Sentimiento Trágico de la Vida* (Madrid: Espasa-Calpe, 1937), especially Chapter III. Eng. trans.: *The Tragic Sense of Life* (trans. J.E. Crawford Flitch) (New York: Dover, 1954).

21. José Maria Gironella, *Los Cipreses Creen en Dios* (Barcelona: Editorial Planeta, 1977), pp. 14–15 (my translation). English version: *The Cypresses Believe in God* (trans. Harriet de Onis) (New York: Knopf, 1955).

22. Rahner, *Grundkurs*, pp. 102–103; English edition, pp. 95–96.

23. See *Inferno*, Canto III.

24. C.S. Lewis, *The Great Divorce* (Glasgow: William Collins Sons & Co., 1946), p. 7.

25. Plotinus, *Enneads* VI. 5. 7.

26. See above, pp. 93f., 151.

27. Our progress thus far roughly parallels Rahner's development of a metaphysical anthropology in *Hörer des Wortes*. Rahner summarizes his anthropology in three major statements: (1) Man is spirit—that is, lives in a continuous process of transcendence (always thematized) toward Being as such (pp. 86f.). (2) Man is that being who stands in free love before the God

of a possible revelation (p. 133). (3) Man is the being who must listen in history for the historical revelation of God, possibly expressed in human "word" (p. 200).

28. Rahner, *Hörer des Wortes*, p. 115.

29. See above, pp. 18, 19, 113ff., 127f.

30. For the concept of "proportionate" being, as above, pp. 136, 138.

31. Karl Barth, *Kirchliche Dogmatik*, I. viii–ix, quoted in Henri Bouillard, *The Knowledge of God* (trans. Samuel D. Femiano) (New York: Herder and Herder, 1968).

32. See Bouillard, *ibid.*, and also his *Karl Barth*.

33. Bouillard, *The Knowledge of God*, p. 106.

34. *Ibid.*, p. 107.

35. *De Veritate*, q. 2 a. 1 ad 9.

36. *Contra Gent.* I, 30, end.

37. Bouillard, *The Knowledge of God*, p. 108.

38. *Summa Theologica*, I q. 13 a. 5.

39. Bouillard, *loc. cit.*

40. See Emerich Coreth, *Metaphysics* (ed. Joseph Donceel) (New York: Herder and Herder, 1968), p. 183.

41. Bouillard, *The Knowledge of God*, pp. 111–112.

42. Coreth, *loc. cit.*

43. *Summa Theologica*, I q. 3, a. 8; I q. 8 a. 1; etc. See also the article "Teilhabe" in HThG.

44. See above, pp. 129, 136f.

45. Lonergan, *Insight*, p. 665.

46. *Ibid.*, pp. 657–669.

47. As noted earlier, Lonergan reaches God first as Truth, and then as Being, because in Lonergan's cognitional theory being is defined in terms of cognition, and metaphysics rests upon a prior study of cognitional structure.

48. This means that God is *ratio sui*—not, as Heidegger puts it, *causa sui;* God is his own intelligibility, but the word "cause" should be reserved for his relation to the finite.

49. Lonergan himself sometimes refers to God as "a" being—e.g., *Insight*, p. 675; also in "Christ as Subject" in *Collection*, p. 191—although in the latter case the offensive "a" was dropped by the editor; see note 47 on the page cited. The insight that God is "above" being is important in the dialogue with Eastern religions; for Hindus and Buddhists frequently have the impression that the Western "God" is a finite being.

50. When we speak of the immutability of God at this point, it must be remembered that we are proceeding within a "moving viewpoint." Revelation, and in particular the notion of the incarnation, will raise the problem of God's "becoming" or changing in his "other." In any case, what is said here of God's absoluteness remains true, even if it must be completed by further statements in a higher existential viewpoint. See Walter Kern, art. "God-World Relationship," in *SM* 2, p. 406; also Karl Rahner, "On the

Theology of the Incarnation," *Theological Investigations* IV (New York: Seabury, 1966), pp. 105–132, and Joseph F. Donceel, S.J., *The Searching Mind* (Notre Dame: University of Notre Dame Press, 1979), Chapter 7.

51. See Rahner, *Grundkurs*, p. 74; English ed., p. 65.

52. The divine knowledge of the contingent world might also be stated in terms of Lonergan's "principle of contingent predication," which states that whatever is truly and contingently affirmed about God (or a divine Person) is *constituted* by the divine essence, but in such a way that a suitable created term is necessary as a consequent condition. (See *De Deo Trino II, Pars Systematica* [Roma: PUG, 1964], p. 217; *Grace and Freedom: Operative Grace in the Thought of St. Thomas Aquinas*, ed. by J. Patout Burns, S.J. [London: Darton, Longman & Todd, 1971], pp. 68, 88; *Insight*, pp. 661–662.) This means that God remains entitatively the same whatever may be the effects he creates in the world. It also means that the conditions for affirming that God knows or wills or creates any thing, and the conditions for affirming that such a thing exists, are the same. Since the divine essence is a strict mystery, Lonergan's principle of contingent predication is similar to Rahner's *reductio in mysterium:* it recognizes the transcendence of God as unimaginable and ungraspable, and eliminates the problems which arise from attempting to formulate God's knowledge and will in anthropomorphic terms. It therefore provides a language for stating what can be said about such matters as God's "foreknowledge" and human freedom, or the theological problem of grace and freedom.

53. Rahner, *Grundkurs*, pp. 85f.; English, pp. 77f.

54. The concept of creation "from nothing" does not necessarily mean creation in (or "with") time; that is, it does not exclude the possibility of an eternally existing finite world (as Aquinas already saw). An eternal finite world would still be, in every moment of its existence and in every aspect, totally dependent upon God—that is, continually created. Modern scientific cosmology seems to have arrived at a consensus that the universe originated in a "big bang" perhaps some fifteen billion years ago. It cannot yet be determined with certitude whether there is enough matter in the universe for gravity to draw together again the expanding cosmos. If there is not, then the "big bang" must be conceived as the absolute beginning, scientifically speaking. At the present moment, this hypothesis seems to have the greatest weight. If it is discovered, however, that there is much more matter in the universe than is known, it could become plausible to hypothesize that the "big bang" was in fact only the latest in a series of explosions, followed by contractions; in other words, that the universe is a "pulsating" affair (something along the lines imagined in Hindu cosmology). In that case, one could not scientifically speak of a "beginning" to the cosmos. In either hypothesis, the existence of matter and time (whether finite or eternal) demands a creator; and either scientific view is compatible with the metaphysical idea of creation "from nothing" (although not, perhaps, with a fundamentalist biblical view).

55. Rahner, *Grundkurs*, p. 92; English, pp. 84f.

56. *Ibid.*, pp. 67–74; English, pp. 57–66.

57. Gabriel Marcel, *The Mystery of Being*, Vol. I (Chicago: Henry Regnery Co., 1950), Chapter X.

58. Rahner, *Grundkurs*, p. 74 (my translation).

59. See above, pp. 168, 169.

Chapter VII

1. On openness as fact, achievement, and gift, see Bernard Lonergan, "Openness and Religious Experience," in *Collection* (New York: Herder and Herder, 1967), pp. 198–201.

2. See Karl Rahner, *Hörer des Wortes* (München: Kösel-Verlag, 1963), p. 133. Also above, Chapter VI, note 27.

3. On the transcendental precepts, see Lonergan, *Method in Theology* (New York: Herder and Herder, 1972), p. 53.

4. See Bernard Lonergan, *Insight* (New York: Philosophical Library, 1957); on the dramatic bias, pp. 191–206; on individual bias, pp. 218–222; on group bias, pp. 222–225; on general bias, pp. 225–226.

5. Abraham H. Maslow, *Toward a Psychology of Being* (2nd ed.) (New York: Van Nostrand Reinhold, 1968), p. 60.

6. Lonergan, *Insight*, pp. 191ff.

7. *Ibid., loc. cit.*

8. See above, pp. 153f.

9. Mt. 10:39 and parallels.

10. Lonergan, *Insight*, p. 220.

11. Lk. 16:8.

12. See Lonergan, *Insight*, pp. 222–225.

13. Arnold Toynbee, *An Historian's Approach to Religion* (London: Oxford University Press, 1956), p. 268. Toynbee points out that religions have been particularly subject to this form of group bias; see Chapter 10, on the idolization of religious institutions; also his *A Study of History* (New York: Oxford University Press, 1962), Vol. IV, pp. 303–423; VII B, pp. 548ff.; and *passim.*

14. On emergent probability, see above, p. 33.

15. Lonergan, *Insight* pp. 228ff.

16. Rahner, *Grundkurs*, pp. 113ff.; English, pp. 106ff. The Hindu notion of "karma"—the objective and irreversible "fruits" of actions, independent of the subject's moral qualities—if understood in a "demythologized" way, may also be considered a way of formulating the moral impotence of man to live authentically without salvation.

17. See above, p. 164.

18. See above, pp. 143ff.

19. If it is true that physical evil is unavoidable in an evolutionary world, one might be led to ask whether God could not have created a non-

evolving world. It does not seem, however, that we can reasonably answer such a question, for all of our data of experience arise in the actual world, and we have no experience of the possibility of any other. It is true that the *idea* of a non-evolutionary world does not contain any apparent contradiction; but absence of apparent self-contradiction does not constitute real possibility. We cannot say, therefore, that because God is omnipotent, he could, if he wished, create a world without evil; for we do not know whether the concept of a finite world without evil of any kind is the concept of something really possible, or is really only a group of words designating nothing; and if it means nothing, there is no sense in saying that God can perform it.

It is in any case difficult to see how a finite *spiritual* world could exist without dynamism and growth, which would imply some sort of process in the material world on which spirit is dependent (for only God is or can be "pure" spirit, in the sense of having no potency or "matter"). On the other hand, a material world seems to make no sense unless it is ordered to spirit. It is difficult to see, therefore, how a finite and non-evolving world could be possible—even if the "evolution" need not have been of the particular kind our world undergoes.

Another line of thought is suggested by the speculations of modern subatomic physics. If there exists—as one interpretation of quantum theory says—a real, and not merely epistemological indeterminacy or randomness in nature, is this randomness (and therefore the process of "emergent probability" which arises from it on higher levels) the necessary substratum on the material level for the existence of real freedom on the level of spirit? I.e., if freedom is a lack of determinacy, does it demand as a pre-condition a certain lack of determinacy in matter—and therefore an evolutionary process that proceeds according to probability? See Heinz R. Pagels, *The Cosmic Code* (New York: Bantam, 1983), Chapter 8, esp. pp. 109–112.

20. Rom. 8:28. C.S. Lewis in his science fiction/theological fantasy *Out of the Silent Planet* constructs a world without "original sin," in which physical evil exists, but is not alienating for the creature. Rosemary Haughton expands upon the idea that evolution unavoidably contains "physical evil" in her *The Passionate God* (New York: Paulist Press, 1981), pp. 91ff. In a world which is constituted by love, there is always what she calls a "passionate" element, which involves leaving behind and losing, and therefore pain, which is nevertheless not evil, but a means toward a greater good. It is only with the refusal of love that "real tragedy" becomes possible (p. 92).

21. Only a being which is free could separate itself from the goodness of the movement of the universe toward God; only a free being can be "alienated" from the divine love, and thereby cause the alienation of the non-conscious world in relation to that freedom. In this perspective, "physical" evil also takes on a new and tragic dimension as an aspect of man's alienation from God.

22. See Klaus Hemmerle, art. "Evil," in *SM,* Vol. 2, pp. 279–283.

23. See Rahner, "Dogmatic Reflections on the Knowledge and Self-Consciousness of Christ," in *Theological Investigations* V, pp. 201f., 214. Regarding *God's* knowledge of man's future free acts, see above, p. 170 and note 52.

24. Lonergan, *Insight*, p. 666.

25. *Ibid.*, p. 667.

26. *Loc. cit.*

27. There is perhaps some ambiguity in Augustine's terminology regarding the proper moral attitude toward creatures. He has been called "the great corrupter of Christian morals" (Anders Nygren) because he states that creatures are to be "used," and are not ends in themselves. (Kant, on the other hand, in the second statement of the "categorical imperative" insists that the fundamental moral principle is always to treat others as ends, and never merely as means.) The context of Augustine's language must be understood. In accord with neo-Platonic philosophy, Augustine regards turning to creatures as a step from the One to the many. Matter is to a certain extent necessarily negative, for it always bears the danger of immersion in the multiple and hence the loss of man's true end. At the same time, however, creatures are the sign of God, the reflection of his beauty, and the means destined to bring us to him. God is *honestum,* or desirable in himself; creatures are *utiles,* or designed to bring us beyond themselves to another end. Creatures are to be "used" in the sense that they are the means toward God; man must not attempt to find final happniess in them.

Sin, then, is for Augustine not in loving creatures, but in stopping there, refusing to recognize that their goodness is participation in the Goodness of the One, God. More precisely, sin is exactly in not truly loving the things of the world, for true love respects its object for what it is; love refers its object to God (whether reflexively or not), and not to self.

The danger of Augustine's terminology, expecially of the word "useful" applied to creatures, and in particular our fellow persons, is that it may be taken in a purely "pragmatic" sense, in which creatures become *merely* means, with no intrinsic value, and the world is regarded as something to be escaped from. In the absence of the Thomistic distinction regarding "secondary ends," Augustine's Plotinian language may be misleading; but a negative, Manichaean attitude toward the world, or a selfish, manipulative attitude toward our fellow creatures, is definitely not his meaning.

28. Søren Kierkegaard, *The Sickness unto Death* (Princeton, N.J.: Princeton University Press, 1941).

29. What we have said about sin applies properly to sin in its radical form of a *fundamental* option against God: what is traditionally called "mortal" sin. Obviously, however, there will be other options which, while not signifying a turning away from the fundamental drive toward God, nevertheless stand to some degree in tension with it. Such acts are called "sin" by analogy.

30. Lonergan, *Insight,* p. 694.

31. *Loc. cit.*

32. On "heuristic," see above, pp. 41, 130, 135.

33. See Rahner, *Grundkurs,* pp. 264ff.; English, pp. 268ff.

34. In the Christian identification of salvation as taking place through the incarnation, the world is more than the mere locus of salvation; it becomes a radical part of the solution.

35. See above, pp. 30f.

36. Eph. 1:10; cf. Heb. 1:1–2.

37. See Lonergan's long digression on "belief" in the heuristic structure of the solution: *Insight,* pp. 703–718; also *Method in Theology,* pp. 41–47.

38. See above, pp. 172f.

39. See above, pp. 192f.

40. Rahner, *Grundkurs,* p. 92; English, p. 85.

41. *Ibid.,* pp. 135ff.; English, pp. 129ff.

42. On "supernatural intentionality," see Juan Alfaro, *Fides, Spes, Caritas* (Roma: PUG, 1968), pp. 234–278; also see Alfaro's articles, "Faith" II and III in *SM,* Vol. 2, pp. 313–324.

43. Karl Rahner, *Glaube als Mut* (Einsiedeln: Benziger, 1976), pp. 24, 27 (my translation). English version in *Meditations on Freedom and the Spirit* (trans. Rosaleen Ockenden, David Smith, Cecily Bennett) (New York: Seabury, 1978).

44. Karl Rahner, *Do You Believe in God?* (trans. Richard Strachan) (New York: Newman Press, 1969), pp. 112–113.

45. See above, on the paradox of love, p. 153. Rahner develops the line of thought concerning the summons to absolute love of neighbor in the article "Jesus Christ" in *SM,* Vol. 3, pp. 194f. He adds two other approaches as well: the argument from readiness for death and the appeal to hope in the future.

46. On virtually unconditioned value, see above, p. 151.

47. This orientation of man toward God is the "supernatural existential."

48. Rahner, *Grundkurs,* p. 136; English, pp. 130f.

49. *Loc. cit.*

50. See Rahner, art. "Jesus Christ," p. 195.

51. On subjectivity as mediated through the objective, see above, p. 24.

52. Rahner, *Grundkurs,* p. 91; English p. 83.

53. *Ibid.,* p. 90; English, p. 83.

54. *Loc. cit.*

55. As Rahner notes (art. "Jesus Christ," p. 205), a purely transcendental revelation could never be definitive for man in history because of the constitutive unity in man of spirit and matter. Man must constantly strive to express transcendental experience categorically; but of ourselves

we could never achieve a definitive or absolute expression of God's self-gift, which would, therefore, remain always relative and provisional.

56. Lonergan, *Method in Theology*, pp. 105ff.

57. Rom. 5:5.

58. Lonergan, *Method in Theology*, pp. 238ff.